joe esposito

and elena oumano

simon & schuster

new york london toronto

sydney tokyo singapore

good rockin' tonight

twenty years
on the road
and on the town
with ELVIS

SIMON & SCHUSTER
Rockefeller Center
1230 Avenue of the Americas
New York, New York 10020

SIMON & SCHUSTER and colophon are registered trademarks
of Simon & Schuster Inc.
Designed by Karolina Harris
Manufactured in the United States of America

10   9   8   7   6   5   4   3   2   1

Library of Congress Cataloging-in-Publication Data
Esposito, Joe.
Good rockin' tonight: twenty years on the road and on the town with Elvis /
Joe Esposito and Elena Oumano.
p.   cm.
1. Presley, Elvis, 1935–1977. 2. Rock musicians—United States—Biography. I.
Oumano, Elena. II. Title.
ML420.P96E86   1994
782.42166'092—dc20
[B]   94-25560
                                                                        CIP
                                                                         MN

ISBN 978-1-5011-5872-8

This book is dedicated to my good friend,
Elvis Aaron Presley.
For the good times.

acknowledgments

many friends have made very special contributions to my life and to this book. I would like to acknowledge them with love and gratitude. To my wife, Martha, for her love, patience, and understanding; my daughters, Debbie and Cindy, who are always there for me; and my son, Anthony, who always makes me smile. I would also like to thank Debbie's husband, Tom Laemmel, who could be a great writer if he wanted to be, and Cindy's husband, Eric Bahr. Cindy and Eric just gave me a beautiful grandson, Cody. For my friends, George and June Di Domizio, for encouragement and unbelievable help in this entire project. I don't think I could have done it without George. I want to thank my family in Chicago. My sister, Phyllis, and my brother, Frank. I don't know how I would have made it without their help over the years. And still today, they are always only a phone call away. I love you both. And, of course, the rest of the family: Frank's wife, Joyce; Phyllis's husband, Jim Soohen, and their daughters, Elizabeth and Laura; Elizabeth's husband, Pat Grossett, and their son, Ryan; my brother's sons, Steve and Mark; Steve's wife, Heidi, and their daughter, Stephanie; Mark's wife, Yolanda. It's nice to have a big family that's still growing. Also, to my mother, father, and JoJo Esposito, who are up in heaven with Elvis, for all their love and support throughout my life.

Then there's my wife's family, who kept asking me, "When is your book going to be finished?" I kept asking myself the same question. Well, here it is! Thanks for being so patient. For Martha's father, Robert Gallub, let me say once more, this all happened before I met your daughter. To Uncle Arnold Gallub for all his notes of encouragement; to Eugenia, Martha's mother, who still hasn't figured me out, and to her husband, Joe Deveau.

Many thanks to Madeleine Morel, my agent. She must have believed in me to take me on as her client. And Elena Oumano, my cowriter. This wasn't easy for me and I know I made it hard for her. But we made it. My thanks to Gary Luke, for all his patience, his assistant, Saul Anton, and especially to my tireless copy editing supervisor, Isolde C. Sauer.

Now for all my friends who helped me to remember the past. They are Sheila Ryan Caan, Linda Thompson Foster, the late Tom Hulett, Rick Husky, Barbara Leigh, Mindi Miller, Pat Parry, Ann Pennington, Priscilla Presley, Jerry Schilling, Ann-Margret Smith, Myrna Smith. And special thanks to Colonel Tom Parker and his wife, LouAnn.

Lastly, I would like to thank all my other friends who kept me from being a failure. For Roxanne Alvarado, Patsy Anderson, Dick Ashby, Pete and Marie Azer, George and Shirley Barris, Sal and Susanne Bonafede, Stan Brosette, Margie Butler, Bob Cantwell, Tom and Jane Collins, James and Evy Darren, Angelo and Adel Dimitropoulos, Jane Elliot, Linda and Barry Gibb, Paul Gongaware, Ken Gross, Peter Guralnick, Joyce Hagemeister, Brian Jamieson, Joan and Tom Kardashian, Jerry and Joan Kennedy, Gene Kilroy, George Klein, Darwin Lamm, Malcolm Leo, Linda McCarty, Loretta Moschetti, Peter and Mary Pasternak, Ron and Chris Pietrafeso, Patrick Pittelli, Shirley Dieu Powell, Karen and Phil Ramone, Dr. Adrianna Scheibner, Andrew Solt, Juanita Visconti, Jamie Voudouris, Roger Voudouris, and, of course, to all Elvis fans, who are the greatest in the world.

Remember, no man is a failure who has friends.

—It's a Wonderful Life,

a Frank Capra film

contents

preface

my name is Joe Esposito. I was Elvis Presley's road manager, right-hand man, and close personal friend from the time we
were discharged from the Army in 1960 until August 16, 1977, when
I tried to bring him back to life as he lay on the floor of his bathroom in Graceland. That was the worst day of my life. For seventeen years, I had organized Elvis's personal life. I handled almost
every detail surrounding his personal needs during the movie years,
the Vegas years, and the touring years. I even made flight and hotel arrangements for all of Elvis's girlfriends, which would be a
challenge to anyone's organizational skills, because Elvis never saw
one woman at a time, even during his marriage to Priscilla. Three
or four was the average figure. One might be in the air on her way
in, crossing flight paths with another on her way out. A third woman
would be with Elvis in his hotel suite, with perhaps a fourth on
hold in a room a few floors below.

I was Elvis's road manager, but many people misunderstand the
job description and think I claim to have been Elvis's personal man-

ager. No. There was only one personal manager for Elvis. And that was Colonel Tom Parker. Since Elvis's death, the truth about the Colonel's relationship with Elvis has been obscured by a rumor mill that works overtime, manufacturing salable lies to this day.

My years with Elvis were wonderful, exciting times, but the words don't do justice to the experience that I want to share. I wrote this book to tell the truth about life with Elvis—both positive and negative—about the Colonel, about my job, about Elvis's relationships with celebrities and ordinary people. You'll learn about Elvis's complex relationships with his buddies, known as the "Memphis Mafia," and his many girlfriends, the most gorgeous and understanding women any man could ever hope to know.

Nothing in my ordinary background could have prepared me for life with Elvis. I was the picture of an ordinary, happy-go-lucky twenty-year-old on March 12, 1958, when the United States Army called me into service. Two weeks later, on March 24, Elvis Presley was inducted.

chapter 1

GI blues

" hello, I'm Elvis Presley," he said as he shook my hand firmly. "Glad to meet you." Everybody in the Western world and beyond knew who Elvis was, yet he acted as if he needed to identify himself.

"Hello, I'm Joe Esposito from the Twenty-seventh Artillery," I blurted out. "You know, the outfit up the road from the Thirty-second Armored." This was the Army, after all, and that's how one soldier identified himself to another.

A group of eight or so people, mostly other buddies in the service and friends from Memphis, were gathered in the living room of the house Elvis was renting in Bad Nauheim, Germany, a beautiful spa town about five miles from our base in Friedberg, where the streets bustled all day long with health-conscious Germans taking their constitutionals. I was here through my friend Wes Daniels, a photographer for Combat Command C, Public Information Office (PIO), whose assignment was to tag after the Army's top-ranking superstar and shoot him performing militarylike activities.

"Elvis plays touch football on weekends. Why don't you join us? We need more players," Wes said one day. "In fact, let's drop by his house tonight." That's how I happened to be in Elvis's living room.

Seeing Elvis Presley in the flesh was a jolt. On the strength of his physical presence alone, he commanded the room. He was the best-looking man I'd ever seen, startlingly handsome, with classical, chiseled features and an undefinable quality that distinguished him from everyone else. He grew up around black children, and perhaps that influence gave him a stance like that of no white man I'd ever seen. He walked differently, kind of hip and relaxed. He had that snarl to his lip and an infectious laugh.

Wes and I were wearing sports shirts, slacks, and windbreakers—standard civilian gear for off-base military personnel. But Elvis wore a striking maroon velvet shirt, opened at least two buttons down and with the collar turned up. It hung loosely over his green Army fatigue pants. He was Hollywood on top and United States Army on bottom. It looked as if the only thing he'd changed that day was his shirt. He still wore his Army boots with the laces hanging out about ten inches.

Introductions over, Elvis returned to his easy chair and settled into a characteristic pose: left ankle resting on right knee, with the left foot jerking back and forth as he talked. It moved so quickly I thought that any minute the bootlaces would crack like bull whips.

Elvis carried a handkerchief that night, and he made a point of apologizing for his head cold. "Man," he said, "I feel like my head is the size of the pumpkin."

"It *is* the size of a pumpkin," chimed in Lamar Fike. Lamar was big, 250 to 300 pounds encased in black slacks and a black turtleneck.

"You oughta know about size," Elvis countered swiftly. "Man, your pants are bigger than the tents we use on maneuvers." Everyone laughed. Lamar was a friend of Elvis's from Memphis. If Lamar had been able to drop one hundred pounds, he would have been a good-looking guy. He just loved food too much. Whenever we went out to eat, he ordered two of everything. Instead of lifting his feet when he walked, Lamar shuffled. Like Elvis's other friends from Memphis, Lamar didn't have a specific job. He ran errands and did other favors like shining Elvis's shoes and taking his dates home. Most important was his role as court jester to the King, making Elvis laugh. Elvis felt sorry for Lamar because he had few friends. He kidded Lamar, but Lamar never seemed to get upset. I realized soon enough that Elvis and Lamar were enjoying their favorite sport, a fast-paced duel of quips and barbed insults.

The room was arranged for conversation, with some chairs and a sofa forming a large circle. The sofa held two or three people. The rest of the guys and a few girls, mostly silent, occupied about half a dozen chairs, some of which looked as if they'd been brought in from the kitchen. Lamar had arranged himself directly opposite Elvis, as was his habit, probably to keep clear of a friendly slam to his arm, belly, or legs.

A tall, red-headed guy with a long, powerful-looking torso paced the room like a muscular caged cat, sitting down for only a few moments at a time. That was Red West, Elvis's friend since they were students at Humes High School in Memphis, where Red was a star on the football team. Elvis never forgot that Red had saved him from having his long hair shorn off by a gang of school bullies. Red had suffered an even more deprived childhood than Elvis. He spent a lot of time at Elvis's home and became very close to Gladys Presley. When Elvis began performing in small clubs around the South, he asked Red to accompany him. Girls were already going crazy over him, and tanked-up boyfriends didn't take too kindly to the threat of his sex appeal. Elvis usually talked his way out of combustible situations, but with Red by his side, he felt more secure. Red was a genuine tough-guy and conferred tough-guy status on Elvis by association. When Elvis began to record with RCA Records and star in Hollywood movies, he took Red along so they could share the good times. Then Red joined the Marines in 1956. After Red finished his tour, Elvis invited him to Germany. That first night, Red showed little of his feelings or personality. He was polite, but not particularly warm or friendly. He remained silent, roaming the living room and occasionally helping Elvis demonstrate karate moves.

Elvis rotated around the room for karate partners. He wanted to be fair and not hurt anyone's feelings by showing favoritism. He recruited several people: Rex Mansfield, a soldier the Army kept with Elvis from the time of their induction; Charlie Hodge; Wes; and even me.

"Just come at me," Elvis urged as we hesitated, unwilling to attack full force and risk injuring him. "Go ahead, just come at me like you were going to put a knife in me." Despite his head cold, Elvis struck dramatic karate poses, demonstrating each move first in slow motion, then at normal speed. "Man, I'm going to get good at this stuff," he vowed enthusiastically. "One of these days, I'll be busting boards, maybe even concrete blocks."

Then, to everyone's delight, he headed for the upright piano positioned along the wall near the front entrance of the house. As he walked over, he bent forward to peek out the front window at that night's crowd. He turned to Red, winked, and flashed his devilish grin. "Some nice stuff out there," he commented. "I guess I'll go out and sign a few autographs later." A moment later, he'd changed his mind. "Nah," he said, "I'm not feeling all that good tonight. Elisabeth, would you go out and tell them I'm not feeling good and won't be able to sign autographs?"

Elisabeth Stefaniak, Elvis's pretty assistant, was eighteen years old and lived in the house. She seemed to be always hovering within easy contact. Despite her loose-fitting clothes, I could see she had a voluptuous body. Elvis had met Elisabeth two months after he arrived in Germany, while on maneuvers for special training in Grafenwöhr, in the hills near the Czech border. Elisabeth had learned that Elvis liked to go to the movies on base and that he always came in after the movie started and left just before it was over. One night, while Elisabeth was waiting at the back of the theater, Elvis entered with Rex Mansfield and another soldier. When Rex got up to go to the bathroom, Elisabeth asked him to deliver a note to Elvis. Rex passed the note, then came back to escort Elisabeth to a seat next to Elvis. After the show, Elvis walked Elisabeth to her family home, a few blocks away. It was cold, so he put his arm around her shoulders to keep her warm. But he was a gentleman, saying goodbye at her door and giving her a little peck on the cheek. He wrote down her telephone number and asked if she would meet him the next night at the theater. They became good friends. He even dropped by her home every so often to have dinner with her family and play guitar. A few days before Elvis was to return to Friedberg, he asked Elisabeth's parents to let her work for him as a secretary/interpreter and run his household. Two days later, Elisabeth was installed in the house in Bad Nauheim.

After several visits to Elvis's house, I discovered that Elisabeth never joined the conversations. She was always in the shadows, available and waiting. Elvis became attached to certain girls, but if they weren't around, he'd just be with someone else. That someone else was often Elisabeth. The entire time he was sleeping with her, Elvis was having other affairs right in front of her. He would spend an evening with a girl in his bedroom, the girl would leave, and he'd call in Elisabeth to sleep with him. This arrangement continued even after Elvis became involved with Priscilla. Elvis never slept alone. He had a severe problem with sleepwalking and someone had to be there throughout the night to make sure he didn't injure himself. Even other guys and I slept in the same room with him on occasion.

That first night I was there, Elisabeth didn't seem at all upset when he took a second look out the window and changed his mind again. "No, that's not right," he said. "Don't do that, Elisabeth. Go out and say I'll sign a dozen photographs or so at about nine o'clock."

Then he settled himself on the piano bench. I thought he only played guitar, so I was surprised to see how skilled he was on piano. Every so often, he stopped playing to pick up a handkerchief and blow his nose.

"That's using your head," said Lamar. Elvis shot a glance at Lamar, struck a few chords for effect, then counterjabbed: "That's right fat-ass. I do use my head for something other than a food funnel." He laughed wildly at his own wit, while we provided the echo and Lamar emitted a nervous giggle. Elvis pounded out some more fast-chugging rock 'n' roll. I couldn't help wondering if the fans crowded by the gate in the freezing cold could hear this rare live performance.

Elvis didn't sing his hits like "Hound Dog" or "Heartbreak Hotel" that first night I met him. In fact, he rarely did offstage. Instead, he ran through a raucous selection of rhythm and blues, while Charlie Hodge, a musician and GI from the South whom Elvis met on the way over to Germany, tapped his feet, and Lamar slapped his enormous thigh. "Man, hit those keys, El!" they yelled in encouragement. As you came to know Elvis, the progression went from "Elvis" to "El" to "E," the most chummy nickname. This first night, I used "Elvis," and over the months, I worked my way to "E."

He pounded out an irreverent version of "Mona Lisa," Conway Twitty's big rockabilly hit. After he played it, Elvis seemed irritated. He was sure it would have been a big hit for him, he said. If only he wasn't stuck in Germany, far from RCA's recording studios. He consoled himself with a soulful rendition of "Danny Boy," milking every drop of sentiment from the classic, mingling delicacy of feeling with waves of emotional power.

Having set a new mood, Elvis rose from the piano bench and walked across the room to a framed quotation on the wall: "The Penalty of Leadership," by Theodore McManus. It referred to the responsibility that weighs heavily on a leader's shoulders. Elvis gazed for a moment at the quotation, then turned dramatically to address the room.

"Man, when you're the guy on top of the pile, there's nowhere to go but down, and there's nobody up there you can talk to," he observed. "As it says on the wall right there, you're all alone . . . all alone." He worked himself in even deeper, spinning out a depressing monologue on the distinction between being alone and loneliness, as everyone in the room leaned forward and listened closely.

"You see," Elvis explained, "loneliness can happen to almost anybody. You can be in a crowd of people, and still feel lonely. It's just that you decided to be lonely. You can change that easily. But being alone. Man, that's something different. You have no control over being alone. I mean, *really* alone, like a general or some top dog leader. That's really being alone because there is no one else up there with you. That's the difference between being alone and being lonely."

"Yeah," Lamar said, staring morosely at the drab gray carpet that covered all but the edges of the floor. "I know what you're saying, man." Lamar was taking his cue and feeding into Elvis's mood. Elvis's reaction was equally predictable. He leaned over and delivered a friendly whack to the top of Lamar's head, hard enough to stir the raven-black hair.

"Don't worry, Lamar," he quipped. "You'll never be alone. There's no way you'll ever climb to the top of anything. There's just too much of you to climb."

Suddenly, he turned serious again. "You see a lot of things and you learn a lot of things in Hollywood," he went on, pausing to light up a Hav-a-Tampa cigarillo. "One thing I learned is that when you're hot, you're hot. Nothing is hotter than a hit. But look out! Nothing's colder than a miss. Jerry Lee Lewis was hotter than a fire-cracker; then he got ice-cold. It can take a lifetime of trying, of hit-ting the road, playing any date you can get. You get lucky and you're heading up the charts. Things look great. Then, bam! It's suddenly quiet. Then it's cold." Elvis sighed, expelling a cloud of cigar smoke. "I hope it doesn't happen to me, at least not now, when I'm so far from home and the fans. I love those fans, but they're fickle. Two years is a long, long time."

Elvis was on a roll. "It's a fickle world out there," he concluded, shaking his head. "And it's not much better in the record business. Man, if you can get to the top of the charts for a couple of weeks, you're really doin' something because they get tired and forget in just a couple of weeks. Two years is a long, long time." He fell silent and gazed down at his Army fatigue pants and the boots with their half-done laces.

"Talk about weird!" Lamar burst out in a clumsy attempt to lighten the mood. "We met some real weird people out there in Hollywood. Right, E? How about that director with the riding crop? That guy paid a flunky to follow him around with a stool just so he could prop up his foot while he gave instructions to the cast or crew. Remember that guy, E? Wasn't he something?"

"Yeah," Elvis agreed. "He was riding high at the expense of some poor slob. There ain't enough money in this world to make me take a job like that. I'd rather starve than to be put down like that. Here's this big-shot director, walking around with a riding crop, whacking his leg and pointing to a spot on the floor. Then this guy runs over with the stool and sets it down. Christ, what makes a man so mean?"

"You know who else is mean?" Lamar volunteered.

"Uh-oh, now what kind of bullshit are we going to hear?" Elvis groaned, but he settled back in his armchair, and rested his left an-kle on his right knee.

"Frank Sinatra!" Lamar pronounced triumphantly.

"You're on your own there, Lamar," Elvis said. "Don't pull me into what you heard. I think it's a bunch of crap."

Lamar heaved his bulk out of his chair, took the stage in the center of the room, and launched into his Sinatra impression.

"First, nobody except a few close friends can call him Frank," he said. "He tells people, 'My name is Mr. Sinatra to you and don't forget it!' Mr. Sinatra!" Lamar snapped his fingers, trying to imitate Sinatra's air of entitlement. "One guy has the job of carrying a bottle of Jack Daniels," he went on. "Another guy has to see that there's ice in a glass. And still another guy carries a white tablecloth. When Frank, I mean Mr. Sinatra, sits down, nobody is allowed to do anything until Mr. Sinatra snaps his fingers."

"You'd never see me do that crap," Elvis commented. "Except maybe to keep Lamar in line." He snapped his fingers. "Down boy, down," he said with a grin. The room exploded in laughter.

I stared at Elvis, still marveling that I was actually in his living room. I remembered the Army chaplain's speech a few months earlier when I was a raw recruit at Fort Hood. "Oh, by the way," he added after his lecture on being careful about women and diseases in foreign countries, "I guess a lot of you know Elvis is being inducted on March 24. If anyone meets him, just tell him chaplain 'so and so' said 'hello.' "

"Fat chance," I'd thought. "Elvis won't really be in the Army and even if he is, he'll be holed up in a dressing room."

But Fate was at work. Elvis had processed through Fort Chaffee, Arkansas, where the media took miles of newsreel footage showing him receiving his uniform and equipment and barbers shaving off his fabled pompadour and sideburns. From there he was sent to Fort Hood, where more than twenty thousand men were receiving basic training. I was one of the twenty thousand, but I didn't meet Elvis there. We didn't get within a handshake of each other, although I saw him a few times. You couldn't miss him. Whenever his girlfriend from Memphis, Anita Wood, visited on weekends, a big gleaming red Lincoln convertible cruised the base with the top down, a gorgeous blonde at the wheel, and Elvis—the only recruit allowed to drive around Fort Hood—in the passenger seat. And every so often, I saw him doing basic training along with everyone else.

Elvis was assigned to A Company, Second Medium Tank Battalion, Second Armored Division. I was also in the Second Armored Division, but I was assigned to the First Artillery. Elvis was in the tank unit, and I was in the self-propelled howitzer unit. Except for the poor guys in the infantry, most of us got to ride around making noise and stirring up dust with our "Hell on Wheels" routines.

We were notified of our assignments after six months of basic training. Elvis and I were both assigned to Combat Command C, Ray Barracks, Third Armored Division, one of the divisions commanded by General Patton during World War II. Our new home would be Friedberg, Germany, a short distance from Frankfurt. Elvis was scheduled to leave the same time I was, but in August, his mother died of liver disease. Devastated, he went home. By the time Elvis arrived in Germany a few weeks later, I was already assigned to an easy job as a payroll clerk in the finance office. I was working late in the office one bitter cold day with my buddy and roommate George Di Domizio. As I looked out my window, I saw thousands of German kids below, milling around the gate of Combat Command C.

"What's going on?" I asked George.

"Elvis is coming," he said.

"Great, wonderful," I thought. "Some excitement to relieve the boredom." Although I was somewhat of a fan, as an Italian guy from Chicago, my allegiance was to the Frank Sinatra–Dean Martin school. After dark, busloads of GIs began pulling up to the gate. There was no way a girl could distinguish one GI from another because they were all wearing the same uniform, but the girls screamed and carried on as if each were Elvis.

I saw Elvis around the base over the next few months. Some people think he didn't live in the barracks because he had special privileges, but anyone could live off-base if they had family. Soldiers with dependents were given a housing allowance. Most recruits brought their wives, but Elvis's entourage included his grandmother, Minnie Mae; his father, Vernon; and friends from Memphis to keep him company, Lamar Fike and Red West. Cliff Gleaves came over after Red went back to Memphis. They weren't on payroll, but Vernon gave them a very small allowance.

Elvis reported to our base in Friedberg every morning. When he arrived, the rest of us were always standing at attention outside the barracks, which we were told had housed Hitler's SS troops during World War II. As we stood there, panting from our mad dash for roll call, Elvis would cruise by in a Mercedes or the sporty white

BMW he had bought directly from the company. He was always late, and he always tossed a sharp military salute to the officers as he flashed them the famous Elvis grin.

Elvis was assigned to the Third Armored Division in Friedberg as a jeep driver. His duties were basically reconnaissance and included driving to the "front lines" and scouting the situation. The Cold War was raging at the time, and no one knew when things might heat up. We all had live ammo nearby.

After anyone has been in the Army for a set number of months, he is automatically promoted from private to private first class. After that, promotions become a matter of merit rather than seniority. As an office worker, I became a spec four after the usual interval and so did Elvis, in June 1959. I topped out at spec four, but Elvis went on to become a sergeant, a rank that very few two-year draftees ever reach. He got his triple stripes on January 20, 1960. There could have been a little favoritism at play, but Elvis was a good soldier. He worked hard, even at such menial jobs as sandpapering the exhaust pipe of his jeep and KP. Most important, except for the late arrivals at roll call, he didn't goof off or screw up. He wanted the respect of the officers, and they gave it to him—not because he wanted it, but because he earned it.

It was rumored that a deal had been struck between Elvis and the Army: Elvis wouldn't be a pain in the ass and the Army wouldn't be a pain in the ass. Elvis wanted to play it straight as best he could, and the Army wanted to make sure there was no unfavorable publicity. As I understood from my friends in the Public Information Office (PIO), a brigadier general at the Pentagon was assigned to Elvis. This general was not always on post, but he was always nearby, attuned to any matter involving Elvis Presley. If a sergeant decided to get cute and give Elvis a bad time, he was told to lay off immediately. There was to be no harassment, and the reward for the Army was that Elvis played ball.

The highlight of that first evening was Elvis's animated stories about show business. The group of awestruck recruits hung on his every word. The life Elvis was describing was light years away from the Army routine or our own humdrum realities back home.

One story he told that night I would hear many times again through the years. The Hollywood people hated Colonel Parker, Elvis said, laughing gleefully. They'd rather see the devil himself than the Colonel arriving for negotiations. When the Colonel was making the deal for *Love Me Tender,* Elvis's first movie, the producers wanted to pay him as a contract star, according to the custom of that time. They offered seven hundred dollars a week, not a bad salary for 1956, plus the car of his choice, and they implied that they'd supply him with all the women he could handle. Elvis thought that was fantastic and wanted to go for it. What more could any young, red-blooded, all-American male ask for? But the Colonel said no. He wanted a piece of the business; Elvis had to have a percentage of the gross profits. That kind of deal was unheard of in Hollywood at the time, particularly for a movie unknown. Elvis loved to reenact the scene that followed between the Colonel and producer Hal Wallis.

"Life is simple," the Colonel said. "My guess is that the only reason you want Elvis in this movie is that he'll attract a crowd that will buy tickets. Is that why you want him?"

"Yes," Wallis conceded grudgingly.

"Well," the Colonel continued, "if Elvis is bringing people to the box office, shouldn't he have a part of the business?"

"No, you just can't do it that way," Wallis protested. "That's not the way it's done."

The Colonel was immovable. "Then I guess you don't need us because you can do it another way," he said. He signaled to Elvis, and the two of them left Wallis's office. Several hours later, they received a call asking them to return.

"It's crazy, it's unheard of," Wallis groused, "but you've got a piece of the action."

Elvis made more money on his first movie than all the contract players at that studio put together and most of the stars. That first movie contract was a big, big deal to Elvis. In later years, he would own a full 50 percent of the net on his movies (which the Presley estate retains to this day). However, that wasn't the case with the early ones. He also told us that night about how he got together with the Colonel.

In 1955, Bob Neal, who was acting as Elvis's manager, was shopping for a better contract than Elvis had with Sam Phillips of Sun Records. Neal knew the Colonel from way back, so he called on him for advice.

"Is there any way you can help us get a better deal for Elvis?"

he asked. "He's got a bad deal with Sam Phillips, only 2.5 percent royalties."

"Let me try RCA," the Colonel offered. "But I've got to have some idea of the price Phillips wants for Elvis." Phillips wanted thirty-five thousand dollars for the master tapes and all rights. The Colonel called his friend Steve Sholes, a vice president in RCA's record division. "Five thousand is the best we can pay," Sholes said. The Colonel called Bill Bullock, another RCA vice president. "Colonel, I think he's going to be great," Bullock said, "but we've never put up more than fifteen thousand. That's all we'll go." The Colonel negotiated them up to twenty-five thousand dollars, then told RCA that if Phillips didn't receive a five-thousand-dollar deposit in cash or cashier's check by Friday, he couldn't hold off making another deal. RCA didn't take the bait. The Colonel withdrew his own funds from his bank and sent Phillips a five-thousand-dollar deposit. The next day, Saturday, he called the two RCA vice presidents at home.

"This is your last chance," he warned. This time they went for it.

"We'll be there Tuesday to make the deal." Phillips got his thirty-five thousand, and the Colonel was reimbursed. But the agreement stipulated that the money RCA paid to Phillips was only an advance on Elvis's future royalties. Elvis would have to pay RCA back, except for five thousand dollars they gave him for a car—the pink Cadillac that he presented to his mother, who couldn't drive. A few weeks after the agreement was made, the Colonel read an article in *Variety* stating that RCA had paid Elvis thirty-five thousand dollars, plus five thousand for a car. No mention was made of the fact that Elvis had to earn back that amount before he saw any income from the records he made. The Colonel got on the phone to George Merrick, the president of RCA corporation, who was in Hawaii.

"*Variety* called asking for my story about what your RCA people told them," he said to Merrick. "I'm going to have to tell them that Elvis has to pay the money back."

"I'll call you back in an hour," Merrick promised.

Less than sixty minutes later, the Colonel's phone rang. "Tell Elvis it's a bonus," Merrick said.

• • •

One of the most ridiculous rumors I've ever heard concerning Elvis and the Colonel was that the Colonel persuaded the U.S. Army to draft Elvis because he was wild and unmanageable. That night in Germany, Elvis told us that he was at the Beverly Wilshire Hotel in Hollywood with the Colonel when the draft notice was delivered to Graceland. Vernon called the Colonel and asked him to break the news to Elvis. Elvis asked the Colonel to announce it during dinner with his Hollywood cronies—Nick Adams, Vince Edwards, Jack Simmons, and other young actors. Certainly, there were times during the early days when the Colonel had to hunt down Elvis when he was supposed to be onstage. Usually he found him dreaming in a movie theater. But there was never any reason to lock Elvis away in the Army for two years, away from the stage and the studio where he could make money. Years later, when I asked the Colonel about the rumor, he laughed. "Why would a manager with thousands invested in his artist want to have that artist drafted?" the Colonel asked. "He would have to be crazy! No one could predict how two years in the Army would affect Elvis's career. The public could have easily forgotten him."

Thanks to the Colonel's tireless and inventive promotion throughout Elvis's Army stint, by the time he was discharged, he was more popular than ever, even though he had recorded only once during his entire tour of duty. That session was arranged during one of Elvis's weekend passes, from June 10 to June 12 in 1958, in Nashville, Tennessee. D. J. Fontana, Elvis's drummer, was the only musician at the session from the original group of musicians that disbanded when Elvis was drafted. The new musicians were recruited from the top sidemen at the time: Chet Atkins and Hank "Sugarfoot" Garland on guitar, Floyd Cramer on piano, Bobby Moore on bass, and Buddy Harmon on bongos and drums. The Jordanaires sang backup. In one night, they recorded five songs that would become smash hits: "I Need Your Love Tonight," "A Big Hunk of Love," "Ain't That Loving You Baby," "A Fool Such As I," and "I Got Stung." They were released during Elvis's two years in the Army along with other tunes like "Hard Headed Woman," "One Night," and "King Creole" that he had recorded in 1958, before he was drafted.

My favorite of the showbiz tales Elvis recounted that night didn't concern the Colonel. It was about Elvis's affair with the movie star Natalie Wood, the breathtaking brunette with large, melting brown eyes and a petite, exquisitely proportioned figure. "I went to bed with Natalie Wood," was how he put it. One morning, he had to play a sad scene in the movie he was making at the time, but he had trouble projecting that emotion. "You know, guys," he confided to the film crew, "I'm having trouble acting sad, because last night I was in bed with Natalie Wood. How can you be unhappy after that?"

"E," Red broke in suddenly. He'd just returned from a brief foray out to the gate where he checked out that night's crop of fans. "There's a USO hostess out there who is heading out to Berlin tomorrow. She'd really like to see you, maybe get an autograph." He winked broadly and turned to escort the girl into the room. We drew in a collective breath. She was stunning, darkly beautiful, a taller version of Natalie Wood, no less. Elvis leaped karate style from his armchair and met her halfway across the room. He flashed the smile, shook her hand, and drawled another charmingly bashful introduction: "Hello, I'm Elvis Presley. Glad to meet you." I'd never thought people could blush all the way down to their ankles, but this girl did. If the scene had been from a movie, the soundtrack would have swelled with girl-meets-boy violins.

Clearly overcome, she sat down quickly next to me. We smiled at each other and introduced ourselves. Her name was Sue Anderson. "I like this life," I thought to myself. Elvis picked up the thread of his Hollywood stories with even greater energy.

"Yeah, there are some weird people out there," he said. "But there are some great ones, too. Robert Mitchum is one of the good guys." Elvis abandoned his chair to stand in the center of the room. "Mitchum came over to see me on the set one day after he heard I'd been drafted. 'I've got some advice for you, Elvis,' he told me. 'Don't go. Just don't go. If I were in your shoes, at the top of your career and getting hotter, there's no way they could get me in the Army. I'd hide as long as I could. When they caught me, I'd grab hold of the wooden rail on my front porch so hard that it would take the medics weeks to pull all the splinters from under my nails.' " Elvis accompanied the story with a comical imitation of Mitchum showing him how to hang on for dear life.

"Another piece of advice Mitchum gave me was to make up stories for reporters," Elvis continued. " 'Never tell the truth and never tell the same lie twice,' he said. 'Just make up any old story. Those reporters will make up most of the stuff anyway. You might as well have fun with them.' " Elvis laughed as he recounted some of the fabrications Mitchum had passed on to reporters over the years. "He'd tell them one time that he was an orphan and was not going to give up until he found out the truth about his parents. Another time he said his dad spent most of his life in prison. Still another, he said he'd been in prison himself, as had his wife. Anything that came into his head during the interview was fine.

"Mitchum is right," Elvis concluded. "I hate to give interviews because they talk with you for an hour, then pick one little thing and make it the headline. This one female reporter really pissed me off. We must have talked for an hour about my music, about where I think we're headed with rock 'n' roll, how I feel about movies, and on and on. The last question she asked was what books I'd been reading lately. I told her I didn't get much time to read because of my heavy schedule. When the story came out, the headline read 'Elvis Doesn't Like to Read Books.' Isn't that a kick in the ass?" he concluded, slapping the heel of his boot for emphasis.

"Hey, Charlie," he interrupted himself. "Let's do some gospel." Charlie Hodge was a soft-hearted, good ole boy from Decatur, Alabama, about five foot two but well-built for his size. Charlie had been in show business all his life, singing in gospel and country groups. He was based in another town not too far from us and visited on weekends. As Elvis walked back to the piano, he directed a smile at Sue. The Robert Mitchum story was designed to warm Sue up; the gospel music would melt her down. Charlie and Elvis sang a few selections, closing with "How Great Thou Art," his favorite. Elvis packed the lyrics with passion, ended by banging out a few chords, then stood up to stretch and yawn. He blew his nose once more, then announced that he'd better hit the sack. Tomorrow was going to be an early day because his unit was doing a special field exercise.

"Red said you wanted an autograph," he said to Sue. She blushed an even deeper scarlet. "Come back with me, and I'll find a photograph for you." She rose from her seat and wobbled on high heels around the hallway toward the bedrooms, and out of sight.

"Let's get some pizza," Lamar suggested to the group. "Anyone up for that? But I'm in tap city." Tap city was GI code for being broke. Most soldiers were in tap city from about midmonth until the next payday. It was only five days until payday, so few of us had money. But thanks to some gambling winnings, I had ready cash and volunteered to pay. Lamar then made sure that Elvis was busy with Sue and wouldn't be rejoining the group, and we headed out for Beck's Bar a few blocks away.

"Elvis is going to call in sick tomorrow," Lamar predicted confidently as we filed out the side door into the cold night. "He's going to say that he doesn't feel well and has to spend the day in bed. I don't blame him. Did you guys get a load of that USO girl? Man, if the guys back home knew we had that kind of stuff in uniform, they could knock off the draft. Guys would volunteer by the trainload."

A few hours later, I tiptoed quietly into my barracks room where I was sure George was sleeping soundly. I hadn't even switched on the lights when I heard, "Well, how did it go?"

"I thought you were sleeping!"

"Asleep, hell! What is Elvis really like?"

"Well, I couldn't get over how down to earth he is," I said. "He really made me feel at home, and he told us all about Hollywood. He invited me to play touch football next weekend. Why don't you come?"

"Man! Joe, that would be great," George enthused. I was too excited myself to fall asleep right away. I lay in my bunk, going over the events of the evening. I must have dreamed the whole thing, I concluded. How could I have been back there in Elvis Presley's living room, talking about movie stars, and still come away with the feeling of having hung out with an unassuming, regular guy?

chapter 2

parisian nights

football's team play, body contact, and release of energy help guys get to know each other quickly. Elvis and I really hit it off the next time we met, at his Sunday afternoon tag football game in a little park near his house. After that day, I became part of the group that gathered almost nightly in Elvis's living room and every Sunday afternoon on the soccer field. It included Elvis's Memphis buddies and new Army friends like Rex Mansfield and Charlie Hodge; my roommate George; and another Army buddy, Billy Greene.

We played football, joked around, and flirted with girls. Except to duck into the movies at another base, we rarely went out, and we never ate out with Elvis because he was a very particular eater—strictly meat and potatoes—and everything had to be well-done to the point of being charred. He refused to eat seafood because he'd never had it when he was young, and he loved to pick from everyone else's food. But God help you if you wanted something from his plate. He hated anyone touching his food, he once told me, because when he was small his cousins would come over and eat his food, and he'd leave the table hungry.

As I remember Elvis today and try to understand him, I realize how much his early life had shaped him, down to his eccentric eating habits. Elvis had been poor but overprotected and, as an only child, lonely. His mother made sure her son was well-raised, according to strong Christian ethics. The facts of his early life explain much about the man he became: his giddy, almost hedonistic enjoyment of material riches and his extravagant gifts to those who were as poor as he had been; his unfailing courtesy to everyone, regardless of wealth or class; his need to be surrounded by old friends with whom he felt comfortable; and his avoidance of powerful people and self-styled intellectuals.

"Man, I can't stand people who go around thinking they're better than someone else because they went to better schools or have more money or read the latest book," he once told me. Yet Elvis's withdrawn childhood personality masked a secret yearning for the limelight and for constant attention and approval.

"I love to get people excited," he confided. "I don't know where I got it, I don't know how long I'm gonna have it, but as long as I do, I want to spread it around. People need excitement and I can give it to them."

Elvis was crazy about a TV show of that time called *The Millionaire.* Each week an ordinary person with a problem answered a knock at his door to find a messenger in a suit who announced that he was presenting the person with one million dollars from an anonymous donor. The only string was that the recipient couldn't reveal the source of his sudden wealth. Naturally, every week the poor clod blew it by blabbing to someone. That show struck a chord in Elvis. "It doesn't take much to change someone's life," Elvis said, then related some of his own "shock treatments." One incident in particular stands out in memory.

"One day we were walking down the street in Beverly Hills and I started handing out one-hundred-dollar bills to total strangers," Elvis said. "No questions. Just hand them the bill. They looked up, recognized me, and in a few moments, a crowd had formed. Each time we had to hightail it out of there before a riot broke out. I got a big kick out of their expressions, though. Man, you know they were telling their friends and families about that for weeks, maybe months. God, but I love those double takes!"

When I first met him, I thought Elvis was generous because he needed to buy friends, that his bursts of generosity were a way to shake off loneliness. But now I think differently. Elvis didn't pass out money just to massage his ego. He got a genuine thrill from making people happy, and he was always a bit amazed at the public's reaction to his presence. He couldn't resist testing it every so often. Elvis wanted to make a difference in people's lives, especially his fans, to whom he was always grateful. He often said that if it weren't for them, he would still be driving a truck.

"My fans expect me to do the things they wish they could do—if they'd had the breaks I have," he said. "A lot of my fans have a rough life. They see me as someone who was lifted from poverty and dropped in a world of glamour and excitement. My job is to share that glamour and excitement with them. When I'm onstage, I want to create excitement. I want each person to feel I'm performing for him or her, and even when I'm offstage, the show goes on. The clothes I wear, the cars I drive, my style of living—they're all part of what my fans expect from me."

"Most people get kicked around in life," he continued. "They just don't get the breaks. I love the idea of overwhelming a total stranger with a gift like a new car, just because they happened to be nearby. It's an incredible kick. No drug can get you as high. It's the same thing I feel when I'm onstage and every eye is on me. I'm giving it all I've got and they're loving every move, every sound. Man, there's nothing better!"

Every Sunday we strolled a few blocks to the football field. I loved the ritual of preparing for the games. We always started the afternoons in the living room, shooting the breeze. At about 2:00 P.M., Elvis would duck into his bedroom and reappear a few moments later wearing a black sweatshirt. A small white handkerchief tied around his neck added that extra touch of style, equivalent to his raised shirt collars. He was always on the black team because he thought that was a hip color then. Years later, he came to prefer white because of its spiritual connotations. The sweatshirts were always piled along the entrance hallway, next to several duffel bags full of fan mail that arrived daily. Elvis recruited me for his team in that first game. "Here, Joe," he said. "Grab a black shirt." Then we walked to the soccer field that stood in the shadows of the large buildings that housed Bad Nauheim's healing baths. On Sundays, the town's pace slowed, and the audience for our games never numbered more than fifty people.

We got going at about two-thirty. Elvis always played quarterback, and particularly enjoyed mapping out the plays. One of the players, Billy Greene from Philadelphia, was a world-class soccer player who played on the All Army Soccer Team in the Pan Am trials. He inspired Elvis to inject a little soccer strategy into our football game that day.

"Hey, Bill," Elvis said in the huddle. "Here's a crazy idea that'll knock them out. You drop back from the line of scrimmage and I'll toss a short pass off to you. Then, you kick it across the field to me as I'm heading down the sideline."

It worked! Elvis caught the kick and ran in for a touchdown. There was a lot of bitching among the white team, but the guys in the black sweatshirts, who were laughing their way up the field, insisted that the play counted. Whenever Elvis made up the rules, everyone went along, especially if laughs were involved.

For the most part, Elvis played seriously. As with everything else he developed a passion for, however fleeting, he had to be the best. Elvis was a true competitor. He wanted to be the best football player, and sometimes seemed to think he actually was. He wasn't a natural athlete, but he became damn good, because he played for hours and hours until he found his special talent. His greatest assets were his heart and guts. He could throw the ball really well, but he wasn't a runner. Elvis wasn't a great blocker either, but he went in there and got knocked on his butt, then jumped right back up. Everyone always made a big deal about every move Elvis made and was careful not to scratch his face or injure him in any way. After the games, we would go back to the house to drink Cokes and order pizzas.

During the week, Elvis performed all the duties expected of any ordinary GI, except one. He never had to endure mail call, which for me was one of the worst aspects of Army life. Everyone gathered around the mail clerk as he read off names in no particular order. You hoped for at least one letter, maybe even a parcel. But as each person received his mail, the crowd gradually dwindled, along with your hopes. Finally, if you had no mail that day, you found yourself standing with one or two others, trying to act nonchalant. After the last name was called, the clerk headed back for the mail room. The losers in the mail call game had to walk past guys with faces buried in letters from loved ones, while we consoled ourselves with lines like, "Ah hell. I wasn't expecting any mail anyway. I haven't been writing, so it's no surprise that I don't get mail."

An Army mail clerk told me that Elvis often received more mail in a day than the entire Thirty-second Armor Unit together, nearly one thousand men! I couldn't help but comment that first Sunday on the amazing volume. "Yes, the fans really want to help me by keeping in touch," Elvis said. "Man, I may not be the best singer in the world, but I sure have the best fans. I hope they'll remember me after all these months. Man, there's no way I could possibly read all that mail, let alone answer it. I'll read some of the letters, but some are a little weird."

I asked what he meant, so he showed me a letter from a fan in Belgium who wrote that Elvis was the Messiah sent to save the world. Elvis shook his head after I read it. "Yeah, man. This isn't the only letter that talks about me being the Messiah. I don't know where they get that stuff. Hell, I'm just a singer who got some breaks. I'm no Messiah. It's weird. I don't know where they get that stuff."

Elvis kept that letter, and I'm certain he read it more than once. As I got to know him better, I realized that he did have a sense of being anointed somehow. Why me? he constantly asked himself and others. The question would bother him more and more as time passed.

I didn't have the answer, not that day and not now, but like everyone around him, I knew Elvis was special. He had an edge, a provocative intensity reminiscent of James Dean. Elvis had that warm, boyish smile, but he wasn't the kind of guy you ran up to and slapped on the back. Sharing his space was like stepping into the eye of a hurricane: He was a core of deceptive calm that retains a charge of electricity because a storm rages just outside and around it.

Elvis had just begun to study karate when I met him. He had read something about the martial arts, and Lamar contacted a German instructor named Jürgen Seydel, whom we called George. He gave Elvis lessons at the house, and we all became involved in it to some extent, but Elvis got into it whole hog. Karate made him feel tough, though it was mostly show; it gave him the self-confidence he'd lacked as a kid. "Oh, yeah, I could kill this guy in a minute, you know," he boasted. It felt good to be able to say it.

Elvis picked up another of his macho interests, guns, in the Army. Although my Army records showed I had a perfect score with the carbine, it wasn't true. We were both fair-to-middling shots. There are many rules in the Army, and my job as a clerk in the Twenty-seventh Artillery required me to qualify at firing the carbine. When I was in training at Fort Hood, my job called for me to have an M1 rifle, the standard killing machine for most soldiers at the time. I qualified as a marksman with an M1.

One day in Germany, we got word that all the clerks had to go out to a rifle range and qualify with the carbine. The idea of leaving the office and hunkering down on the cold ground at the rifle range didn't appeal to anyone. But we followed orders and out we went. I couldn't have cared less whether I hit the target. Amazingly enough, instead of getting the white flag known as "Maggie's drawers"—a signal that the shot was a total miss—I got a signal that it was a bull's-eye. My slugs kept hitting the dust and the flags from the guys at the target zone kept signaling perfect shots. I guess the guys wanted to do me a favor, so I wound up with a perfect score in my record.

On my next visit to Elvis's house, I told him about my perfect carbine score. He was impressed, clearly interested in guns and my supposed skill with them. I could see Elvis doing mental calculations about me, the Italian kid from Chicago who turns out to be good with a gun. From then on, every so often Elvis would ask me questions about the Mafia. "Hey, Joe, do you know any of those Mafia guys from Chicago?" he'd ask. Or he'd make comments like, "Hell, I guess everyone in Chicago must be part of the Mafia."

Now that I think about it, I gave Elvis other reasons to link me with the Mafia. My buddy George and I liked bragging to Elvis about our gambling adventures—good filler material between his much more exciting Hollywood stories. Elvis embellished our anecdotes when he repeated them to others. The difference between what we did and what Elvis *said* we did was about as great as the difference between me hitting the dirt halfway to the target and the flag coming up bull's-eye. One day, a few of us got to talking about killing. Elvis looked me straight in the eye. "Joe, tell me the truth," he said. "Could you kill a man?" It seemed like a strange question coming from a guy wearing a military uniform and serving on foreign soil.

"Hell, yes," I answered. "We've been trained to kill. That's our job. I hope all of us are able to pull the trigger when the time comes. I'm ready."

"Bullshit aside," Elvis said. "Could you look a guy in the eye and blow him away?"

"If that's my job, then that's what I do," I replied. I thought he was talking about military duty. But now I realize Elvis was asking me a much larger question. I think he was asking a guy from Chicago whom he suspected of Mafia connections how he felt about killing someone. And the answer he heard was that if it was my job, I could kill. Just like the Mafia hit men. I'll never know, but I suspect Elvis asked me to work for him partly because he thought that if the situation called for it, I could be cold-blooded. He loved that notion; it fed straight into his hyperactive fantasy life.

He often asked me about the personal lives of Mafia bosses. He was particularly intrigued by the way they segmented their lives into neat compartments. "They have it made," he said. "They have a safe, comfortable family life with a respectable wife who takes care of the house and raises the kids. And they have a wild life with beautiful women, fast cars, and lots of excitement. Man, that's living." Elvis was fascinated with the Mafia's code of strict but contradictory ethics, one he would later adopt for himself. He wanted the wife, kids, the warm security of family life, and the pride of being the head of the household. And when he finally married, he didn't abandon his pursuit of the "wild life." All of us would live double lives then: Our wives and children in one carefully insulated compartment, while we cavorted all over the country with the many women who gathered around Elvis, attracted like gorgeous moths to his flame.

At times, Elvis even seemed to model his entire lifestyle on the Mafia, modifying it according to my reluctant answers to questions like, "Hey, Joe, how do you explain a godfather who thinks it's okay to make lots of money from illegal gambling, prostitution, and loan sharking, but it's not okay to deal drugs?"

"You're asking me?" I usually responded. "How do I know what goes through anybody's mind?"

But he kept after me. "No bullshit, Joe. You know those guys, why do they draw the line at making money off drugs? Hell, I hear there's lots of money to be made."

"Maybe the difference is that people don't get hurt as much, except for broken knees, when dealing with gambling, prostitution, and loans," I offered. "Drugs can do a lot of damage."

Elvis had a dark sense of humor, and the idea of broken knees struck him as comical. For the moment, he was satisfied with my explanation. But he returned to that subject from time to time. I suspect our conversations helped him draw his own boundaries, and later, create the rationalization for his own drug abuse. Elvis knew the sordid tragedy and humiliation of being part of a family that had suffered from the effects of drinking. Both parental lines were studded with alcoholics, and his mother died of liver disease after a lifetime of heavy drinking. The result was that Elvis was as adamant a teetotaler as a Puritan, even though he later became addicted to prescription drugs. In his mind and in the minds of many others, including doctors, prescription drugs were okay. Street drugs and alcohol were not.

Although we always had fun, Elvis often seemed keyed up, almost tense. He either sat in that characteristic ankle-over-the-knee pose, his foot wiggling as he talked, or he roved around the room, pausing briefly to fiddle with various objects. Because he was trying to calcify his knuckles for karate-style board chopping, he often interrupted his monologue to bang his hand on a wooden table or another hard surface. That never failed to inspire another story about a master who destroyed various objects with a single karate chop. One night he told us about a guy who was so good he could slice the horn off a charging bull. Whether or not that was true, Elvis vowed, "That's what I'm going to do, I want to be that good!"

The nightly group sings by the piano were Elvis's only vocal practice. One night, after yet another rendition of "Mona Lisa," Elvis worked himself up into yet another fury over not being able to record the song. He struck the piano keys with increasing force, his eyes turning to slits and his face growing redder and redder. Then he flung an ashtray against the wall. It was one of the few times in the early days that I witnessed the volatile Presley temper, a sudden storm that usually cleared as quickly as it came on.

"It was too fucking late," he muttered as he sat down and recommenced banging away on the piano keys. "And this is my kind of music!"

Aside from playing piano and singing during our nightly bull sessions, Elvis didn't perform before an audience during his entire two years in the Army. There was one notable exception I'll never forget: Christmas 1959. Elvis decided to invite me and a small group of regulars to a special Christmas party held in a small but pleasant social room in a building the Army rented in Bad Nauheim for Special Forces whose dependents resided off-base. The star of the first part of the show was Charlie Hodge. Charlie played the piano and guitar and sang, occasionally getting one or two of us to join in. Elvis sat with me and a few others at a table, thoroughly enjoying Charlie's performance and urging him on with comments like "Hey, Charlie, do the one about Santa hanging his balls on the Christmas tree!" Then Elvis stepped onstage to join him.

They jammed together on gospel duets and whatever else they felt like singing. It was the first time I'd seen Elvis perform on a stage, and he was truly magnificent. Everyone, onstage and off, was having a great time. Charlie and Elvis finished their performance, then someone put a stack of forty-fives on the turntable. A few guys and girls started to dance. I rarely saw Elvis dance offstage in all the years I knew him, but that night he put in a few hours on the dance floor, slow dancing and jitterbugging. I was surprised to notice that Elvis's jitterbug style was rather clumsy. Onstage, his feet, legs, arms, and head all moved in time with the music. But when he danced with a girl, Elvis seemed to lose touch with the rhythm. Not that his dance partners cared a bit. They were dancing with Elvis.

The highlight of the party was a surprise distribution of gifts from Elvis. The guys each received a beautiful, personally engraved Ronson butane lighter, the Varaflame model, which still looks sharp today, even after thirty years. Most of us smoked at the time, so it was the perfect gift. Mine read: "To Joe from Elvis. Christmas 1959."

The party was such a success that we arranged to hold Elvis's birthday party in the same room a few weeks later, on January 8, 1960. Charlie began the show again, and, after a little while, Elvis joined in. We hadn't known what to give the guy who had everything, but we finally gambled that a trophy recognizing his skill at football might be the perfect gift. About ten of us pooled our money for a total of thirty-five dollars spent on a birthday present for the most famous person in the world. We bought a trophy and had it engraved, and I was elected to present the gift. I performed my duty with a bit of fanfare, but it was a risk. If he didn't like the idea of a trophy, putting him on the spot would make a bad situation worse. I gambled and called for everyone's attention as Elvis came forward to accept the gift.

"On behalf of the Bad Nauheim Sunday Afternoon Football Association, I'd like to present you with this trophy as the most valuable player," I announced. Elvis read the inscription aloud: "ELVIS PRESLEY. MOST VALUABLE PLAYER. BAD NAUHEIM SUNDAY AFTERNOON FOOTBALL ASSOCIATION. 1959."

Elvis beamed a huge smile. The group broke into loud applause.

"Man, I couldn't be happier with any gift," said Elvis. He was so carried away by the spirit of the occasion that he made an impromptu acceptance speech ending with: "Even if you gave me a new Cadillac, you couldn't make me happier than I am now." He held the trophy high, like an Academy Award winner. "This is going to get a special place in my trophy room at Graceland!" he promised.

Not long after his birthday party, Elvis went on maneuvers, the field trips where soldiers sleep outdoors and play Army games. Of course, as clerks, George and I seldom went. A few days after he left, we heard that Elvis had been hospitalized. Apparently, it had rained heavily the night before and there had been a strong wind. Elvis had pulled his poncho over his head because he was in an open jeep. But he had kept the jeep running and was overcome by carbon monoxide. He had passed out, then slumped over and fallen out of the jeep into a pool of dirty water. Luckily, a gust of wind had blown the poncho off his head, and he was revived. He came down with a severe sore throat, and the Army doctors were concerned about the possibilities of bronchitis, carbon monoxide poisoning, and damage to his voice. Elvis was very prone to tonsillitis, so they talked about removing his tonsils. No one wanted to take responsibility for possibly damaging Elvis's priceless singing voice, so it was never done.

As soon as we got the news, George and I rushed to the hospital. Outside the room, the atmosphere was funereal. Everyone was serious and somber, warning us to visit for only one minute because Elvis was very weak and others wanted to see him. Fearing the worst, we opened the door gingerly.

Elvis was propped up on a nest of pillows, smiling and perky. Pretty nurses swarmed around his bedside, giving him massages and ministering to his every need. The impression I got was that he wanted to shorten our visit not for the sake of his health, but to allow him more time with the nurses. For the three or four days he was in the hospital, he actually had affairs with nurses in his room. He never explicitly said so, but the expressions on his and the nurses' happy faces spoke volumes.

Aside from the nurses, there were two other primary sources of women for Elvis. One was the visitors who, by prior arrangement, joined the group. Either the guys brought them to meet Elvis or they were picked up at the local beer gardens. Then there were the thirty to a hundred people—mostly women—always outside Elvis's gate. I remember a pair of beautiful blond sisters who came over from England and rented a room in the house next door just to be near Elvis. It wasn't long before they were plucked from the crowd. That night at around ten o'clock, Elvis faked a yawn with a devilish expression. "I guess I'll hit the sack," he announced. "I've got a big day tomorrow." Then he disappeared. The sisters knew by prior eye contact that they were the chosen ones, so they followed him into the bedroom. On other occasions, if the girl didn't get the message, Red said something like, "Elvis wants to see you for a second." But those sisters definitely got the message. "Man," Elvis said the next day, "It's crazy!" But he never revealed what went on in there. Elvis rarely went into details about his sex life. "It must have been great for you as a single guy to have all these fantastic girls available," guys have said to me over the years. But in the Army days at least, it wasn't. As I read the social interaction among Elvis, the girls, and the Memphis buddies, this was a lose-lose situation for the guys. Elvis said he would never go after a girl who liked someone else because it was unfair competition. What girl would choose Joe Esposito if she could be with Elvis Presley? If a girl seemed to like one of his friends or vice versa, Elvis ruled her out of that night's competition, and she realized pretty quickly that she was out of the running for Elvis. She could stay, but she wasn't going to be Elvis's girl. So the girls usually remained aloof toward us. It was okay. There were many other ways to find girls in Germany.

Though he wasn't too pleased about it, Elvis also attracted men. A so-called holistic doctor from South Africa named Monsieur Laurenz, whom we referred to by the considerably less grand "Larry," came to the house regularly to give Elvis massages, facials, and nutritional supplements. One day, he tried to seduce Elvis. Failing, he threatened to go to the media with a story that he and Elvis had had an affair. We later discovered that Larry had thought this would be a good way to raise money for his hair transplant operation! No one knew what to do, so Lamar called the Colonel in the States at two o'clock in the morning, and Elvis got on the line to ask the Colonel to take care of the situation. I don't know how, but the Colonel squashed the sleazy blackmail attempt.

At heart, Elvis was an innocent. Overprotected by his mother, labeled strange by his peers because of his long hair and weird clothing, he was suddenly transformed at age nineteen into an international superstar and a fabulously wealthy man. In an instant, it seemed, he became an object of passion for millions of women and a figure of envy for an equal number of men. Now money was for spending and women were for getting. This was never more apparent to me than during the trip Elvis, Lamar, Cliff Gleaves, Jürgen (Elvis's karate instructor), and I took to Paris right after his birthday in 1960, ostensibly so Elvis could study karate with a renowned Korean instructor named Murakami Tetsuji, who taught at Paris's Club Yoseikan.

The first time I assumed the role of organizer of Elvis's life was just before that leave in Paris. We were about to leave for the train, when Elvis couldn't find his military identification card. He couldn't cross the border without it, so I raced over to the office where I worked, typed out a fake card, and signed the commanding officer's name. As we walked out the door, his father handed all the money to me and asked me to keep an account of our expenses. I paid all the bills in Paris—hotel, restaurants, and shows. When we got back to Germany, I turned over all the receipts to Vernon. He was thrilled to death. He finally got receipts for his money, the first time ever.

We had a private compartment on the train, and when we arrived at the station in Paris, we spotted two generals hailing a cab. Barely concealing our laughter, we saluted them as we—a bunch of draftees—climbed into a limousine and drove through the streets of Paris to the Hôtel de Galles. Here I was, a twenty-two-year-old high school dropout who'd never been out of Chicago until the Army took me out, luxuriating in a magnificent suite of rooms on the top floor of the finest hotel in Paris. "Order anything you want," Elvis said, flashing that crooked grin and executing a grand sweep of his arm. "Just order."

Elvis instructed me to make reservations for the famed Lido show. A few German girls we knew from Frankfurt happened to be in Paris, as was another Army friend, Currie Grant, and we took them along. Elvis put on his blue dress uniform, proud to be a soldier. The rest of us didn't own dress uniforms, so we wore regular suits. As we were leaving the hotel, I noticed the lobby was filling with young girls. Word had gotten out that Elvis was staying at the Hôtel de Galles. But the girls didn't bother him, they just kept their distance and watched us leave. Elvis asked the driver to give us a little tour of Paris before we went to the Lido. "Look, Joe," he said, reaching from his backseat to the front and tapping my head, "there's the Eiffel Tower." The highest-paid tour guide in the world was showing me Paris, the City of Light, the most romantic city in the world! We drove past Notre Dame Cathedral. "Hey, let's stop and see if the Hunchback's home," Elvis suggested. The chauffeur thought Elvis's remarks were very funny.

After an hour's sightseeing, we arrived at the Lido, where the manager was waiting to escort us to our stageside center table. Everyone's eyes were on Elvis. It drove home what I'd nearly forgotten, that my Army buddy was a world-class celebrity—a strange feeling. We were mesmerized by the procession of long-stemmed, bare-breasted beauties onstage. Throughout the show, I noticed the dancers kept glancing at our table, stealing looks at Elvis. He leaned across to me.

"What do you think of the show so far?" he asked.

"I keep thinking this is just a wonderful dream and I'm going to wake up any time now," I told him truthfully.

"This is only the beginning, Joe," he said. He was getting a big kick out of my enjoyment.

Of course, we went backstage to meet the showgirls and the singer, Lynne Renauld, whose voice Elvis loved. The girls were thrilled to meet Elvis. To our surprise, half of them turned out to be English. "What are you girls doing after the show?" we asked. They usually frequented Le Bantu, a female impersonator club, they said, so we invited all thirty of them to meet us there after their second show.

Le Bantu was a showbiz dive, packed from stem to stern with even more gorgeous women than the Lido. Unfortunately, they all turned out to be expert female impersonators, including one of the most beautiful creatures I'd ever seen. As we sat around talking, a few of us, especially Cliff Gleaves, were knocking back drinks.

"Elvis, don't you want a drink?" I asked.

"Order me a Coke," he said.

"Don't you want a real drink?"

"No, I don't drink alcohol."

"Not even a beer?"

"No," he said. "My relatives drink enough for me. I saw too many drunks in my younger days. That's why you'll never see alcohol in my house. I don't allow it."

I thought about it, and realized that I hadn't seen any alcohol in the house, not even a beer.

"I don't like to drink myself," I told Elvis. I could still remember getting drunk on beer with some neighborhood boys one night, then going home and crawling into bed as the room spun.

At the other end of the table, Cliff was clearly feeling no pain as he grabbed a chair next to a magnificent girl and set about getting acquainted, whispering sweet nothings and nibbling on her ear. When the Lido chorus girls arrived, one of them said to Elvis, "You know, the girl your friend is talking to is not a girl. It's one of the impersonators." Cliff was having a great time, so we enjoyed the romantic scene playing out before us for several moments before Elvis finally told someone to break the news to lover boy. When

Cliff learned he was romancing a man, he jumped from his chair as if he'd been electrocuted, knocking it over. "Get away from me!" he screamed. "Don't touch me! Don't touch me!" Elvis and the rest of us were doubled over, hooting and screaming with laughter.

The Lido girls were between eighteen and twenty-one years old, and lived together in a dormitory. We were having such a great time that they missed their 1:00 A.M. curfew. They couldn't go home, we had a commodious suite, so we gallantly invited them back. We ordered up food, had a good time, and then, whatever happened, happened. I took a beauty from the Lido to bed. Elvis went off to his room with Nancy Parker, an American redhead who ice-skated in the show. Cliff probably talked some girl's ear off. Lamar went to sleep with the newspaper. Jürgen was married, so he slept alone. Of course, there were too many girls, so the extras slept on the couches, chairs, and floor. When I woke up and wandered into the living room, gorgeous women were draped all over the place. As I stepped over their slumbering bodies, I thought I'd died and gone to heaven.

The next morning, we went sightseeing in the limousine. Elvis never went with us, so someone always stayed back in case he needed something. We returned to pick up Elvis for his late-afternoon karate instruction, and then we did some more sightseeing. In the evening we returned to the hotel to prepare for another night of hitting the clubs. I went downstairs to get cigarettes for myself and cigars for Elvis. In the lobby, I spotted a beautiful French woman with dark hair and striking blue eyes sitting in a chair, reading a newspaper. I summoned up my nerve to introduce myself and told her I was on leave from Germany. Her name was Nicole, and she accepted my offer for a drink in the hotel bar. She said she worked as a secretary in Paris and was visiting a friend at the hotel. We chatted for about twenty minutes, and I mentioned I was stationed in Friedberg.

"Isn't that where Elvis Presley is stationed?" she asked casually.

"Yes," I answered, but I wanted her to like me even if I wasn't associated with Elvis. "I see him around the base once in a while," I lied. Then I asked her, "What are you doing tonight?"

"Nothing special."

"How would you like to join me and some friends for dinner and the Lido show?"

"That sounds like fun," she said. I excused myself and said I would be back to pick her up in about thirty minutes. When I got to the suite, I told Elvis excitedly about the young woman and asked if it was okay to bring her along.

"Sure," he said. "No problem."

"She's down in the lobby," I said. "I told her we'd be down in about thirty minutes." I went to my room and sprayed on extra aftershave.

That night Elvis was dressed to kill in his black mohair suit with a white shirt and red tie. We all wore black suits. In fact, our group resembled the Mafia more than a bunch of GIs. We strolled over to where Nicole was sitting in the lobby, and I introduced her to everyone. Her mouth fell open when I presented Elvis. "Nice to meet you," Elvis said politely. Cliff elbowed me in the ribs. "Not bad!" he whispered. Nicole took my arm as we left the hotel, and we all piled into the limo. As we sat at our table—Nicole between Elvis and me—eating dinner and making small talk, I noticed the manager approach Elvis and whisper in his ear. Five minutes later, Elvis excused himself, saying he wanted a word with me in private. We left the table and went into the WC.

"Joe, I've got something to tell you," Elvis said. All sorts of possibilities went through my head, but I knew it had something to do with Nicole. Maybe she was a lady of the night, or maybe she wasn't even a lady!

"The manager just told me that Nicole is a reporter for a big Paris newspaper," Elvis said with a pained expression. He didn't want to hurt my pride. "She's just here to get a story. I'm sure you didn't know, but these things happen around me all the time."

I tried to hide my stung feelings as I apologized to Elvis. "I'll take care of this right away," I promised. Elvis patted me on the back like a big brother, and we walked together to our table to finish dinner. It was hard not to say anything to Nicole, but I was cool. Elvis was great, even extra nice to her. After the show was over, Elvis signed a few autographs for American tourists, and everyone went backstage. I told Nicole I needed to talk to her alone and walked her out to the lobby. We sat down on a couch.

"Nicole, are you a newspaper reporter?" I asked in a normal tone of voice. I was determined that she not see how angry and hurt I was.

"Why do you ask?" she responded guardedly.

"Someone told me," I said. "You said you were a secretary, so apparently you didn't want me to know. You knew that if you had told me, I wouldn't have asked you out. Goodbye, it was nice talking with you." I left her there in the lobby and went backstage where Elvis was talking with some girls and Lynne Renauld in her dressing room. He looked at me as I entered the room and I gave him the high sign. Elvis winked back and I felt better.

We carried on in Paris for nine days straight. Every night the Lido or the Crazy Horse, then meeting the dancers back at Le Bantu. Every night, a different beautiful woman. We all switched partners, but no one dared to hit on Elvis's girls.

Poor Lamar had a hard time getting laid.

"We've got to get him a hooker," Elvis decided after several scoreless days had passed. I called downstairs to the concierge. "Hey, I've got a friend who would like a female companion for the evening," I informed the concierge, rather smoothly, I thought. A half-hour later there was a knock at the door. I opened it to find a stunning nineteen-year-old French girl. She spoke very little English, but when she spotted Elvis, she rushed over and smothered him with kisses.

"Wait, wait, don't do this!" I protested and pointed in the direction of Lamar. "You're for *him!*"

The girl wouldn't take her hands off Elvis, and she flatly refused to go with Lamar. Of course, Elvis didn't want anything to do with her because it would have killed Lamar. So I paid her off and hustled her out of the room. I really felt bad for Lamar.

After nine wonderful days, we boarded the train for Germany to finish two months of service. At one point, Elvis and I were alone in the compartment. Lamar and Cliff were in the dining car and Jürgen was already asleep.

"I don't know how to thank you for taking me to Paris with you," I said. "That was the experience of a lifetime. I could get used to that kind of living very easily." I was already wondering how I was going to return to the life I'd loved so much in Chicago. From the perspective of Paris with Elvis, it seemed dull and humdrum.

"Yeah," Elvis agreed, "but even that gets old after a while."

"Elvis," I began tentatively, "I have a personal question for you, but you don't have to answer if you don't want to."

"Shoot."

"Well, you've been with so many girls. Have you ever gotten one pregnant?"

He smiled. "First of all, Joe," he said, "if I'd slept with every woman the movie magazines say I have, I would have been dead a long time ago. Before I went into the Army, there were three different girls who claimed I made them pregnant. A couple of them even claimed they'd had abortions. But I didn't get them pregnant."

"How do you know for sure?"

"Whenever I'm making love, I make sure I don't come in them. I pull out in plenty of time. If I knew for sure that the girl was having my baby, I would never let her have an abortion. I don't think I would marry her unless I was in love, but I'd make sure the baby got whatever it needed." Despite his sexual escapades, Elvis had a disarming naïveté when it came to women and sex. Deep down, he believed sex and fatherhood were for marriage. He wasn't ready for marriage, though. Not by a long shot. I don't think he ever was. But he already knew who he would marry when that day came.

Fourteen-year-old Priscilla Beaulieu had entered Elvis's life several months before our leave in Paris. They were introduced by Elvis's Air Force friend Currie Grant, in August 1959. Currie visited Elvis from time to time and even joined us for a few days in Paris. He was based in Wiesbaden, where Priscilla's father, Captain Joseph Paul Beaulieu, was stationed, and he told Elvis about this gorgeous fourteen-year-old brunette he'd love Elvis to meet. "Sure, why not?" Elvis said, so Currie brought Priscilla over one evening. I'll never forget it. She entered the room, wearing a little blue sailor outfit with a white collar that has been written about many times, her long brown hair curled in ringlets. Elvis jumped up to introduce himself. "Where have you been all my life?" he teased with a sweet smile. Priscilla didn't look as young as fourteen, but no more than sixteen. She was pretty smart, too, but naturally, she didn't say much that night. She was very quiet, very nervous, and clearly felt out of place.

Elvis did his best to put Priscilla at ease. She sat next to him on the piano bench as he serenaded her. They talked alone in his room for a few hours, and then Currie took her home. From then on, Currie, Lamar, or I picked Priscilla up in Wiesbaden several nights a week. Elvis and Priscilla spent hours alone in his bedroom, kissing, caressing, and talking. But after she left, Elisabeth took her place in Elvis's bed.

Priscilla's father (who is actually her stepfather) was a true military man. He was understanding, up to a point. Both Elvis and Priscilla had to work hard to convince Captain Beaulieu that they were just friends. Priscilla never spent the night, but she did arrive home late, often at one or two in the morning. They were just playing music, she assured her anxious parents, and, besides, Elvis was a night person. They might date seriously down the road, but nothing was going on. Elvis could talk anyone, particularly female, into anything.

Every Sunday afternoon, Priscilla sat by herself on the sidelines watching the football games. I still have that image clear in my head. I've never seen anyone before or since so absolutely fragile and beautiful, like a precious China doll. Elvis handled Priscilla with great tenderness and delicacy. But I remember one comment that veered from his usual reverence. "She's a beautiful girl," he said, "I wouldn't lay a hand on her." Then he added, "But to have her sit on your face!" Their "affair" continued for approximately four months, until Elvis was discharged from the Army. He liked Priscilla a lot, he told me. He thought she was gorgeous, and he hoped there could be a future to their relationship, but he couldn't be absolutely sure because she was so young.

A few weeks before he was scheduled to leave Germany, Elvis asked Elisabeth if she would work for him in Memphis. She declined the offer. Elisabeth had other plans. None of us had ever suspected that all the time she'd been living at Elvis's house, she'd been having an affair with Rex Mansfield. Elisabeth and Rex were too concerned about upsetting Elvis to let anyone know about their feelings for each other. Soon after we were all released, they married in the States, and we never saw them again. Elisabeth sent Christmas cards every year to Elvis's grandmother Minnie Mae, with whom she was very close, but the rest of us never heard a word.

By the time our group of Army buddies began dwindling away, as each finished his service and was sent home, Elvis and I had been friends for about six months. One dreary evening, Elvis asked me to take a ride with him. It had rained earlier, and the cobblestone streets of Bad Nauheim were slick. In the gray chill, the town looked like a set from an old Humphrey Bogart flick. Elvis's mood matched the town's. As he drove his white BMW 507 sports car through the streets, he expressed deep fears.

"I hope they remember me when I get back to the United States," he said doubtfully.

Just then, we came to a stoplight and pulled up next to a car full of Germans. They looked over and waved happily to Elvis, who, to their delight, waved back.

"See," I joked, "if they don't remember you back home, you could always come back here. They love you."

"I'm really going to miss Priscilla," Elvis went on. "She has been a godsend to me for the past few months. I don't know what I'm going to tell Anita when I get home. I know it's going to get out and the newspapers will have a field day."

"Well, I'm sure everything will work out for the best," I tried to assure him. Words of wisdom from a twenty-two-year-old. "E, what about your dad?" I asked. "Is he going to marry that woman Dee?"

Vernon had met Dee Stanley just as she was extricating herself from a troubled marriage to an Army sergeant also stationed in Germany. Dee was shapely, blonde, and certainly pretty enough. From the back, she looked like an eighteen-year-old. But she was an empty-headed flirt, who seemed too interested in Elvis.

"He told me that he wants to get married right after I'm discharged from the Army," Elvis said. He didn't seem happy at the prospect.

"What do you think of her?" I prodded. "I don't know her very well."

"I have my doubts," Elvis answered. "I think she's only marrying him because he's my daddy, but if she makes him happy, that's all I care about. There's one thing she'll never have to worry about."

"What's that?"

"I'll never call her Mom," Elvis said. Then he changed the subject. "What are you going to do after the Army?" he asked.

"Go back to Chicago and pick up where I left off."

"Would you like to work for me?" he asked.

I was thrilled. "Are you kidding?" I yelped. "Of course, I would love to. What would I do for you?"

"You could be my right-hand man," he said. He flashed me that grin. "The Chicago Mafia loses one. The Memphis Mafia gains one. Hey, that sounds pretty good. 'The Memphis Mafia.' Joe, you are now part of the Memphis Mafia. Hell, you *are* the Memphis Mafia. We'll have a lot of fun."

We laughed, but the name wasn't a bad idea. It would be a great way to signal the transplanting of a big-city Chicago guy to the old South. Plus Elvis enjoyed an entourage. It meant power and style from the outside, and even more important, it supplied the comfort of uninterrupted companionship. I told Elvis that night that within the real Mafia, respect for the boss was an absolute requirement. Any breach of respect, no matter how slight, was treated harshly. Elvis liked that. He had learned about respect from his parents. He never failed to show it to people at every level, and he demanded it in return. He knew he could count on me to base our relationship on respect, Mafia-style, and he could count on my loyalty, another critical Mafia element. Add to that my alleged killer instincts, and Elvis's not-so-secret desire to play godfather was fulfilled.

As Elvis savored the possibilities of donhood, my mind raced: Hollywood! John Wayne! Marilyn Monroe! Frank Sinatra! Beverly Hills! People and places I had only dreamed about, and Elvis was going to make it all come true for me! I couldn't wait to get back to base and tell George. By the time we returned to Elvis's house, he was in a lighter mood. I think it made him feel better to see how excited I was about working for him. About eight fans were waiting for him by the gate. We got out of the car, and Elvis stopped to sign autographs. I stood on his right, wearing an ear-splitting grin.

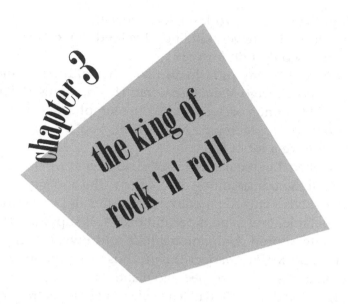

chapter 3

the king of
rock 'n' roll

I returned to Chicago, where my family threw a big welcome home party for me filled with the prettiest girls in the neighborhood. At first, I thought they were happy to see me, but I
realized all they wanted to know about was Elvis. The girl I'd left
behind informed me that she just wanted to be friends, but I sur-
vived. One night I went with some buddies to the corner pool hall
where the older guys had ignored me before I was drafted. Now
that I was the neighborhood celebrity, they all wanted to be my
friend. I realized that as long as I worked for Elvis, I would never
know whether people were being nice to me because they liked
me or because of my connection to Elvis. What the hell, I decided.
As long as they were being nice, who cares?

Elvis flew to Fort Dix for his formal discharge, then took a train
to Memphis where the Colonel had put together a gala welcome
home festival. Elvis hated press conferences, but he endured several, which I watched on television. The reporters plied Elvis with
questions about Priscilla. "I met this little girl named Priscilla, and

they made a big thing out of it. I liked her," he admitted with a shrug. "She was nice," he said. He refused to elaborate.

After Elvis had been home for a few days, I left for Memphis with my brother, Frank. It was my first plane trip ever! We arrived in Memphis on a beautiful sunny, cool afternoon. When we asked the taxi driver to take us to Graceland, he assumed we were fans. He pulled up to the famous tall iron gates embellished with musical notes and two iron likenesses of Elvis, and a gentleman asked what I wanted. I introduced myself. "They're expecting you," he said in a thick Tennessee drawl, then said he was Uncle Vester, Vernon's brother. "Just go to the front of the house, someone will meet you there." I thanked him and got back into the taxi. We drove up the long, circular driveway. At Graceland's front steps, Alberta, a large black lady with a warm smile who worked for Elvis as housekeeper/cook, was waiting to welcome me. I paid the stunned driver. "Tell Elvis welcome home," he managed to say.

Elvis had bought Graceland in 1957 for his parents. Today, the beautiful antebellum mansion is shaded by tall graceful trees. When I arrived at Graceland, the seedlings had yet to be planted. Frank and I grabbed our luggage and followed Alberta past four white Grecian pillars and through the front door. Elvis was upstairs sleeping, Alberta said, so she gave us a brief tour. As we walked through Graceland's foyer, I saw the formal dining room to the left with a large black marble table surrounded by six black-and-gold high-backed chairs. The carpeting was a plush white, and the floor directly under the table and chairs was tiled in black marble. To the right of the foyer was the living room, also carpeted in white and decorated in blue and white. The fireplace was white marble and smoked glass, and there was a plush white couch at least twenty feet long. At the far end was the music room, which Elvis had converted from the original owner's sun room. It featured a gleaming white baby grand piano. Alberta took us downstairs to show us another of Elvis's favorite relaxation spots, more private than the music room—a sumptuous two-room den he'd built in Graceland's basement. One room housed a pool table, which Alberta said he used often. The walls were covered with the many plaques and awards he'd received in his brief, meteoric career. The other room contained Elvis's huge collection of gold records, accentuated impressively by indirect lighting. Over the years, the garage would shelter hundreds of cars. Elvis also loved animals and accumulated a "zoo" that included at various times monkeys, a turkey named Bowtie, ducks, peacocks, parrots, myna birds, mules, dogs, horses, and a chimp named Scatter, who had his own house that was heated in winter and air-conditioned in the summer. If a pet died while Elvis was away, his father and the Graceland staff kept the news from him until his return.

After we toured the first floor and basement, Alberta showed us to our room on the second floor, near Elvis's bedroom. It was an ordinary room, decorated in Graceland's blue-and-white color scheme. We put our luggage on the twin beds, then went downstairs to the kitchen, where Alberta fried us a couple of hamburgers.

"Alberta, what time does Elvis get up?" I asked.

She laughed. "Mr. P. gets up whenever he wants to."

After lunch, Frank and I walked around the grounds. It was March, still winter, and nothing was very green yet. We strolled down to the kidney-shaped swimming pool, and Frank took pictures for our friends and family back home. Then we went to our room to unpack. At 4:00 P.M., Alberta knocked on our door. "Mr. P. is awake," she announced. "He will be downstairs in about thirty minutes." When Elvis came down, he was wearing a pair of black slacks and a sharp black-and-maroon sports shirt.

"Well, you made it!" he said with a big grin.

We shook hands, and I hugged him. I introduced Elvis to Frank. "Welcome to Graceland," Elvis said. "After I have some breakfast, I'll show you guys around the house."

"Go ahead and have your breakfast," I said. "We'll be in the kitchen."

"No, come into the dining room while I eat," he insisted. We followed him into the dining room and sat with him while he ate his bacon and eggs, talking all the while. Afterward, Elvis gave us a guided tour. We didn't mention we'd already seen the house while he was asleep. Frank stayed a few days, then flew back home to Chicago, leaving me to adjust to Elvis's inverted schedule, staying up all night and sleeping all day.

Beautiful women with charming southern accents swarmed all over Graceland, including Elvis's local steady, Anita Wood, a shapely, effervescent little blonde who worked as a radio disc jockey and television dance show host. Anita was curious about "this girl Priscilla saying goodbye to you at the airport and all the talk about her in the papers." Just another fan, Elvis told Anita, very nice but no big deal. In private, he confided his real feelings. "I miss Priscilla," he said. "I have to call her." He called Priscilla in Germany once in a while, but it would take a year and a half to persuade her parents to allow their daughter to visit him.

Elvis didn't know how to tell Anita about the girl he'd met in Germany. He was clearly in love with Priscilla, and I doubt he had ever been in love with Anita. She just happened to be his favorite girl at the time. Anita was pressuring him to get married, and that didn't help their relationship. But he didn't like to hurt people, and there was no convenient way to get out of this entanglement. He had never broken up with a girlfriend before.

Those first two weeks in Memphis flew by. Every night fifty to one hundred people came to the house to party on the patio behind the house, next to the swimming pool. A white wooden fence strung with red, blue, and chartreuse lights encircled the multi-leveled brick and flagstone patio and a pool lit from below by fluorescent chartreuse lighting. At one end of the patio stood tall, graceful columns. The guests sat on the lounge chairs scattered around or danced to the music pumped out of the large jukebox set against one wall. It wasn't unusual for one or two or more guests to wind up in the pool sometime after midnight. Elvis usually installed himself in a lounging chair at the front of the patio with Anita snuggled up to him.

We often ended an evening by renting the Memphian Theater after midnight in order to avoid autograph seekers and fans. The first time I went, I noticed that Elvis took his seat, and everyone sat behind him, never in front. We could just walk up to the refreshment counter and order what we wanted. Elvis took care of the tab, which averaged around four hundred dollars a night. He loved movies and watched his favorites over and over, reciting all the dialogue along with the actors. Other nights he rented the roller rink or Liberty Land, the local amusement park, and we rode the different amusements—especially the bumper cars—for six or seven hours until dawn. He was making up for lost time, two years in Germany and an entire childhood. Whatever Elvis wanted to do, he did. Whatever he wanted to buy, he bought. We were our own crowd, and together we enjoyed movies, the bumper cars at the amusement park, and roller skating at the rink. We returned to Elvis's childhood with him, and as his playmates, we had a great time fulfilling the fantasy of a childhood that should have been.

As the sole Yankee in Elvis's court, I was not exactly welcomed with open arms. But the Memphis boys and I learned quickly to get along. Besides me, the only people put on payroll after the Army were Elvis's cousin Gene Smith, Lamar Fike, and Sonny West, Red's good-looking, slightly calmer cousin. I replaced Gene, who had grown up dirt poor in Tupelo just like Elvis. Elvis trusted his cousin, so Gene accompanied Elvis on the road during the first few years of his career. In those early days, if you wanted to get to Elvis, you had to go through Gene. The problem was that Gene didn't talk very well, and Elvis's situation became too sophisticated for him. In addition, Gene was a strange guy. He always carried a brief-case, which is normal in itself, but if you opened it, all you'd find inside were door handles and pliers.

Vernon was often at Graceland, but since his marriage on July 3, 1960, he lived in a house near Graceland with Dee and her three boys, David, Rick, and Billy. Elvis liked Rick, the middle son. Billy, the oldest, was a colorless personality and overattached to his mother. David, the youngest, resented Elvis because he over-heard him putting down his mother. Of course, Dee tried to force the other two on Elvis, which didn't help. Vernon was a tall, lean, handsome man, with a long, chiseled face crowned by a mane of distinguished-looking silver hair. Everyone said Elvis looked just like his mother, but as I came to know them, I realized that Elvis's smile and many of his mannerisms were inherited from his father. A lot of the guys were imitating Elvis then, turning up their shirt collars in the back and trying to walk like him. Elvis had a dis-tinctive off-center walk that also involved a wiggling finger action. I remember watching Vernon walk one day. "Jesus Christ!" I thought to myself. "I don't believe this! Even his father is acting like Elvis!" I didn't stop to consider that Elvis might have gotten it from Ver-non. Vernon had grown up the hard way, and though most of the guys, myself included, considered him cheap, he just wanted to save his son's money. Vernon was the kind of guy who bought a chair at Sears rather than the Design Center, whether that chair was going into Graceland or a little shack.

Elvis was good to his "Daddy" and wonderful to Grandma Minnie Mae Presley, who always had a room in his houses. Grandma was a tall, thin, stooped woman with razor-sharp faculties that included a dry sense of humor. Her hair was always done neatly and a fresh apron always covered her dress, even though she no longer stirred pots in the kitchen. If we found her there, we teased her.

"Oh! Are you eating again?" we'd ask.

"Oh, shut up and leave me alone," she'd snap back, and we'd all crack up, including Grandma. She passed her days in her rocking chair watching television, a chew of snuff lodged between the inside of her cheek and her gums. Her vision wasn't very good, and she wore dark glasses because bright light bothered her. The TV's reception was bad, so she could barely see what was on the screen.

"Grandma, can you see that television?" Elvis finally asked her one day.

"It's okay, son," she said. But he bought her a great big new one. Anything she wanted, Elvis got for her. But Grandma rarely asked. He coddled her like a big baby and called her all sorts of baby names, especially "Dodger." Even if Elvis was running late, he made sure to stop in Dodger's room for a talk. In later years, when we were touring, we'd be in a rush to fly off somewhere, but Elvis always had to spend time with his grandma before he left. He wouldn't leave until he was finished visiting and made sure she'd be okay while he was gone.

I met Elvis's Memphis buddies, like Alan Fortas, who'd tried to go into the Army with Elvis via the Buddy Plan. Alan was low-key and amiable, a big stocky football player, and a genuinely good person with a great sense of humor and a sharp mind. His uncle was Abe Fortas, the Supreme Court justice, and Alan himself later became an important bonds salesman for banks. Elvis liked and trusted Alan, and Alan thought the world of Elvis.

George Klein was another of Elvis's good friends. As Memphis's top radio jock, George had a keen appreciation of Elvis's talent. They knew each other from Humes High School where George had been president of Elvis's class. But they didn't get to know each other until after graduation. When George started working at a local radio station and Elvis started recording, they became close. George harbored show business aspirations himself, and he even cut a song on the Sun Records label in Memphis. If Elvis needed something done in Memphis while he was off shooting a movie in Hollywood, he called George, who was always happy to take care of it. When George told Elvis he was planning to marry his girl, Barbara Little, Elvis acted as best man and paid for the wedding, which was held in his Las Vegas Hilton suite. I made all the arrangements, including plane tickets and hotel rooms for friends and family.

Elvis and George even had their noses cosmetically altered together in the fifties by Dr. Morry Parks, Hollywood's reigning plastic surgeon at the time. Cosmetic surgery for men was still rare, and Elvis was uncomfortable about having the procedure done, as it seemed less than masculine. So he enlisted George as a surgical partner to justify his own operation. "If you can do it, then it's okay for me to do it." You can see that Elvis's bridge is thinner and more refined in the later pictures than in the earlier ones.

After a few weeks of partying, the first order of business was recording a new album in Nashville. A lot had changed in the music business since Elvis was drafted in 1958 and that made him unsure of his success. Eddie Cochran and Buddy Holly had died in the same plane crash. Fats Domino and Jerry Lee Lewis were no longer popular. Little Richard had become a preacher. Before the Army, Elvis would duck into a studio with D. J. Fontana, Scotty Moore, and Bill Black. They'd sing and play, and record the results on tape. Those tracks lacked polish, but they were rock 'n' roll pared down to its rawest and most visceral. This time, he recorded with state-of-the-art equipment and the best studio musicians drawn from Nashville, the capital of country and western music. The sound would be much cleaner, and perhaps more appropriate for a new era in rock 'n' roll. Although Elvis lacked formal musical training, he was a true natural musician, capable of working with the best and getting the results he wanted. My first job as Elvis's official right-hand man was renting a Greyhound bus to take us to Nashville and reserving hotel rooms for the two days we would be recording in RCA's studios, March 20 and 21.

The sessions for *Elvis Is Back* were almost as dynamic as a live show. Elvis didn't just clap on a pair of earphones, plant himself in front of a microphone, and sing. He couldn't help moving with the music, and he drove the engineers crazy as he constantly moved toward and away from the mike. It seemed that he accidentally kicked over a stool or the mike stand or something with nearly every take. But those were minor distractions from the spectacle of Elvis and his musicians plunging deep into outlaw rock 'n' roll territory, then returning to wring every last sticky-sweet drop of emotion from the love ballads. Elvis preferred recording everyone at once because he never knew what sound he would finally aim for until he was able to try out different ideas. "I want voices here," he'd say at one point, directing the backup singers. Then he'd tell the musicians what he wanted. The conventional method today is to record each instrument and vocal on separate tracks, then mix them together. But what you gain in control, you lose in the magic that happens when people come together to make music.

I particularly remember the session when Elvis recorded "Fever." He announced, "I want all the lights in the studio turned down real dim. I want the mood right." We even turned down the lights in the engineer's booth. Elvis assumed a straddle stance in front of the microphone, bowed his head, and closed his eyes in concentration for a few moments, then sang the hell out of that torch song.

Elvis clowned around a lot between takes and during re- hearsals. He sang off-key deliberately, or belted out a long note and ended by falling on his butt, or ripped through the piano scales and tumbled off the stool. He changed the lyrics, or broke from the song they were recording into a favorite like Ray Charles's "What'd I Say." At first, I thought he was just goofing off, but there was another reason he did it. He wanted the musicians to tap their natural talents fully, and the clowning helped them relax. He knew they were a little nervous about working with the biggest record- ing star in the business. He knew what he was doing. Elvis was al- ways serious about his music, but he thought that making music should be fun. The sessions began at eight or nine each night and we didn't leave the studio until four or five in the morning. At the end of each night, Elvis played the tracks he'd recorded over and over and over, until you knew every word by heart.

During those Nashville sessions, I met Freddie Beinstock, who ran Elvis's two music publishing companies; Colonel Tom Parker,

Elvis's manager; and Tom Diskin, the Colonel's right-hand man. The Colonel was an imposing man, thick through the middle and solidly built, with a cigar permanently clamped between his jaws and a baseball cap permanently perched on his head. He was a bit leery of this Yankee Army buddy Elvis had hired so impetuously to head his organization. He obviously didn't trust me, but he was polite and businesslike, issuing orders in a perfunctory, almost military manner. He was more relaxed with Lamar and Gene, whom he knew better.

As soon as I saw the Colonel and Elvis together, it was apparent to me that Elvis had a great deal of respect for his manager, even more than the usual courtesy he extended to his elders. They loved to joke around with each other. Elvis was always tickled by the Colonel's accounts of his carnival days and loved hearing his favorite stories over and over, especially the one about sparrows who became canaries for the show through the help of a can of yellow paint.

Many people still don't grasp the Colonel's managerial style. He did a great job with Elvis, and they worked as a team. Elvis told me repeatedly that he trusted the Colonel completely. For many years, he even bragged that they didn't need a contract. A handshake and trust was fine for them. For a few years after Elvis got back from the Army, the Colonel often stopped by Graceland to have dinner with him and the Memphis Mafia. After dinner, Elvis sometimes asked us to leave the room so he and the Colonel could talk business. When they were finished, Elvis often poked his head out of the dining room to call us back in and regale us with the latest deal the Colonel had just completed. I remember one in particular, a great deal for five movies. We all let out a whoop, then offered the Colonel our congratulations.

"Just remember, boys," the Colonel cautioned, "if we didn't have Elvis, I couldn't make these deals, and we wouldn't be having dinner in this beautiful home."

Years later, when Elvis grew more and more dependent on drugs to regulate his life, he socialized less with the Colonel and his assistants. They preferred to avoid each other, especially when Elvis wasn't looking and feeling his best. By default, I became a convenient conduit for their messages to each other. Elvis and the Colonel knew they could depend on me to pass on information and smooth any rough edges. The Colonel would call when he wanted to inform Elvis about a matter, and I knew when the time was right to deliver the message. In the last few years, it sometimes happened that the Colonel wanted to talk directly with Elvis and Elvis would simply refuse.

"Joe, just ask him what he wants," Elvis would say.

To keep the waters calm, I'd resort to white lies. "Elvis is busy right now, Colonel," I'd say. "He asked if you could tell me what it was you wanted to say to him."

Sometimes the Colonel would tell me. Other times, he became angry at me, the bearer of bad news, as well as at Elvis. As smart as he was, I don't think the Colonel knew how to handle Elvis in certain situations.

"Just tell Elvis to call me when he's not too busy," he would snap.

In spite of those bumpy spots and the mistakes all human beings make on occasion, today, after many years of experience in show business, I rate Elvis and the Colonel as the greatest show business team of all time. Tom Parker was an extremely shrewd businessman who enjoyed outwitting his opponents. He was tough on people, but only when he believed they deserved it, and he had no patience with inefficiency. He wanted matters taken care of as they should be, without excuses. Just do it. He never intended to be abrupt. His manner merely reflected his organized way of thinking: "We do this, this, this—and that's it!" The Colonel never said, "Well, when you get a chance . . ." You had to know him to appreciate him fully. If he liked you, he liked you very much, and he was always there for you. Elvis and the Colonel both prized loyalty in all aspects of life, and each appreciated that trait in the other.

We wrapped the first two days of work on the album, then left Nashville by bus for the Fontainebleau Hotel in Miami Beach, where Elvis was taping a Frank Sinatra television special, "Welcome Home, Elvis."

The Colonel initially offered the "Welcome Home, Elvis" appearance to Jackie Gleason because Gleason had featured Elvis on his weekly show before Elvis was drafted.

"Great idea," Gleason said. "I love it!"

The Colonel named his price. "I want $125,000."

"You gotta be out of your mind!" Gleason screeched. "One hundred twenty-five thousand dollars!" No one had ever paid such a high sum for a single night's performance. It was like asking for several million dollars today.

"You're asking way too much money," Gleason argued.

"What are you talking about?" the Colonel countered. "If I was *your* manager, I'd ask $125,000 for you!" That shut Gleason up, but he still refused to pay. So the Colonel took the deal to Sinatra.

We traveled twenty-four hours straight before arriving at the Fontainebleau, the showpiece of Miami Beach's fabled Collins Avenue. The hotel was a pair of blue-and-white towers planted on a wide expanse of sandy shoreline and rising and blending into the tropical sky. Balconies overlooking the wave-tossed ocean jutted from the upper-floor suites. Elvis and I shared a five-thousand-square-foot, two-bedroom penthouse suite. The Colonel and his staff were down the hall, and Gene, Lamar, and Cliff Gleaves had rooms adjoining Elvis's suite. Altogether, we occupied half the floor. Sinatra and his group had the entire top floor of the other tower.

Elvis and I quickly settled ourselves in and headed downstairs to the hotel's Grand Ballroom for a meeting with Frank Sinatra and his group, men I'd idolized all my life. Joey Bishop, Sammy Davis, Dean Martin, Peter Lawford were all there, all sporting their signature casual, sophisticated style—beautifully tailored slacks topped by button-down-collared shirts and luxurious cardigan sweaters. Sinatra also wore a baseball cap. Elvis was dressed in a beige sports jacket and wearing a black fedora. Sinatra was friendly to Elvis in the manner of the kindly veteran with the up-and-coming youngster, but there was no trace of condescension. Sinatra respected Elvis's abilities, and as a former teen idol, he understood the peculiarities of the younger man's position. Elvis was the object of the same outlandish adulation Sinatra had received from the bobbysoxers of a generation earlier. Besides, Sinatra was acutely aware that having Elvis on his television special was a smart move. It would attract a whole new audience—millions of Elvis fans.

Elvis was shy and somewhat deferential, but this was due more to his southern manners than to Sinatra's status. And Elvis had reason to be nervous. He had never done a television special before, let alone costarred with a titan like Frank Sinatra. Dean Martin was more approachable, very friendly and laid-back, as was Sammy Davis Jr. Sammy had absolutely no pretensions, and he and Elvis became great pals. Sammy was the kind of guy who always approached you first. "Hey, Joe, how ya doing?" he called out whenever we ran into each other over the years. But at this first meeting, I was completely awestruck and tongue-tied.

Sinatra walked Elvis to the middle of the stage to a music stand and microphone. He handed Elvis a lyric sheet and then asked, "Well, Elvis, how does it feel to be back onstage after two years."

Elvis grinned. "Ask me after the show," he replied. Sinatra chuckled, setting off ripples among the rat pack and the Memphis Mafia.

"Hey, I do the jokes here!" Joey Bishop quipped.

"Oh, I was wondering what you were here for," Dean Martin chimed in.

"All right, you guys," Sinatra said. "Let's rehearse."

"Yes, Francis, whatever you say," Dean Martin answered. We took seats in the audience to watch.

"All right, Sergeant Presley," Sinatra began. "These are the lyrics for our duet. I'm going to sing 'Love Me Tender' and you're going to sing my old hit, 'Bewitched.' " It may have been my imagination, but I thought I detected a bit of ego in Sinatra's failure to describe "Love Me Tender" as Elvis's hit.

Sinatra gave the high sign to Nelson Riddle and his orchestra began playing. Sinatra and Presley were singing as a duet for the first time, and I believe it was the first time Elvis ever sang with a full orchestra. After an hour, Sinatra decided they'd rehearsed enough. Elvis deferred to Sinatra, and it was apparent Sinatra would have it no other way. He was the veteran, after all, and it was his show. Sinatra always performs in a tuxedo, which meant that everyone had to wear a tuxedo for the show. "If you want everybody to wear tuxedos," the Colonel told Sinatra, "you have to buy them. The boys don't have tuxedos." Sinatra may not have been used to such ultimatums, but the Colonel was immovable. Sinatra sent tailors to our rooms to fit us for tuxedos.

We didn't see much sunshine that time in Miami Beach. Hotels lined Collins Avenue, each with its own superb nightclub featuring the day's top entertainers: Tony Bennett, Alan King, Red Skelton, and others. Many Mafia bosses had vacation homes in Miami. The

Mafia had a large investment in the town in those days, and they built the larger hotels with gambling in mind. The large meeting rooms were designed to convert easily into casinos, and the Mafia was pushing hard to get gambling legalized in Florida. I won't mention names, but we met a few top-ranking wiseguys at the Sinatra show. Elvis seemed to enjoy his up-close and in-person view of the real Mafia, but there wasn't enough time for more than an exchange of greetings. We were smart enough not to introduce ourselves as the Memphis branch!

One evening after rehearsal, Lamar, Charlie, Gene, and I were sitting out on the balcony, talking over the day and admiring the ocean. Elvis came out of his bedroom all dressed up in his black mohair suit, black shirt, and white tie. He looked like one of the godfathers himself.

"Well, guys, I feel like going out tonight," he said. "Joe, call the concierge and find out who's got a good show in town. Tell him to make a reservation for us." The concierge told me about a local performer whose name I no longer recall, but I was assured he put on a great show. I made reservations for 8:00 P.M. and called for a limousine to pick us up at 7:00. Then I went out to the balcony to tell Elvis that the concierge had recommended a local performer. "Great," Elvis said. "I'd rather see up-and-coming performers. You guys go get ready."

Elvis was always interested in seeing new talent, particularly pull-out-the-stops singer-dancers who put their all into a performance. He also loved passionate pros like Sammy Davis Jr., Jackie Wilson, Bobby Darin, and James Brown. He particularly liked gospel and rhythm and blues artists who feel the music *then* sing it. He hated mechanical performers, the type who sang the song the same way every time. Elvis's enthusiasm for other performers was undampened by insecurity. He never seemed threatened. "Joe, there's enough room in this business for all the talent," he said. Elvis knew that he could learn from other greats. Besides, he was always doing audience research and picking up whatever worked.

When we came off the elevator into the hotel lobby that night, Elvis was besieged by autograph seekers. He signed scraps of paper and assorted articles of clothing for about twenty minutes.

"Elvis, we've got to go," I said. "We'll be late for the show."

"That's okay," he said. "Without my fans, we wouldn't be here."

He wouldn't leave until he satisfied every one.

We arrived at the club about half an hour late. All heads in the crowded room turned toward Elvis as we threaded our way to a table down front. Elvis loved making a grand entrance. And I certainly felt important by association. I even thought I noticed people looking at me as I trailed directly behind Elvis, perhaps thinking: "I wonder who that guy is with Elvis?"

It happened that we were seated next to a table full of young ladies, who could very well have given the maître d' a generous tip to get there. Elvis was seated with his back to the girls, but after we ordered drinks, he struck up a conversation with two of them and bought their table a round. They were from Atlanta, Georgia, on layover from their jobs as stewardesses for American Airlines and scheduled to fly out at eleven the following morning. Elvis tried to keep the conversation minimal out of respect for the performer onstage, who he knew was watching him. You could tell he was performing to our table, directing his attention to Elvis. After the first show, the waiter delivered a message: "Mr. Presley, the performers would like to invite you and your friends backstage." By now, Elvis was mobbed by fans.

"Please tell them we'll be back after I get through here," Elvis said. "Joe, ask the girls if they would like to join our party." Elvis had his eye on a pretty redhead named Diane, and I was interested in a cute blonde named Cindy. Elvis signed autographs for fifteen minutes or so, then we went backstage. He told the performers how much he enjoyed their show, and the star asked if Elvis planned to stay for the second show, which he promised was completely different. We stayed, this time with the girls at our table. Elvis sat next to Diane, I sat next to Cindy, and the other girls mixed in with Charlie, Lamar, and Gene. The chemistry between Cindy and me was bubbling. We were laughing and having a good time, while Elvis was engaged in what looked like a deep conversation with Diane.

"Why don't we go back to my hotel and have a drink," I whispered in Cindy's ear.

"Okay," she agreed with a sweet smile.

I leaned over to Elvis to tell him I was going back to the hotel. "Fine," he said, then shot me a sly grin and winked.

The limo driver drove us back, then returned to the club. Cindy and I went up to the suite. I ordered drinks and we sat out on the balcony, enjoying the beautiful, balmy night. "You know, Cindy," I said, "only a month ago, I was a GI, stationed in freezing cold Germany. Now here I am in Miami Beach at the Fontainebleau Hotel, having drinks on a balcony overlooking the Atlantic Ocean with a very pretty lady." I leaned over and kissed her. One thing led to another, and we ended up in my bedroom.

"Joe," Cindy said suddenly, "you wouldn't happen to have any Tampax?"

"I ran out last night," I joked. She laughed, and I called downstairs to the bell desk to send up a box. When the bellman reached our floor, the security guard stopped him.

"I have a package for the Presley suite," the bellman said.

"We're not allowed to take any packages into the suite without checking with the Colonel," the guard answered.

By now it was about 1:00 A.M., and the Colonel and his staff had been asleep for about three hours. The Colonel and I were just getting to know each other, and he still regarded me with suspicion. Now the security man was ringing his doorbell with a package of Tampax and the bellman in tow. A sleepy Colonel answered the door.

"What is it?" he growled.

"The bellman has a package for Joe Esposito, and we were told all packages had to be cleared through you."

"Well, you got the wrong information," the Colonel said testily. "But now that you've woken me up, let me have it." The Colonel gave the bellman a couple of bucks, then looked in the bag. I heard a knock on my door and figured it was the bellman. But there was the Colonel in his bathrobe, looking extremely peeved. "I've got a package here for you," he barked. "Next time go down and get it yourself!" He turned and stalked back to his suite. I didn't even say thank you, because I didn't know what to say. Before this incident, it had been just "hello" and "yes" between us. Our relationship nose-dived, but the Colonel never mentioned it to anyone, and we eventually came to get along very well. We're close friends today.

•   •   •

The night of the show, March 26, Elvis was struck with a se-vere case of stage fright. He hadn't faced an audience in over two years. He didn't admit it, but he was sweating and pacing back and forth in the dressing room. At least a dozen times he asked me, "How much more time?" I didn't know if this was normal or not, but it didn't feel too good to me. I was getting nervous myself, but I couldn't say that to anyone, especially not to Elvis. The best I could do was check my watch and tell him the time left, all the while trying to quiet the butterflies in my own stomach. Grand en-trances onto the floor of nightclubs were fine, but when it came to making stage entrances, I didn't want to be in his shoes.

Elvis had to make his entrance in dress blues, then perform in a tuxedo instead of his usual slacks and shirt. He was a bit stiff dur-ing the early part of the show, but he gradually relaxed and even seemed to enjoy himself. The smiles came more easily and more often. Elvis rarely admitted to stage fright, and it was unusual for him to suffer a bad attack like the one that night. But no matter how many times he performed throughout the next seventeen years, he was always revved up just before he walked on stage. I always sensed a quiver in his muscles as I walked him to the wings, but that burst of welcoming applause from the fans rarely failed to convert his nervous energy into an electrifying performance.

The audience that night was packed with friends of the per-formers and other movers and shakers. None of us knew many people in Miami, but the Colonel had friends in the crowd dating back to his youth as a barker in a carnival and the early days of his management career when he handled successful country and west-ern singers Gene Austin and Eddy Arnold. It was a great show, par-ticularly when Elvis and Frank sang a duet on "Witchcraft" and "Love Me Tender," and the two melodies meshed and harmonized. Sinatra moved his shoulders up and down to the rhythm. "I move my body like Elvis," he joked, "but in a different area." Onstage, they created a nice rapport, but Elvis and Frank never got along all that well, despite the close friendship Elvis would share with Sinatra's daughter Nancy. They seemed to circle each other like a pair of wary tomcats. Perhaps it was the competition for women and attention between two macho superstars.

When we had finished the show, we drove back to Nashville

for two more days to complete the record. Elvis recorded twelve songs in a total of four days. Today, it takes six months or more to make an album.

Elvis Is Back was his first LP in true stereo, and it contained some scorching rhythm and blues numbers, especially the final track, "Reconsider Baby," one of Elvis's favorites. Some of the demo records for the album were produced by the musical prodigy and future rock 'n' roll legend Phil Spector, who later produced the Crystals, the Ronettes, the Righteous Brothers, and the Beatles.

Elvis himself may be the most underrated record producer in the history of rock 'n' roll. Despite credits on each album to various RCA producers, Elvis was the real producer of his music. He produced in order to protect what he'd sung. RCA's producer was always present, but Elvis controlled his recording sessions. Even Sam Phillips of Sun Records acknowledged Elvis's production skill. "I never told Elvis to do anything," Phillips always said. "I just encouraged him when he was going in a direction I thought was contemporary." Elvis was a perfectionist. In later years, he told me several times that he suspected that RCA, or someone else involved in mastering his recordings, was altering his final mixes. That was the biggest source of contention between Elvis and his record company. After a night of recording five, six, or seven songs, he had them all mastered on acetates. When a record was released, he always matched each track with those acetates. I recall one time when we hadn't believed him. "You guys thought I was crazy," he said, "but listen." He played his mix and then he played the final product. It was true. They had messed with his tapes. In that particular instance, the "uh huhs," Elvis's signature vocalizations, were emphasized. They were supposed to be subtle, Elvis said. But the record company always pulled his voice out front in the mix. They thought the music was too overbearing and that fans just wanted to hear Elvis. That mix was corrected before the record was released, but in other instances, by the time Elvis heard the changes, it was too late. Elvis didn't become a huge recording star by accident. He understood the heart and soul of rock 'n' roll, and he always remembered exactly what he had recorded. But the record company followed the same reductive thinking that would later guide the producers of his movies: People just wanted to see Elvis on screen; it didn't make a difference if what surrounded him—

the script, the direction, and the other actors—were good or bad.

Elvis Is Back is technically polished, and it was a success, reaching number two on the *Billboard* Bestselling LP Chart. But something had been lost on the way to progress, the rebel edge and restless spirit of the pre-Army Elvis. Two years of military life had tamed the young man who once sparked so much social upheaval and controversy. The old sound was gone and it would never come back.

The biggest reason for the change in Elvis's music had to do with his publishing companies, Gladys Music and Elvis Presley Publishing. In the early days of his career, Elvis's publishing wasn't a big business. But once people around Elvis realized how much money was involved in publishing songs, they hired writers. Elvis no longer dipped into his own treasure trove and recut favorite records he'd held on to from high school. Big Mama Thornton had blown his mind performing "Hound Dog," inspiring him to record his own version. But he no longer could do that. Nor could he stroll into the Home of the Blues, Memphis's black record store, and pick through the bins for rhythm and blues gems. Elvis's music was big business now. If you own a piece of the publishing and you're paying staff to write songs, those are the songs brought to you. Others just don't get through. So he depended on the publishing people to bring him a selection from which he chose what he wanted to record. Elvis's writers brought him many good songs over the years, but even better songwriters weren't able to get to him. If Elvis was aware of any change in his style, he never mentioned it to me.

Elvis rarely spoke about musical styles, his own or those of other singers. His primary interest was heart, how much a singer put into a song. "You gotta feel it before you can send it," he often said." Yet few people around Elvis really grasped the quality of his passion and the great gift of his ear that allowed him to naturally adopt the sounds of Memphis—the music he heard on the radio, in record stores, and from the R&B acts that played there. As a child, Elvis was drawn to blues and gospel quartets. He sang gospel in church, and he loved the rhythm and blues he heard his black neighbors sing. As a poor white southerner, the first radio he ever heard was tuned to the Grand Ole Opry. Elvis's talent was such that he could sing anything he chose. His personal style, physical and vocal, accommodated all those influences. It was natural for him to pick up all sorts of traits from everywhere and then automatically, unconsciously, incorporate them into his personality. Elvis drew from the truck drivers he worked with after high school, from actors he admired on the movie screen, and from his favorite singers. He never deliberately stole from a performer, but he absorbed influences so well that they became part of him.

Elvis epitomized a generation that was struggling to carve an identity separate from the mainstream postwar society enamored of modern assembly line production, gray flannel suits, and cookie-cutter suburban lifestyles. Conformity was the buzzword of the day. But the rebellious among the youth were discovering music as a break from conformity, particularly intensely visceral rhythm and blues artists like Roy Hamilton, Bo Diddley, and their white imitators. When Elvis was growing up, Memphis venues presented segregated shows, one for whites and one for "coloreds." Elvis attended those shows and learned a great deal. Even his dress style—the collar turned up in back, for instance—reflected the happening Beale Street esthetic. Elvis merged that hip African-American influence with white youth's burgeoning craze for such screen idols as Marlon Brando and James Dean, who personified their own alienation. Movies like *The Wild One* and *Rebel Without a Cause* captured the vague but powerful yearnings of an entire generation. At the time, the aura of volatile unpredictability and sexuality that surrounded those singers and actors was social dynamite.

After we finished *Elvis Is Back* in April, we returned to Memphis for a few more weeks of partying and a show at Ellis Auditorium, with George Jessel as MC, and a great band—Boots Randolph, a famous Nashville saxophone player, and Bobby Moore on bass—backing him on all the early RCA tunes. Lean and handsome, his hair partially grown back from the Army cut, he was dynamic and cool without being detached. Afterward, we set off for Hollywood to film *G.I. Blues* for Paramount Pictures.

Elvis was afraid of flying in those days, so the Colonel rented two private railroad cars for the trip: a lounge car with comfortable chairs and couches, game tables, and a hi-fi system, and a sleeping car with a private stateroom for each of us. Elvis's friends came to the train station to see us off, including Charlie Hodge, who had been visiting. We were waving goodbye as the train began pulling out, when suddenly Elvis yelled out the window to Charlie.

"Y'all want to come?"

Charlie's eyes lit up. "Yeah!" he shouted back. "But I don't have anything with me."

"Don't worry about it," Elvis laughed. "We'll buy what you need when we get to California." Charlie jumped aboard. Our Hollywood-bound party now included Sonny West, Gene Smith, Charlie, Elvis, me, and the Colonel and his staff.

We talked, joked, and laughed across the country. But even during the trip out West, the Colonel's promotion machine ran at full steam. In seventeen years, I never saw the Colonel miss an opportunity to promote his star. Hundreds of fans were waiting at each stop, hoping for a moment with Elvis. He walked to the back of the train, said hi, and signed autographs like a politician on a whistle-stop campaign. At one point, a bullet whizzed through the window in the Colonel's sleeping compartment, perhaps someone taking target practice as the train sped by. Luckily, no one was injured, and we soon forgot about the incident.

Elvis disembarked outside Los Angeles to avoid the crowds and the media poised for an ambush at the main station downtown. Sonny, Charlie, and I took the train into Los Angeles. The Colonel had arranged for a car for us and a truck for the baggage. We loaded everything and drove off to meet Elvis and the Colonel at the Beverly Wilshire Hotel, where we lived during our first year in Hollywood.

Production for *G.I. Blues* began on May 1, 1960. Every weekday morning, we reported to the Paramount lot, where we ran into such stars as John Wayne, Dean Martin, and Jerry Lewis. Elvis's friends dropped by our suite regularly. They included television actor and singer Rick Nelson; Vince Edwards, a TV heartthrob at the time; Ty Harding, another major actor, and James Dean's friend Nick Adams, who later starred in *The Rebel* television series. Elvis was particularly fond of Nick. Sadly, he committed suicide several years later, on February 7, 1968.

The first day on set, we met Elvis's costar, the beautiful South African dancer Juliet Prowse, and the producer, Hal Wallis, who had produced *Casablanca* and other major films. I still remember Warren Beatty, who was very bashful in those days, standing at the back of the *G.I. Blues* set, watching. We visited Steve McQueen, Rock Hudson, and others and joked around between takes. For some reason, a lot of royalty visited Elvis on set, including the king and queen of Nepal, Queen Margarethe of Denmark, and Princess Astrid of Norway. Elvis was his usual gracious self, a bit shy, but he handled himself well—exactly as he would with anyone.

G.I. Blues was an eight-week dream shoot. Norman Taurog, a veteran director, was great to work with. It turned out to be a huge moneymaker, but when it opened in Mexico City, riots broke out at the theater, and the Mexican government banned all future Elvis movies. We would work all day, then go back to the hotel and order dinner from room service. Most of the time, we invited girls we'd met at the studio to join us, and sometimes we even went out to a movie. Elvis, the guys, and our dates snuck into Grauman's Chinese Theater after the lights had gone down and the movie had started. We ran out just before it ended and jumped into a car at the curb, just like the Army days. The audiences never knew Elvis had been there. These were fun times, before Elvis decided he couldn't go out anymore, before he began to weary of the constant and insatiable demands of his fans.

While we were shooting *G.I. Blues,* Elvis told me a funny story about the *King Creole* shoot before the Army. Alan Fortas always dreamed of a life in show business, so he accompanied Elvis to Hollywood. Elvis enlisted the director and assistant director to play a little joke on Alan. They told him he was going to act in a scene and to report to makeup. The makeup artists worked on Alan for an entire hour, then put tissue around his neck to keep the makeup from staining his clothes. "Stay near Elvis," the director warned Alan. "We'll call you when it's time for your scene." Alan stuck to Elvis like a faithful dog. Everywhere Elvis went, Alan followed, still wearing the tissue around his neck. He wasn't going to blow his big chance at stardom. "Get away from me!" Elvis kept saying, but he couldn't shake Alan off. Every once in a while, Alan broke away for a second to ask the assistant director when his scene would be shot. "Just wait," the assistant director kept telling him. "I'll let you know when you're needed. Don't worry, just be ready." The charade went on for two entire days. Finally, a few weeks later, they gave him a bit part. The scene ended up on the cutting room floor.

Elvis loved gags. He did most everything on impulse and hardly ever suppressed his spontaneous reactions. He also worked hard to set up situations that would yield big laughs. He was never mean or cruel, but he didn't always recognize conventional boundaries. Elvis was also able to enjoy an occasional joke at his own expense. During *G.I. Blues,* Elvis was deep into karate chopping wooden boards. One day he made an announcement on the set: "I'm ready for a new dimension of board breaking. I'm going to break a board with the tips of my fingers." Elvis was a hopeless showoff who basked in large-scale admiration. He never, ever passed the time of day as part of the crowd. It was only when the performance, onstage or off, ended that his essential shyness emerged. Word got out around the set, and soon over fifty people had gathered to witness the event. Red, who had joined us in Hollywood, held the board. "You have to use your mind," Elvis explained. "It's all mental. You think about the board breaking in half. Then, when you go to hit it, you put the strength of your whole body into it." Elvis squeezed every ounce of drama out of the event, assuming a number of karate stances and holding them with deep concentration, before bringing his arm down with a horrendous karate yell. The board didn't break. Elvis went through the elaborate preparations once again, drew his arm back and came down with another yell. This time it broke. Amid oohs and ahs from the crowd, Elvis swaggered over to his dressing room, the guys in tow. As soon as he was safe inside and the door was shut, he let out a different yell. "Jesus Christ!" he moaned. "I almost broke my fingers!" He had managed to hold in the pain in front of the cast and crew, but once he was with us, he was half-laughing at himself and half-crying from pain, cradling his hand and wondering aloud, "Good God! Am I crazy? I almost broke my fingers!"

I occasionally ran through lines with Elvis between takes, but most of the time, the guys relieved the tedium of moviemaking's "hurry up and wait" pace by flirting with girls and horsing around. Charlie Hodge also kept us amused with showbiz yarns about his adventures with the Foggy River Boys and playing backup for Gene Autry and Roy Rogers. The Memphis Mafia's main occupation was hanging around Elvis and making sure he was happy and everything was fine. My job was to make all of Elvis's arrangements and give the guys the semblance of organization. Elvis wanted a first-class outfit that functioned smoothly no matter where we were: on the set, in public, driving from one place to another, even in the house. He appreciated that I took care of his business the way he wanted it handled. After a short time, we no longer had to talk about what he wanted. It just happened naturally. I knew how to finesse ticklish situations, how to keep Elvis the good guy in circumstances when no one could be the good guy. What I received in return is obvious. Elvis was extremely generous, and I was the "main man," the one you had to go through to get to Elvis. If I wasn't always present for the late-night bull sessions or the clowning, it was because I was busy, wheeling and dealing and making arrangements on Elvis's behalf.

Elvis had formed the pleasant habit of trying to romance his female costars from his first movie, 1956's *Love Me Tender*. He didn't always succeed, though. He had not been able to seduce Debra Paget, his costar in that film. "Debra was in love with someone else, and I couldn't get in the game," he told me. It bugged Elvis, because Debra reminded him of his mother.

Of course, he had no trouble getting dates, and he was still professing his love for Priscilla. He was calling her in Germany and telling me he thought they would eventually marry, but he saw lots of other women. During the *G.I. Blues* shoot, he dated Judy Rawlins, a beautiful actress who played a small part in the movie and later married singer Vic Damone. At the same time, Elvis was having a secret affair with Juliet Prowse, who didn't know about Judy. Juliet was wonderful—very funny, a great dancer, and always cheerful. Her upbeat style and long legs captivated Elvis. They enjoyed huddling together between takes, sharing jokes we couldn't hear. The real reason for the secrecy was Juliet's official engagement to Frank Sinatra, but I don't think Juliet's relationship with Sinatra played a role in Elvis's attraction to her. They were simply forced by circumstances to spend a lot of time together and they hit it off. There was no long-term pressure, because both knew their affair had a limited run. That's how it goes on a movie set. Everyone works so closely together that if there's any chemistry at all between two people, they fall into bed. When the movie shoot is over, the affair usually ends with it. Juliet went on to her next career move and Sinatra, and Elvis to his next movie. In later years, we saw her whenever they played Vegas at the same time, but they never resumed their affair.

After *G.I. Blues* was in the can, we traveled to Memphis for some Graceland-style rest and relaxation. Because of Elvis's fear of flying, in the early sixties we traveled back and forth between Memphis and Hollywood in a luxuriously appointed bus customized specially for Elvis. We took our time, stopping frequently along the way, logging 150 to 250 miles per day over five or six days. A car followed the bus in case it broke down. When Elvis wasn't driving, Sonny West or I—who were better drivers—took the wheel. Late one night in Arkansas, Elvis was pumping gas. An older black gentleman who happened by remarked to one of the guys, "Boy, that fellow sure looks like Elvis Presley." He walked over to Elvis. "Does anybody ever tell you that you look like Elvis Presley?" he asked.

"Oh, yeah," Elvis said, "all the time, but I'm not him." He told the man his name was "Jon Burrows." Sometimes he used "Jon Carpenter," his alternate traveling name, to pull the wool over people's eyes. Other times, of course, he got a kick from admitting his identity and shocking people.

Elvis was a big, happy kid on those trips, carefree and full of fun. He sang as he drove, while Charlie and Red sang harmony. He always had a smile on his face and seemed to not have a care in the world. Even now, I can picture him, singing and driving, wearing his special driving gloves and hat. Like any kid, Elvis loved to dress up, according to the role. He loved his military uniform and in later years, as we befriended police forces around the country, he acquired several uniforms.

Just before dawn, we would check into a motel to grab some sleep, and we were back on the road by dusk. Every few hours, we stopped by the side of the road to toss a football, or let Elvis practice a little karate on us, or just sit under the stars, listening to him speculate about beings from another world. He genuinely believed in UFOs. Outer space was another piece of the puzzle of life Elvis was determined to solve. He made us all lie on our backs and gaze up at the clouds. "See all these pictures in the clouds?" he'd say, pointing out the shapes of presidents' faces and such.

"See that cloud? I'm going to make it move," he'd announce. Sure enough, eventually it would move. Elvis thought it was his mystical powers, not the wind.

Most of the time, we had high-spirited fun of the rowdy young men variety. Elvis loved a good time, and he could make a good time out of a sad situation. His laugh was so infectious that no matter what mood you were in, you laughed with him. He wasn't afraid to let go, just let loose completely and have fun. Passersby probably thought we were nuts and probably never realized that Elvis Presley was the ringleader of the group horsing around by the side of the road.

We made the trip between Memphis and Hollywood at least three times a year. Throughout that time, Elvis deviated only once from the "men only" rule. We brought wives and girlfriends along that time, turning the journey into a family vacation and driving by day and sleeping at night, like normal people do. Elvis and the guys fooled around, waging mock fights across the country, and actually did one another some damage. Elvis's cousin Billy Smith came along, a small, wiry guy with sandy hair like Elvis. They kept punching each other on the shoulder. I had just bought a super eight-millimeter camera, so I shot a lot of film. As I filmed everyone relaxing at the Grand Canyon, Elvis and Billy rolled up their shirtsleeves for the camera, revealing arms that were entirely black and blue. They'd burst all the blood vessels. "This little fellow doesn't know when to quit," I thought to myself. Of course, that was the very quality Elvis shared with Billy and appreciated in him.

They had other traits in common. Billy was a sharp guy with a serious side as well. If there was one relative Elvis truly loved, it was Billy. Elvis took pride in the fact that he had kept Billy with him from a very young age and that of all his cousins, Billy turned out the best. Elvis was more a big brother to him than a cousin. Billy could have had anything he wanted from Elvis, but he never took advantage. When he got married, Billy became a family man and rarely traveled with Elvis again. But he was with Elvis at the end.

On one drive to Graceland from Hollywood, when we reached Fort Smith, Arkansas, we started to receive signals from WHBQ radio from Memphis, where our buddy George Klein was on the air. He was playing "Green Green Grass of Home," Tom Jones's latest song. Elvis flipped over the lyrics and Tom's powerful delivery. "I've got to hear that song again," he said after it was over. When Elvis liked something, especially a piece of music, he wore it out; I remember when he played Roberta Flack's "The First Time Ever I Saw Your Face" over and over. "Hear how clear her voice is?" he'd enthuse to anyone who'd listen. He wore out several records of Charles Boyer's "Softly As I Leave You." In fact, he adopted that song when he returned to live performance in 1969. Elvis even concocted a tear-jerker introduction to it, telling the audience that a man wrote the lyrics when his wife died in his arms. He went so far as to say that the words came to the man just as his beloved slipped away. Elvis also flipped over one of Bill Cosby's comedy albums. He knew every word of Cosby's skit in which God talks to Noah, yet he laughed every time he heard it.

This time it was "The Green Green Grass of Home."

"Joe, get out of the car, get to a phone, and call George and tell him we're on our way home," he told me at the next service station. "I want to hear that song again." I made the call and jumped back into the bus.

"I just heard from a bunch of my friends coming back from California," we heard George tell his listeners. "They just requested that I play Tom Jones's song again." Then he played it.

"I've got to hear it again," Elvis said. It was twenty minutes before we found another pay phone. I got out and called George.

"George," I said, "E wants to hear it again and a few more times after that. So, please, play it as much as you can."

"Joe, I can get into a lot of trouble playing the same song over and over," George said.

"Well, do what you can," I asked.

George came on the air again. "You'd never guess, folks, but I just got another call from the same guy who's coming back from the West Coast." He was hinting broadly so his listeners could figure out that the friend was Elvis. "And he requests that I play this song another four or five times!"

By the time we crossed the bridge from Arkansas to Memphis, Elvis knew the song by heart and was singing along. The first thing we did when we got to town was stop at a record store to buy "The Green Green Grass of Home." Elvis wore that record out.

Elvis was an extremist. He was never simple, not even then.

The uninhibited, fun-loving Elvis was the polar opposite of another aspect of his nature, one that brooded on life's injustices and prodded doggedly at its mysteries. In time, his tendency to extremes would lead to his tragic and untimely end. But for most of the years I knew him, Elvis's open enjoyment of life gave us all the most wonderful times we would ever know.

chapter 4

hollywood

after *G.I. Blues,* we went back to Memphis and plunged into party mode, renting the Memphian Theater for all-night movie sessions, taking over the amusement park or the roller rink, and playing our own version of roller hockey with the simple goal of knocking people down. Billy was one of the toughest players, and he always looked out for Elvis. There was always some new guy trying to make his mark by knocking down Elvis Presley. More often than not, he was blindsided by short, wiry Billy before he even got close.

During that vacation, Elvis was initiated into the Tau Kappa Epsilon fraternity at Arkansas State University, about fifty miles from Memphis. Rick Husky, president of the chapter, hit on the idea of initiating the most famous man in the South as a publicity stunt. Since Rick was a northerner, he asked a few natives for candidates. They all nominated Elvis Presley as the most famous man in the South.

"Fine," Rick said. "We'll initiate him into our fraternity and get some pictures."

"Yeah, sure," his frat brothers laughed. Rick went to his room and typed out a letter: "Dear Elvis, Tau Kappa Epsilon fraternity has just named you 'Man of the Year.' " He mailed it to Graceland. Two days later, he found a telegram slipped under his door: "Elvis will be at Graceland Thursday night at 7:30. Please come." Stunned, Rick raced to a sporting goods store to buy a plaque and pay extra to have it inscribed in time.

That Thursday, Graceland's doorbell rang at precisely 7:30 P.M. I opened the door to find a group of nervous young men in suits and ties. "Elvis will be right down," I told them. After several minutes, Elvis came downstairs wearing a cast on his wrist because he'd broken his pinkie playing touch football. We all filed into the music room, where Rick and his frat brothers took Elvis through the initiation ceremony, complete with skull and crossbones and the usual frat-boy mumbo jumbo. When it was over, Rick, who was now Elvis's official big brother, whispered the secret fraternity word to him. Elvis went through the entire process with the utmost gravity. Occult and mystic ceremonies were right up his alley. He recited the pledge solemnly and even asked questions about the traditions behind all the symbols and phrases. Then his "big brother" fastened his own fraternity pin on Elvis's lapel, until "little brother's" pin arrived. Rick read the inscription on the plaque aloud: "'Distinguished Member of the Year: In recognition of the remarkable achievements in the world of entertainment and as a prominent American, to Elvis Presley, Distinguished TKE Member of the Year.'" Elvis gazed at the plaque for a moment. "This is one of the nicest awards I've ever received," he said sincerely. "The plaque is certainly beautiful, and you can be sure it will occupy a place of honor in my home." He added that the plaque would hang among his most prized possessions—his gold records.

After the ceremony, we went to the living room to chat about Army life, show business, and football. Someone took photos of Elvis and his fraternity brothers, and he held the cigarillo he'd been smoking behind him when the pictures were taken. He didn't want to mar his clean-cut, no-drinking, no-smoking image. He was terrific to those college kids, even more gracious than he'd been to the royalty who visited the *G.I. Blues* set.

• • •

Flaming Star, Elvis's next movie, was originally written for Marlon Brando, who turned it down. It was obvious why. The story was contrived to the point of absurdity. But Elvis enjoyed wearing dark makeup for his role as a half-breed Indian, and we shot on a ranch in the Thousand Oaks section of the San Fernando Valley. Barbara Eden, the costar, was married to Michael Ansara, a hot TV star at the time, playing Cochise in the popular series *Broken Arrow*. Michael showed up every day to keep an eye on things, or maybe to see how Elvis stacked up as a fellow Hollywood Indian. There was never a shortage of women, so Elvis made do with the minor players. He was still calling Priscilla at least once a week, still calling Anita regularly, still following his "if I'm not near the one I love, I love the one I'm near" philosophy.

At first, Elvis was afraid to mount his horse. But by the end of filming, he came to enjoy horseback riding so much that several years later, he bought himself a palomino to ride around Graceland. As usual, the hobby eventually got out of control. Elvis bought horses for all of us, then he bought a ranch to house them and trucks and trailers so we could all live there with him!

The *Flaming Star* shoot was a good example of how strange filmmaking can be. For the climactic death scene, Elvis delivered a long speech to Steve Forrest, who played his half-brother. Steve was supposed to run in from somewhere and beg, "Don't go!" Elvis was supposed to say, "I have to return to my heritage and die!" or lines to that effect. Forrest prepared for each take by doing pushups just off camera. But Elvis's horse was uncooperative and kept rearing. Steve was doing pushups to get into the right sweaty, breathless state while Elvis kept trying to mount the horse and deliver his lines. "Damn you, you're asking for a karate chop," Elvis told the horse. Take after take, nothing worked. Finally, the trainer lay on the ground out of camera range and massaged the horse's front leg. I can still see the scene: a guy lying on the ground rubbing a horse's leg, Elvis in the saddle, caked with thick Indian makeup and delivering a corny speech about going back to the mountains to die, while Steve Forrest panted from all the pushups.

After another break in Memphis, Elvis returned to California for *Wild in the Country*, which costarred Hope Lange, Millie

Perkins, Gary Lockwood, and Tuesday Weld. Philip Dunne directed a script written by Clifford Odets, which he adapted from *Golden Boy,* a novel by J. R. Salamanca. We shot in the Napa Valley and stayed in a nearby motel. Elvis and Tuesday hit it off immediately, but their affair lasted only a short while before it mellowed into a friendship. Tuesday was a free spirit; she would never have put up with Elvis, who liked to control his women. "You stay here, I'm going out tonight" or "Do this for me, I want it done right now" typified his attitude. Tuesday would never fall in with that program. Elvis was raised to believe that the man is the master of the house, and he was never motivated to change. Tuesday hung out with us like one of the boys. She definitely had a wild streak, but she was a pleasure to be with despite her reputation around Hollywood for being "difficult."

Once, on a double date, we were driving—Tuesday next to Elvis in the front, my date and me in the back—and Tuesday began throwing anything she could find in the car at people in nearby cars. Another time, she decided to chuck a quart of milk out the window of our top-floor suite in the Beverly Wilshire just because she wanted to see it splatter.

Wild in the Country was supposed to be Elvis's first real dramatic feature, because it had only four songs. Elvis took the movie seriously, and we curtailed our usual highjinks on the set. But despite its literary pedigree, the script made no sense whatsoever, and the movie failed to establish Elvis as a dramatic actor. Elvis and Tuesday had fun together anyway, and he also spent time on location talking with Hope Lange. He probably had eyes for her, but Hope wasn't the type to go for a casual movie location affair. Elvis was too intimidated by this classy woman to force the issue, so they became friends instead. They giggled together between takes, and Elvis invited her to the house a few times for pizza. I think Hope truly cared about Elvis, and he treated her with great charm and respect.

During the shoot, Elvis developed a huge boil on his rear end. The studio doctor was called to the motel, and he lanced it. When Hope learned that Elvis wasn't well, she came to the motel suite to see how he was.

"What's the problem?" she asked him.

"I got a boil on my ass," he said, trying to play it off as a joke, but clearly embarrassed in front of this cool, elegant movie star.

"Let me see," Hope said.

Before Elvis could stop her, she yanked down the covers and examined the boil. Alan Fortas, Gene Smith, and I almost died of laughter. Elvis turned beet red and jerked the covers back. After a few days, the wound healed, but every once in a while, Hope strolled over to Elvis and inquired with a concerned look, "How's your ass?"

One weekend on location in Napa Valley, we were feeling a little stir crazy, so Elvis, Alan, Gene, Sonny West, and I took a little side trip to San Francisco, about an hour's drive south. The studio travel office made reservations at the Mark Hopkins Hotel, and a limousine picked us up at 7:30 P.M. Elvis took Nancy Sharp, a wonderful woman who was head of wardrobe on the movie. Nancy was blonde and beautiful but very Ivy League and proper, not at all Elvis's usual type, but he liked her a lot. We arrived late Saturday evening, checked in, and ordered dinner. After dinner, Elvis and Nancy retired to his bedroom. None of us had dates, so we hired a taxi and asked the cabby to take us to the most swinging spot in town. By now it was about 12:30 in the morning, and the city was pretty well shut down. But he could take us to an after-hours club called the Broken Drum. Fine. We weren't going to spend our first trip to San Francisco sleeping in our rooms. The club wasn't in the greatest neighborhood, but it was packed with people sitting at small tables, talking and sipping coffee. As soon as our eyes adjusted to the dim lighting, we were heartened to see that the place was full of beautiful women. Then we noticed that they were dancing with each other. It was a lesbian club. Being true macho fellows, we beat a hasty retreat. That was our San Francisco experience.

I was dating Christina Crawford, Joan Crawford's adopted daughter, who had a small part in *Wild in the Country* and later wrote *Mommie Dearest*. Christina was sweet but clearly troubled. After reading her book, I understand why she had problems. The first time I picked her up, I was shocked to see that the daughter of a wealthy woman—Joan Crawford owned Pepsi Cola at the time—lived in a tiny Hollywood apartment with a mattress on the floor and no other furniture, not even a television. She had no money at all, and her mother never helped her. I was happy to learn that she eventually got her life together, no thanks to Joan. Christina and I got along well, but she had an unpleasant clash with Elvis one evening. Elvis picked up a cigar, and as I leaned over to light it for him, she knocked it out his mouth.

"He shouldn't have to light your cigar," she declared.

"I don't mind," I protested.

But Christina was very indignant, and that set off Elvis's quick temper. He pulled her by the hair across the coffee table, and ordered her to leave.

This was way out of character for Elvis. He usually exerted exceptional control. But he was stung at being accused of behavior he proclaimed to detest. When I drove Christina home, she explained that she hated to see people waiting on others because it reminded her of her mother. I felt bad, but I didn't know what to do. When I returned after taking Christina home, I told Elvis about her life with her mother.

"I'm sorry, Joe," he said. "I didn't want to do what I did, but she really got me mad. She had no right to act that way in my house. If she didn't like it, she could have asked to leave."

A few days later, Christina sent Elvis a case of Pepsi with a note of apology. Later, on the set, I saw them talking. I couldn't hear what they were saying, but it was clear that they smoothed the rift because I saw them hug.

During those years, none of us slept more than a few hours at a time. We lived on amphetamines. We woke at five o'clock each morning to report to the set, then spent the rest of our time screwing around. Music blared continuously and at high decibels from our floors. We ferried Hollywood starlets up and down in the elevators all day and night. Elvis was breaking boards in his suite, and trying to teach the rest of us karate. When we weren't trying to break boards, we were running around the halls, waging water gun fights that escalated into full-scale battles involving buckets of water. By then, I had nicknamed Elvis "Crazy" for his wacky sense of humor, and he'd dubbed me "Jaws," after my full jowls.

Finally, the management of the Beverly Wilshire asked, very firmly, that we leave. The final straw came when we were shooting the breeze one day, and word came from the lobby that a young woman claiming to be Tuesday Weld was kicking up a ruckus because security wouldn't let her up to Elvis's floor. They didn't believe she was Tuesday Weld because she was wearing dungarees and didn't look like a movie star. Elvis sent someone down to get her, and when she arrived, she pranced around the room like an angry little cat spitting expletives.

"Those fucking security people," she raged. "I told them I was Tuesday Weld and wanted to come up to see you. The stupid bastards didn't believe me! Fuck! Fuck! Fuck! That just pisses me off!" Elvis sat back and enjoyed her tantrum.

The Beverly Wilshire was the type of hotel where wealthy older people lived all year round. They weren't too pleased with our rowdy bunch. The management didn't want to lose the patronage of a superstar, but the havoc we wrought wasn't worth it. So I met with a real estate agent named Elaine Young, Gig Young's ex-wife, but didn't tell her I was looking for a house for Elvis. She showed me four houses, finally showing me the shah of Iran's home on Perugia Way, in Bel Air. It was located in a private area adjacent to Beverly Hills, overlooking the Bel Air Country Club. When I told Elvis about the place, he wanted to see it. Elaine could barely control herself as she toured the house with him.

Not long after we moved into the shah's house, in November of 1960, Elvis met a girl who would play an important role in his life, one different from that of Priscilla or any other romantic interest. Pat Parry was driving down Santa Monica Boulevard with a girlfriend on her way to a party when she pulled up at a stop light next to Elvis, who was going to the studio to record the *Flaming Star* soundtrack. Pat's sense of humor was as off-the-wall as Elvis's. She didn't scream like other girls. She was determined to be different.

"You look familiar," Pat deadpanned. "Do I know you?"

"I'm Elvis Presley," Elvis said, playing along with an apprecia- · tive grin.

"I'm Pat Parry," the seventeen-year-old replied politely.

That was our first encounter with the girl who became the sole female member of the Memphis Mafia. In those days, we threw parties nearly every night, so Elvis gave his telephone number to Pat and invited the two girls over for the next night. When they showed up, they found eight guys—Elvis, Cliff Gleaves, Lamar Fike, Sonny and Red West, Gene Smith, Charlie Hodge, and me. No women. Elvis gave Pat his standard tour of the house, ending, as was customary, in his bedroom. She was terrified. "I'm a nice little Jewish girl," she whimpered. Elvis laughed and decided to adopt Pat as his little sister.

When we first met Pat, she was studying to be a hair stylist. She spent all her free time with us but wanted to retain the semblance of a private life. She refused to go on permanent salary. The first time she cut Elvis's hair, he gave her $750. From then on, Pat never accepted any payment. "I eat here every night, you buy me stuff, I travel with you," she said. But Elvis lavished presents on his little sister. Over the years he bought her a car, a fur coat, diamonds, even her first Jewish star. Elvis wore a Jewish star himself, along with a cross. "I wear a star with a St. Christopher medal on the back and a cross because I don't want to be shut out of Heaven on a technicality," he said, only half-joking. More seriously, he told me, "I think there is only one God, but different people worship Him in different ways. Who's to say who's right and who's wrong? I think everyone is right if they just believe in God."

Pat worked all day at a salon in Beverly Hills, and showed up at Elvis's house at about four or five o'clock. She stayed until about one in the morning, then returned to her small apartment. On weekends, she traveled with us to Las Vegas or Memphis, then came back to Los Angeles to work a three- or four-day week.

"Patty, why are you with us?" Lamar once asked her. "We love you, but don't you think you should be out there getting a life?"

"Leave me alone," Pat said. "I'm having a great time. I'm going to date nineteen-year-old guys when I'm traveling with Elvis Presley?"

Every morning at breakfast, she heard our tales about the girls of the night before. Pat vowed never to be like those girls. Thanks to her upbringing with the Memphis Mafia, Pat remained a virgin until twenty-one, a ripe old age in Hollywood. The sole drawback was that she often found herself in the uncomfortable position of having to lie to our wives and girlfriends, who also were her friends. We'd be about to leave for a trip and Elvis would put out the word: no wives. Pat had to pretend she was going somewhere else on her own, though she was really traveling with us. When she returned on the same date, she had to greet us as if we hadn't been together all that time.

"Deny everything, Patricia," Elvis told her. He always called her Patricia.

"What if I get caught?" Pat wanted to know.

"Deny it!" Elvis repeated.

"Whaddya mean deny it?"

"Just deny it! Are you their friend or my friend?"

That was the clincher. She had met Elvis first, he always reminded her, so she was *his* friend. Bottom line: Pat wanted to be with us, and Elvis wanted her there.

Initially, Pat didn't know the rules. Anita Wood came to town during the time Elvis was dating actress Sandy Ferra. Pat had just graduated from hairdressing school, and she was doing Anita's hair.

"Who has Elvis been seeing?" Anita casually inquired.

"Well, he's just seeing this one little girl, Sandy Ferra," Pat said.

Later that afternoon, Elvis ordered Pat to his room. He shut the door.

"You want to be around us, you've got to learn to never, ever, ever, say anything about women or anything else we do in private," he said sternly.

"I didn't know," Pat apologized. Anita was very crafty; she'd worked Pat like a pro.

"They'll try," Elvis warned dramatically, as if he were playing a scene in a spy movie. "They'll try everything to get information out of you, but don't ever let them."

That was the one and only time Pat blew it.

By now the Memphis Mafia also included a young friend of Elvis's from Memphis named Jerry Schilling. They had met on a basketball court just after Elvis recorded his first single and remained friends ever since. Several years later, Jerry was on his way home from Arkansas State University where he was a senior, studying to be a football coach and a history teacher. He ran into Elvis and the guys coming out of the Memphian Theater at about three in the morning. Jerry and Elvis stood in the parking lot catching up on news, and Elvis asked if Jerry wanted to work for him. They were leaving for Hollywood that afternoon to shoot another film. Jerry had always fantasized about working for his friend. It took a split second for him to forget about college and teaching history to high school kids.

For the first two years, Jerry was so shy he barely uttered a word. But as a seasoned jock, he helped organize the touch football games we played in a secluded neighborhood park we discovered at Sunset Boulevard and Beverly Glen. Elvis invited his Hollywood friends: actors Rick Nelson, Ty Harding, Max Baer Jr., Michael Parks (who was supposed to be the next Jimmy Dean), Gary Lockwood, Pat Boone, Dennis Crosby (one of Bing Crosby's kids), and Kent McCord. Word got out, and more and more people, especially women, began showing up. At one game, Elvis injured his ankle. Pat Parry and Brandi Marlowe, a five-foot-tall stripper with an amazing body, took him to UCLA's medical center, where he entertained the staff and patients by racing his wheelchair and doing wheelies up and down the hospital corridors. Usually, though, the games ended with drinking Cokes out of the back of a station wagon, flirting, and more horsing around. Then Elvis would invite everyone back to the house, where he wound up at the piano, leading us in group sings of favorites like "Beyond the Reef" and the Hawaiian songs he loved.

Blue Hawaii, shot in 1961, was either the last of Elvis's reasonably good films or the first of the clunkers, depending on your point of view. But even if the early movies had been as godawful as the later ones, Elvis wouldn't have minded much because the first four or five years were so much fun. Just as we were preparing to travel to Hawaii for the *Blue Hawaii* shoot, the Colonel learned of a stalled attempt to build a memorial for the USS *Arizona,* the battleship that was sunk on December 7, 1941, killing thirteen hundred crew members, when the Japanese bombed Pearl Harbor. In honor of their memory, it has never been untombed. The Colonel came up with the brilliant idea of doing a benefit to kick off the fund-raising effort. "What the hell," the Colonel reasoned. "You're going to be there anyway. Paramount pays for your transportation to and from Hawaii. We'll pay for the band and do a show."

Elvis would do anything for his country. "Man, America is the best country in the world," he was always saying. "Where else can a poor country boy like me get so lucky in such a short time?" All of us were proud to wave the flag, but none more than Elvis. That's why he went into the Army without complaining.

We arrived at the airport and were greeted in true Colonel Parker style by an entourage of hula dancers, a Hawaiian band, hundreds of leis—the works. A full-scale motorcycle escort worthy of the president sped our limousine to the hotel. We checked into the top floor of the twelve-story Hilton, at the time the tallest building in Hawaii. The next day we did the show and raised sixty-seven thousand dollars, a great deal of money then for a single show. Thanks to Elvis and the Colonel, the USS *Arizona* Memorial is one of the most popular tourist attractions in Hawaii.

Part of the reason we raised so much money was that the Colonel made all of us buy tickets. Even Elvis had to buy his own ticket. "No free tickets" eventually became the strict rule whenever we toured. No matter what, someone paid for each and every seat. Elvis bought twenty per show. I know because I always wrote out the check to the box office. The Colonel did the same. If you wanted a friend there, you paid for him. That way no one was offended, and no one could take advantage of Elvis. Of course, we gave away tickets, but they were paid for either by the Colonel or by Elvis.

It was the Colonel's idea to do a lot of benefits, and it was a good deal all around. Elvis got favorable publicity and did good works at the same time. The Colonel and Elvis put on the best charity shows because they shouldered all the expenses, and no one was paid. I've heard a lot about the Colonel's fifty-fifty split with Elvis, yet I've never heard anyone mention that 50 percent of those expenses were paid out of the Colonel's pocket. Years after the *Arizona* benefit, the Colonel learned that the *Potomac,* President Roosevelt's yacht, was about to be destroyed. He bought it in Elvis's name for fifty-five thousand dollars and put in twenty thousand of his own money. The yacht was a valuable part of American history. America signed the peace treaty for World War II on the *Potomac,* and it still contained historical documents. It was severely decrepit, and the cost of rehabilitation was twenty-two thousand. The Colonel decided to paint only the side facing the dock, at a cost of six thousand dollars. "We'll put ropes on the other side where you can't see it," he reasoned. That was the most Elvis ever spent on a donation, but he received worldwide publicity in exchange. We flew in from Vegas for the dedication ceremony and then flew right back. The Colonel and Elvis intended to donate the ship to the

March of Dimes because President Roosevelt had suffered from polio. But the charity refused the yacht; they didn't know what to do with it. So they gave the *Potomac* to entertainer Danny Thomas's St. Jude Hospital for Children. Thomas sold the boat and used the money for the hospital.

"Don't we get something?" Vernon always asked.

"We're getting goodwill," the Colonel told him. "That's what we need." The Colonel had honed his keen promotional skills on the carnival circuit, where the barker's pitch makes or breaks an act. Because Tom Parker didn't think like everyone else in the music industry, he revolutionized it.

After the *Arizona* benefit, we stayed for the *Blue Hawaii* shoot, one of the greatest times we ever had. For four weeks we filmed all day on a sunny private beach that belonged to the Coco Palms, a quaint little hotel composed of individual huts and outdoor showers. Elvis dated his costar Joan Blackwood, and I tried, unsuccessfully, to get next to Darlene Tompkins, another of Elvis's costars. Every night, the cast and crew partied until the wee hours. The strain began to show in the early morning shots, so Hal Wallis, the producer, ordered a 10:00 P.M. curfew for the actresses. We skirted that snag by dating girls who weren't working on the movie. Hal Wallis didn't dare give Elvis a curfew. Despite our carousing, *Blue Hawaii* was one of Elvis's most commercially successful movies.

Elvis loved Hawaii. The weather was fabulous, and the people treated him with respect. Unlike mainland fans, who hounded him wherever he went, the Hawaiians left Elvis alone. He made two more films there: *Paradise, Hawaiian Style* and *Girls! Girls! Girls!* It was the location for the famous 1973 "Aloha from Hawaii" television special. A group of ten or twelve of us began taking vacations in Hawaii. I noticed that every time we were preparing to go there, Elvis switched into an especially buoyant mood. On the flight over, he walked around the plane and chatted with strangers. He became a different person. "When I get off the plane in Hawaii," he told me, "it's like a big weight is lifted from my shoulders."

Girls! Girls! Girls! deserves mention if only because it is the sole film record of Elvis in a *truly* excited state. One day, Elvis was preparing to shoot interior scenes with Laurel Goodwin on Paramount's lot. He dressed in the black trousers made for the scene, without putting on underwear. Elvis rarely used underwear.

"Hey Joe, these pants don't feel right," he complained. "They're rubbing me the wrong way."

The dance scene with Laurel was complicated. Elvis had to sing and dance, and the apartment was rigged for special effects, including a coffee table that bounced around the floor and a ceiling that crashed down a few seconds after Elvis and Laurel jumped backward, out of the way and onto a floor model record console. At some point during all the wiggling and jumping, those pants really rubbed him the wrong way, and "Little Elvis," as he called it, became erect. With so much going on in the scene, the director, Norman Taurog, didn't notice. When Elvis came off the set, he headed for the nearest chair and sat down fast.

"Did you see that?" he whispered to me.

"See what?" I asked, trying to hold back the laughter.

"Did you see what happened below the belt?" he answered, concerned but a bit proud. "Damn pants were rubbing me the wrong way and I couldn't stop the feeling. Geez, I hope they don't have to reshoot this. The ceiling might get me this time."

Of course, I had alerted all the guys. It had taken all of our concentration not to yell out wisecracks during the filming. Elvis couldn't wait to see the dailies the next day to see if the camera had caught what happened.

"Hot damn!" Elvis yelped when the dance sequence came on screen. "Will you look at that? I was hoping it wouldn't show because the pants were black. But there it is, sticking out like a sore thumb . . . well, sort of like a sore thumb."

After we got over cracking jokes, we agreed to keep quiet and see what would happen. They do a lot of shooting and you never know how the editing will go and what eventually winds up in the final cut.

"Don't worry, E," I couldn't resist saying. "Maybe they'll be able to cut it out in the editing."

"Man, I hope they don't see it and decide to cut it off before we get out of here," Elvis came back.

I couldn't believe it when the movie came out. There was Elvis, dancing around the apartment with Little Elvis at attention and aimed directly at Laurel! Of course, you had to be looking for it to notice. I'm guessing that only the few of us who knew were looking in that area and saw Little Elvis in action.

Working and living together so closely for long periods meant a lot of wear and tear on the nerves. Elvis was very demanding. I was on call twenty-four hours a day, seven days a week. He needed to know that he could get hold of you at any time. I think it was a security issue, but I'm sure he didn't realize how difficult it could be on occasion, that we had our own lives outside of our time with him.

"Elvis, I need to get away from everyone and relax," I told him once. "I think I'll go to Hawaii for a while."

"Joe! Great idea!" Elvis said. "Let's all go to Hawaii!" I wound up working for two to three weeks, organizing a vacation for Elvis Presley and twenty friends. At first, I was upset, but then I realized, what the hell, he's my friend and we always have a great time together in Hawaii.

Las Vegas was another favorite vacation spot. I met my future wife, Joan Roberts, in Vegas during one of our two-week vacations that stretched out into six. Las Vegas was a great town then, still small enough to be warm and familiar, yet charged with an exciting, brittle electricity. It was a twenty-four-hour playground, and all the hotels were still owned by individuals, not by corporations as they are today. Each bore the stamp of its owner's distinct personality. We always set up headquarters in our friend Milton Prell's Sahara Hotel, where we dallied day and night with an endless chorus line of Vegas cuties. The lounges promoted great shows then, headlined by such performers as Fats Domino, the Four Aces, Diana Washington, Della Reese, and Don Rickles. All the big stars of the day played the hotel showrooms—Sinatra, Tony Bennett, Nat King Cole—and each show opened with fourteen to twenty magnificent showgirls. We were determined to meet every single one. Each girl seemed to have her own special way of being a woman, and we loved the thrill of the chase. Every night we went to a different club, got to bed at 6:00 or 7:00 A.M., slept all day, then started again. We took tranquilizers to sleep and Dexedrine to wake up. Elvis became so rundown that he kept getting nosebleeds and we eventually had to call a doctor.

"Why is my nose bleeding?" Elvis asked innocently.

"Because you have to rest," the doctor replied patiently. "You can't just keep going. Your body is telling you to lie down and take a little rest."

We took off a couple of days and started all over again.

In those days, the dancers were required to stay in the hotel lounges between shows to mingle with guests and ensure that gamblers didn't defect to other casinos. Being familiar with that rule, we used it to our advantage. "See those five girls over there," we'd say to the maître d'. "Ask them if they would like to join us for a drink after the show." Or we just went backstage. That was how I met Joan, a former Miss Missouri in the Miss Universe contest.

She danced in Dean Martin's show at the Sands. We always had a ringside center table, so as she danced by on a large ball wearing a little poodle outfit, I grabbed her ankle. After the show, we met her and the other dancers in the lounge, and I made a date for the next night. We spent the rest of my free time in Vegas together. Elvis volunteered to come along when I picked her up for our first date because he knew I wanted to impress her. We took the Rolls-Royce, but later, Joan confessed that she'd mistaken it for an old car. At least she was impressed with our courtly manners. We fell in love and married in 1962. I moved out of Elvis's Bel Air house, and we took an apartment nearby. But whenever we were in Memphis, we stayed in our room at Graceland. About ten months after our marriage, we had our first daughter, Debbie. I loved my daughter more than I could say, but my life was full of too many temptations. I'm afraid I wasn't the best of fathers. I was never home long enough to enjoy my child. Joan did all the work of raising her and our other daughter, Cindy, who was born three and a half years later. To this day, I hold a lot of guilt about that.

Meanwhile, Elvis was juggling women. He phoned Priscilla regularly, still saw Anita Wood, and dated other girls, mostly Hollywood starlets and hopefuls. Like all of us, Elvis felt no guilt. It was easy to attract women and it was fun. They wanted him, and he wanted them. Anita and Elvis almost broke up when she discovered a letter in which Priscilla had written to Elvis that if she was ever to visit him as he'd asked, he would have to convince her father first. Anita confronted Elvis, they argued, and she left Hollywood in a huff. Not long afterward, Elvis gathered together Pat and the other girls who partied with us. "I want you to know something," he announced dramatically. "I met this girl in Germany and we've been talking on the phone a lot," he said. "I'm bringing her here." No girls except Pat were to be allowed in the house during Priscilla's visit, he said. The parties would stop, and the guys would bring their wives to the house every night. During Priscilla's visit, Elvis's home would be family-oriented.

Elvis had finally convinced Priscilla's parents to allow their precious sixteen-year-old to visit. He'd called her father in Germany and somehow persuaded him that his little girl would be safe in Hollywood. Vernon and Dee would chaperon, he assured Colonel Beaulieu, and she would stay at the home of our good friends, Shirley and George Barris, the man who designed custom cars for Hollywood celebrities. Elvis had tremendous persuasive powers. He just turned on the charm and people did what he wanted. Something about Elvis was totally believable.

Joan, who was pregnant with Debbie, was assigned the job of "taking care of Anita" in Memphis. Elvis usually spent the Fourth of July at Graceland, but he was staying in California for Priscilla's visit. Anita Wood was waiting for him at home, so we figured that if Joan went to Memphis, Anita would believe that Elvis was not far behind. I asked Joan to leave St. Louis, where she was visiting her family, and go to Graceland to keep Anita busy. The heat would be off, and Elvis could deal with the fallout later. Anita, Vernon, Dee, and Joan took an overnight trip to a fishing camp and occupied themselves with various other activities.

When Elvis finally arrived at Graceland, he told me that he and Anita had a serious talk about their future. "I told her that I wasn't ready to settle down," he said. "I told her that I knew she wanted to get married and have a family, so it was better if we stopped seeing each other and went on with our lives." Anita later married Johnny Brewer, a former football player with the Cleveland Browns, and she and Elvis remained good friends until his death.

When Priscilla arrived in Los Angeles in the early summer of 1962, two years had passed since she and Elvis had seen each other in Germany. I went to the airport and picked up a nervous girl of sixteen who confided that she didn't know what to expect. On the way back to the house, I gave her a short tour of Los Angeles. By now Elvis had moved to a large Italian villa on Bellagio Road in Bel Air that had been purchased by Mrs. Reginald Owens for the express purpose of renting it to Elvis! It was very grand, and even came with a butler.

Priscilla looked adorable with her hair caught up in a long ponytail ending in a curl, but Elvis asked Pat to go on payroll during Priscilla's visit so she could do Priscilla's hair every day. Exaggerated cat-eye makeup and big hair, along with lots of false hairpieces anchored in place with gallons of hair spray, was the style of the day. Elvis liked to see Priscilla in what Pat calls "that big boombah" and decked out in the flamboyant outfits Elvis preferred. During the day, she hung around the set, then Elvis squired her around Hollywood, showing her the sights and taking her shopping for expensive clothes. We drove to Las Vegas in Elvis's customized bus and stayed at the Sahara. Elvis took her to all the shows and bought her more wild clothes at Suzy Creamcheese, the famous Vegas boutique. They even gambled together. All this at sweet sixteen.

Of course, Priscilla was impressed with everything. She was young, naive, unspoiled, and unaware of much of what was going on. She spent a lot of time with the wives, so she never saw our real Hollywood lifestyle, although she was a faithful reader of *Photoplay* magazine, and she'd seen the stories about Elvis and other girls. Priscilla questioned him about Juliet Prowse and Tuesday Weld. "Oh, don't believe that stuff in the papers," Elvis assured her. "They all do that in Hollywood. It's for publicity." Priscilla stayed only one night with the Barrises, then moved in with Elvis and slept in his bed. But they didn't make love, Priscilla has told me, and I believe her. Elvis was grooming her for the job of Mrs. Presley. He literally gave her instruction on how to be the perfect wife and mother. When Priscilla left, Elvis called her several times a week, although not every day. They never wrote because Elvis was not a letter writer. I think he wrote six letters in his life: three to Anita Wood, one each to Alan Fortas and George Klein while he was in Germany, and one to President Nixon. But that's another story.

The next step was to campaign for permission for Priscilla to live in Memphis. He was falling in love, so he wanted Priscilla near. Elvis also relished a challenge, and this was as formidable a task as any he'd ever faced. But when Priscilla finally broached the subject to her parents, her father had a fit. "No way in hell," he shouted. "Are you crazy? You're sixteen years old! You have to stay here and go to school." Elvis summoned all his charm for the job. "Please," he begged Colonel Beaulieu. "I'll make sure she lives with my father and his wife, right near Graceland. I'll make sure she goes to Catholic school." I think he also promised her father that he would eventually marry her. Ann, Priscilla's mother, was excited about Elvis and Hollywood and more inclined to let her daughter go. Finally, Colonel Beaulieu agreed to another visit, at Christmas.

It was not until 1963, when Priscilla turned seventeen, that her father allowed her to live in Memphis. Living with us had to be a great strain. She was so young and desperately trying to appear older. And when Elvis was home, she had to stay up all night to keep him company, then go to school in the morning where she was finishing her senior year. After school, she had homework, but by then, Elvis was up, and the night was just beginning. Priscilla functioned on zero sleep. At first, she did stay at Vernon's to keep her promise to her parents. But Priscilla spent most of her time with Elvis, and before you knew it, she was permanently installed at Graceland. I assume her parents knew because she moved in less than a month after she came to Memphis. Elvis still didn't make love to her. He was waiting until they were married.

In the beginning, Priscilla had a hard time adjusting to our rough teasing, Memphis Mafia style. We hurt Priscilla's feelings one day, so Elvis dressed down the entire group while Priscilla cried upstairs. He reminded us that she was very young and we couldn't treat her so harshly. Joan commented that she felt like a child who had been snitched on, but our relations improved, and Joan in particular came to be like a big sister to Priscilla.

We were in Hollywood a lot then, doing three pictures a year. Elvis left Priscilla in Memphis and took off for the West Coast for two or three months at a time. "Okay, we have to go to work!" he would say, and she waited for him to come home. Every day Priscilla went to Catholic high school in her prim little school uniform, packing a little .25 automatic Elvis gave her for protection.

The same year Priscilla came to live in Memphis, Elvis filmed *Viva Las Vegas,* one of his biggest productions. We stayed at the Sahara in Vegas for about three weeks of shooting at the Flamingo and Tropicana hotels and other locations. Ann-Margret, a rising star who was being touted as the female Elvis Presley, costarred beside him. They sizzled together, on screen and off. Elvis was on cloud nine with Ann, and his happiness was contagious. They spent a lot of time alone, which was highly unusual for Elvis. She insisted that he pick her up by himself instead of sending someone else, and he was happy to comply. Elvis was riding a Harley motorcycle at the time and got Ann into riding bikes. If we weren't shooting in the evenings, they went riding in the desert. Sometimes, the four of us went out to dinner and then hit the nightclub lounges. But more often than not, Ann and Elvis went off by themselves. "Okay, you guys, disappear," Elvis said whenever Ann came over. Elvis usually wanted us around, so it was obvious something special was happening. I don't know what went on behind closed doors, but I do know that they were mad about each other, and their affair received a great deal of publicity.

The only problem on the *Viva Las Vegas* shoot involved the director, George Sidney. He was an older man who was in love with Ann-Margret himself and favored her too much in the shots. He saved the closeups for Ann and relegated Elvis to long shots. Needless to say, the Colonel had a talk with the producers and put a stop to that. One day, while we were filming in Hollywood, Elvis paid an unexpected visit to the Colonel's home. Marie, the Colonel's wife, called him at his office on the Paramount lot. "Elvis and all the boys are out front," she told her husband. The Colonel hurried home.

"Ann-Margret's sitting in my car, and the boys are in the other car. I want you to do something for me," Elvis said. "I'm very unhappy and if I don't get to feel better, we're going to go back to Memphis."

"You're on a picture!" the Colonel reminded him.

"I don't care," Elvis retorted.

The Colonel decided he'd better hear Elvis out.

"I want you to manage Ann-Margret," Elvis said. "She doesn't like her managers anymore. I'll pay you extra."

"Elvis, how are you going to pay me extra?" the Colonel asked. "What the hell are you talking about?"

"She's out there, crying," Elvis said stubbornly.

"Look, I can't do it," the Colonel insisted.

Elvis's eyes narrowed. It was apparent that explanations would go nowhere, so the Colonel had to maneuver subtly.

"I'll do it," he said, nodding indulgently and keeping a close watch on Elvis's expression. "But the only way I can is if I spend 50 percent of my time on her and the rest of the time on you." Elvis shot a suspicious look at the Colonel, then thought a moment.

"Let's forget the whole deal," he finally said.

Spending time on Ann was okay, but taking the time away from him was not. It would be too great a sacrifice.

The Colonel believed in Elvis wholeheartedly. Unlike other big-time managers with a stable of seven or eight clients, at 15 to 20 percent each, the Colonel devoted himself to Elvis twenty-four hours a day. "I was offered a lot of entertainers," he told me. "But I only want one—Elvis. I don't need anybody else." After Brian Epstein died, even John Lennon visited the Colonel in Palm Springs to ask if he would manage the Beatles. Tom Jones and many other major stars asked as well. But the Colonel always said no.

Despite his heady romance with his twin soul, Ann-Margret, Elvis was careful to keep in regular touch with Priscilla. However, by now Priscilla was very concerned and upset.

"What about the newspaper pictures of you and Ann-Margret? You're out motorcycle riding with her!"

"I was giving her a ride home and they took some pictures of us," Elvis answered in a tone of pained patience. "It was no big deal." But it was a big deal. Elvis and Ann-Margret were enmeshed in a true love affair. Yet Elvis still felt strongly for Priscilla. He didn't boast about his affairs, but it was clear that he was well pleased with himself. He had a compliant young beauty stashed away back home in Memphis and a fabulous lady in Hollywood.

Elvis knew the affair with Ann-Margret had to end. He and Ann had many conversations about Priscilla, and Ann told me herself that they both agreed their relationship couldn't last. She had a wonderful career ahead of her and wouldn't give it up. She would be famous and have to work on movies for two and three months at a time, just as Elvis did. He wouldn't be able to take that. And there was Priscilla, waiting at Graceland. Ending the affair was the smart thing to do, but Ann and Elvis remained close friends until the day he died.

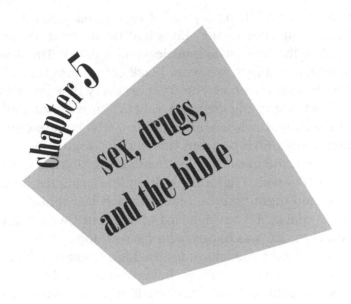

chapter 5
sex, drugs, and the bible

in a total of fourteen years, including two spent in the Army, Elvis made thirty-three films. I was present for twenty-eight of them. From 1960 until 1970, our lives were ordered by a regular rhythm: two or three months of shooting in Hollywood or on location, then several weeks vacationing in either Memphis, Las Vegas, Palm Springs, Colorado, or Hawaii. The Memphis Mafia began playing bit parts in Elvis's movies, which helped break the tedium a bit. The guys were always on the set anyway, and Elvis didn't mind us making extra money. I played a soldier in *Kissin' Cousins,* a carnival barker in *It Happened at the World's Fair,* and a service station attendant in *Clambake,* and in *Stay Away, Joe,* I repossessed Elvis's car.

By the early sixties, the Memphis Mafia had developed into quite a collection of characters, some of whom my friend George Di Domizio labeled accidents. But they were just good ole boys, poorly behaved kids who entertained Elvis with their screwups, and his relationship with them was a volatile mix of business and friendship. Elvis loved having a pack of men to back him up. To give his group a sharper image, Elvis had us all wear identical clothes, as well as the same style bracelets and watches. That lasted about eight months. At first, we wore black cotton jumpsuits. But stretch materials hadn't been invented yet, so every time you raised your arms or sat down, the crotches split. Then we switched to black mohair suits with white shirts and ties, which were equally uncomfortable. Next, Elvis decided we needed a logo. After many days of discussion, he and Priscilla decided on "Taking Care of Business"—"TCB"—with a lightning bolt underscoring the initials. Someone had told them that the lightning bolt was a Mafia sign meaning "Do it quick." I'd never heard of that, but I wasn't about to argue with Elvis. He was happy with his new logo.

Priscilla designed a medallion for the logo, and Sol Schwartz, a friend who had a jewelry store in Beverly Hills, made them up in fourteen-karat gold with beautiful custom-made chains. Soon afterward, Elvis came up with a pendant for the women reading "TLC," for "Tender Loving Care." At first, only our immediate group wore the medallions, but Elvis never did anything halfway. He had to give all his friends medallions, and before you knew it, everyone was wearing one. There's no telling how many he had made over the years, over two hundred at least. We even had them made for our kids.

The only problem the guys had was money. No one was on salary before Elvis was drafted. Elvis took Gene, Red, Cliff, and Lamar on the road with him and paid all their expenses. But they were never salaried. Even when Lamar, Red, and Cliff were in Germany, they weren't paid. I was the first to be put on salary, in 1960, at sixty-five dollars a week. Elvis never thought about money. He just assumed everyone was fine. If you needed money, you asked, or he just gave you something, like a car. Elvis simply lacked a concept of what it took to live. He had grown up poor, so the minimal salaries he paid the guys seemed substantial to him. Vernon handled Elvis's money with a cautious eye, and he wasn't about to tell Elvis to give the boys a raise. When we were in Hollywood, about three times a year, some of them lived with Elvis. But when it was time to go back to Memphis between films, they had to pack up all their belongings and put them in trailers, which they hauled behind their cars. Several of the guys had homes there, others didn't. At the time, Graceland had three bedrooms, but Elvis had the whole top floor for himself. The basement had another bedroom, his grandmother occupied another room, and there was a maid's room off the kitchen. So every time this group of four to twelve guys arrived in Memphis, they had to hang around for two or three days, looking for apartments while all their belongings were packed away in a U-Haul. When we returned to California to shoot another film, the guys who didn't live there had to find a place. All this on about eighty-five bucks a week.

Everyone was afraid to talk to Elvis about the problem, because they knew Vernon wouldn't be happy to hear the guys wanted more money. Finally, one summer day in 1962, the guys called a big meeting with Elvis at the house on Perugia Way.

"Elvis, we don't have enough to live," someone finally said. "Rents have gone up."

"Why didn't you guys tell me?" Elvis asked, astonished. He'd had no idea. From then on, he paid for apartment rentals whenever someone had to live on his own. Vernon had known all along what had been going on. It was the Colonel's job to make money, Vernon's to keep it, and Elvis's to spend it.

Even during the movie days, the Colonel's group and ours were separate and distinct. Colonel Parker and his assistants never stayed on set, but he visited frequently to check things out and hold a short business conference with Elvis. Most of the time, he was busy making deals in his office on the studio lot. We were on location in Crystal River, Florida, in July 1961, shooting *Follow That Dream,* when some townspeople asked the Colonel if Elvis would do an autograph party. He named a price of ten thousand dollars, thinking that would dissuade them. But they actually went for it, and Elvis had to do the party. The Colonel gave Elvis all the money. "I knew I had to give him something to sit down for two hours," the Colonel told me.

If Elvis had filled half the requests he received for interviews and promotional work, he would have quit show business in his first year. One time in New York City, Elvis tried to back out of a scheduled press conference. "Look, if they ask anything you shouldn't answer, I'll cough," the Colonel promised. After the conference, a reporter approached the Colonel. "You better get some cough drops," he said. "I know what you were doing." That was the exception. Usually, the Colonel was able to engineer a situation to Elvis's benefit without anyone realizing what he was doing.

One day, Lamar Fike inadvertently helped the Colonel pull off one of his schemes at the Crystal River location for *Follow That Dream*. When the Colonel had arrived on set, he noticed that the producers had dared to give Elvis the same-size trailer as the other principal players. He immediately ordered a twenty-seven-footer for Elvis, seven noticeable feet longer than the others, and without asking, billed the cost to the producers. The day the trailer was to arrive, the Colonel knew there would be tension. He needed a diversionary tactic.

I was sitting next to Lamar when the assistant director came over. "We're breaking for lunch at twelve at the schoolhouse about a mile down the road," he said. "Let the Colonel know." When the Colonel showed up a few minutes later, Lamar said, "Colonel, Bert said we're breaking at noon for lunch at the schoolhouse about a mile down the road."

The Colonel exploded. "Jesus Christ!" he yelled. "That's it! Lamar, from now on you're in charge. You make all the goddamn decisions. Nobody talks to the Colonel. Forget the Colonel!" As he ranted and raved, poor Lamar couldn't understand what he had done and kept pleading, "What did I do? I'm sorry."

"No, no, no," the Colonel sputtered. "That's all right. Lamar, you're in charge of this goddamn operation. Forget the Colonel! What's the Colonel got to do with it? They want to talk to you! That's it! I'm out of here!" The assistant director informed the director of the outburst, and everyone became frantic. The Colonel was pissed off! This could mean disaster! No one dared bring up the matter of the trailer. The Colonel might blow up completely and pull Elvis from the picture. Mission accomplished.

Actress Joanna Moore was due on location after the other major players, but her reputation for being rather promiscuous preceded her. We were all craning our necks to get a good look when Elvis was introduced to Joanna, a petite, shapely girl with big brown doe eyes. Sure enough, they went off together. The next day, the newspapers reported that they "discovered" each other and shared a romantic luncheon on his yacht. The "yacht" was a twenty-one-foot speedboat we'd brought up from Memphis.

The affair lasted only a few days, but Joanna fell madly in love with Elvis. She was a strange girl who gave the impression of being emotionally fragile. She moved too quickly, spoke in a tense, high-pitched voice, and was overly effusive to Elvis and the guys. Elvis liked Joanna, but after those first few days, he wasn't really interested. He was involved with another actress in the movie, Anne Helm, a voluptuous, down-to-earth woman with an easy personality and a ready smile.

One night, Joanna suddenly showed up at our door at about eleven o'clock. Charlie and I were watching television, and Elvis had already gone to bed because we had to be at the studio very early the next morning. The doorbell rang, and when we both went to see who was leaning on it, there was Joanna, looking terrible, as if she'd just climbed out of bed.

"Joanna, what are you doing here so late?" I asked.

"I have to see Elvis," she said, slurring her words. I thought she had tossed back one too many.

"Elvis is asleep," I told her. "Can't it wait until tomorrow?"

She began crying and demanding to see Elvis, and then she tried to force her way into the house. Charlie and I grabbed her, and she passed out in our arms. Charlie went to the kitchen to get a wet cloth, while I stayed with her. We revived her and I asked what was so important that she had to see Elvis that night.

"Elvis got me pregnant," she sobbed. "And I took a bunch of sleeping pills. I have to talk to him!"

"We better take her to the UCLA Emergency Room right now," Charlie said. We put her in my car and rushed her over.

We informed the doctors what she'd told us, and they pumped her stomach. After several hours, a doctor came out and told us everything would be fine. Charlie and I got back to the house at about 2:30 A.M. I couldn't sleep, so I lay in bed until the sun came up, then met Charlie in the dining room for breakfast. We were having coffee when Elvis entered and took in the grave expressions on our faces.

"Okay, what's wrong?" he asked.

We told him about our night.

"Why didn't you guys call me?"

"We didn't know how she would have reacted if she saw you," I said.

"We just thought it would be better if we took care of it," Charlie explained.

"Make sure you guys call and find out how she's doing today," Elvis said. "I knew that girl had problems. That's why I stopped seeing her." He was concerned about Joanna, but not surprised. I called the hospital later that morning, and the nurse told me Joanna was doing well. As for the alleged pregnancy, the doctors had found no signs of it. We never heard from Joanna again. She later married Ryan O'Neal and had two children, one of whom is the actress Tatum O'Neal.

Elvis seemed to appreciate the way I handled his business, and the first few years I worked for Elvis were amazingly smooth. It wasn't until August of 1964 that we had our first argument. On our way back to Memphis after completing *Girl Happy* for MGM, we stopped over in Amarillo, Texas, and I called the Colonel to let him know where we were. We slept all day, and when we awoke that evening, thousands of fans were massed around the motel. A local radio station had announced Elvis's presence, and Elvis was steamed. The only way they could have known was if the Colonel had tipped them off. But Elvis blamed me for having called the Colonel. He knew I always checked in with the Colonel so he could find us in case of an emergency, but he chose to ignore that fact and jumped all over me. I was just as angry, and quit on the spot. I left the room, packed my bags, and put them in the car. Elvis drove the bus to Memphis, and I rode in the car. When I reached Memphis, I checked into the Howard Johnson Motel down the street from Graceland. I stayed an extra day, hoping that Elvis would want to talk. But he didn't. Elvis never, ever admitted he was wrong. At least I never saw him make an open admission. He preferred to find a way to make things right—usually with a spectacular gift—without admitting his error, like companies that agree to an out-of-court legal settlement without formally admitting to any wrongdoing.

I flew back to Los Angeles to my family and called every friend

I had in the business. Some helped, others didn't return my call. That's Hollywood. I did extra work in several films and television shows, and those four months were probably the closest I ever came to being a real husband and father. At Christmas, Elvis sent me a small check as a present. I called to thank him, and we talked.

"What are you doing?" Elvis finally asked.

"Extra work," I said. I swallowed my pride. "Do you think you could use me in the same job?"

"Sure," Elvis said. "No problem."

If you read Marty Lacker's book, he tells a different story. Marty had taken my place and organized every aspect of Elvis's life—no matter how minute or trivial—down to a ludicrous level. He planned menus for dinner a week in advance, made out shopping lists, which he took to the supermarket himself so he could save twenty bucks, and he circled all the television shows in *TV Guide* he thought Elvis might enjoy. If anyone—and that included all the guys—wanted to talk to Elvis, they had to come to Marty first so he could relay the message. Some of them later told me that toward the end of Marty's brief reign, Elvis began complaining. "I'm tired of this guy mumbling in my ear," he said. "Tell him to brush his teeth." One night, they left the house in Palm Springs without telling Marty, who was asleep. Elvis loved pranks like that and he did them either out of anger or just for fun. Many times, he pulled an intimidating tantrum, then, without breaking stride, glanced over at me and winked. I suspect he had learned one of the Colonel's most effective tactics, emotional diversion. The Colonel was amazingly inventive in conjuring up ways to throw people off-balance and keep them there, because—as he pointed out—the more off-center your adversary, the more options you have.

My return was greeted with a collective sigh of relief from the Memphis Mafia. Marty grumbled a little over his demotion, but it didn't take long to get back into the swing of things. I must admit, I was glad to see Elvis. I knew he was happy to see me too, but he never said it. He liked everyone to think that they were expendable. That, too, he probably learned from the Colonel.

Part of the reason we argued was that by the mid-sixties, making movies had become less fun and more of a chore to Elvis, and he was becoming frustrated. Except for the rare exception, like 1958's *King Creole,* Elvis's talent was wasted in a series of movies where one plot blurred into the next. Only the title, location, cast, dogs, cats, and kids changed. All he had to do was show up and be himself. Essentially travelogues tacked onto the same boy-gets-girl story, the movies were really vehicles for the soundtrack albums, an even dozen Elvis songs—poorly composed and poorly recorded.

So most of the recording sessions after 1960 were soundtracks. At three films a year, with a dozen songs per film, that added up to three albums every year. The songs were usually written to underscore various scenes, such as Elvis serenading a beautiful woman while driving a race car or singing to a little kid in a playground. It's hard to write good rock 'n' roll to suit such unrealistic, corny situations. The Colonel asked Elvis if he wanted to perform on weekends, but Elvis felt he would be too worn out to face the camera early Monday morning. Between film shoots, he wanted to forget about the movies, do nothing but rest and play.

Nevertheless, Elvis had three number-one hits in 1960: "Stuck on You," "It's Now or Never," and "Are You Lonesome Tonight?" In 1961, one Elvis song reached number one—"Surrender"—and "Little Sister" reached number two. But in 1962, he scored only a single number-two hit, "Return to Sender." The downhill spiral would continue until 1969, when Elvis's moviemaking period came to an end and he recorded a total of thirty-five tracks at American Studios in Memphis—the first time he had cut wax in that town since his days with Sun Records.

By 1965, Elvis hadn't scored a hit record in three years. *Tickle Me,* his latest movie, was a flop. The Beatles dominated pop culture the way Elvis had several years earlier. Every piece of music the Beatles put out burned up the charts. They were the hottest thing since . . . well, Elvis. But he would never admit they were good, which was unusual for him. They must have reminded him of his early days, and he probably was a little jealous of the intensity of their popularity. This was the first time that someone other than Elvis had made such a powerful impact on the public. Obviously, they were a threat.

The Fab Four were scheduled to play the Hollywood Bowl that year, and when they landed on the East Coast, they held a press conference. A reporter asked what they wanted to do most in the United States. "Meet Elvis Presley," all four Beatles agreed. The Colonel immediately arranged for a meeting with Brian Epstein, their manager. We had just returned from location for *Paradise, Hawaiian Style,* and were in the midst of shooting interiors on the Paramount lot. The Colonel phoned me on the soundstage.

"Joe, tell Elvis I need to see you. Come to my office."

The Colonel always kept an office on the lot where we were making a movie. It was written into the deal, and the walls and ceiling of each were decorated in an Elvis motif, plastered with Elvis posters and photographs, and autographed photographs signed to the Colonel from presidents of the United States and such famous movie stars as Clark Gable, Frank Sinatra, Bette Davis, and Doris Day. When I walked into the Colonel's office, he was seated behind his large desk, a giant Havana poking out of the corner of his mouth while he talked a mile a minute to a large man in a dark blue suit with long blond hair.

"Joe, I want you to meet Malcolm Evans," the Colonel said. "Malcolm is the road manager for the Beatles and a big Elvis admirer." We shook hands, and for some reason, I liked him immediately.

"Please take him to the set and introduce him to Elvis," the Colonel said.

Malcolm's eyes lit up. He hadn't expected to meet Elvis right away.

"Is this your first time in the United States?" I asked, as we walked to the soundstage.

"No," Malcolm said. "I was here last year when the guys played. The Beatles were hoping to meet Elvis then, but I guess the Colonel and Brian couldn't work it out."

"Well, you're going to meet him now," I assured Malcolm. He was actually getting nervous, talking more and more rapidly and asking one question after another. He asked how I liked working for Elvis, and before I could answer, he asked something else. He ducked into the bathroom twice before meeting his idol, and I noticed that, after the second time, he had combed his hair and straightened his tie. This man worked with the Beatles and hung out with rock 'n' roll superstars, but he was reduced to a quivering mass of nerves at the prospect of meeting Elvis Presley.

"The Colonel and Brian are setting up a meeting for the boys,"

Malcolm said excitedly. "I think we're going to visit Elvis at his home."

We paused for a few moments outside the soundstage. The red light over the door was on, signaling that cameras were rolling for a take. When the light blinked out, we headed for the set where they were shooting. I spotted Elvis in his chair.

"Elvis, I want you to meet Malcolm Evans, a friend of the Colonel's," I said. They shook hands and exchanged pleasantries.

"Are you from England?" Elvis asked.

"Yes," Malcolm answered. "I'm here on business."

"Malcolm is the road manager for the Beatles," I told Elvis.

"Oh, right," Elvis said. "The Colonel told me that you guys are coming over to the house one night next week. I'm looking forward to meeting them." Elvis seemed as enthusiastic about meeting Malcolm as Malcolm was about meeting him.

The assistant director called Elvis for a scene with his costar Suzanna Leigh. Elvis excused himself, shook Malcolm's hand again, and said he'd see him next week. I introduced Malcolm to the Memphis Mafia. We watched Elvis do the scene for a few moments, and then I walked him back to the Colonel's office. Actually, Elvis was just being polite to Malcolm. He had no desire to meet the Beatles. A few days later, the Colonel called me into his office again.

"Joe, I talked to Elvis about the meeting with the Beatles," he said. "He wanted me to get him out of it, but I told him no way. It's all set for next week. I'll get together with you tomorrow to make all the arrangements."

On August 27, the evening of the meeting, I met the Colonel at Elvis's house at 525 Perugia Way in Bel Air. Two limousines would take the Colonel and me to the house the Beatles were renting in Coldwater Canyon, then we'd all come back to Elvis's house. As we left to pick them up, fans were gathering on the street in front of Elvis's house. Word of the meeting had leaked out. At around 7:30 P.M., we arrived at the Beatles' place, a modern house perched high in the hills with a panoramic view of Los Angeles. Security guards opened the gates and we drove through the crowd of girls screaming "John (and Paul and George and Ringo), we love you!" Malcolm met us at the door with Brian Epstein. We shook hands and Malcolm introduced the Colonel and me to the Beatles. The house was full of people I presumed were their friends or people working on their tour. In fact, it looked just like one of our parties. The Beatles seemed very nervous to meet the legendary Colonel, who had a reputation of being unfriendly. They were so restrained and polite that I thought to myself, "These aren't the same hip, wisecracking guys I just saw interviewed on TV!" But the Colonel was very nice to them and offered each Beatle a cigar. After a few moments, we left.

The Colonel rode in the first limo with Brian, John, and Paul. I was in the second one with George, Ringo, and Malcolm. When we arrived, over a thousand kids were waiting, crowding the street that led up to the house and perched on the walls that surrounded it. Flashbulbs popped every few seconds, and the air was filled with screams. It felt like going onstage for a show. We dashed into the house and were met at the door by Alan Fortas, Marty Lacker, and Jerry Schilling. Elvis was waiting in the den with other friends and family: Priscilla, Joan, Sonny, Richard Davis, Billy and Jo Smith, Mike Keaton, "Chief" Ray Stitton, Pat Parry, and Tom Diskin, Colonel Parker's assistant.

The Beatles walked in, and Elvis rose to greet them, wearing a short black jacket over a red silk shirt and black pants.

John stretched out his hand. "Oh, you must be Elvis," he said. Everyone laughed.

"Oh, you guys must be friends of Malcolm's," Elvis came back. More laughter.

Paul and John sat on the couch next to Elvis and Priscilla. Ringo went over to the bar and started a conversation with some of the guys. George floated around the room, trailing clouds of pungent marijuana smoke and enjoying a party of one. The television was on, but the sound was turned off. The jukebox was playing oldies: Chuck Berry, Fats Domino, Jackie Wilson, but no Elvis or Beatles songs. No one was talking. Every time a song finished, an awkward silence hung over the room. It seemed as if no one wanted to start the conversation. Elvis was uncomfortable. John and Paul were just staring at him, as he sat on the edge of the couch, playing with the rings on his fingers.

"This silence is killing me," he said, and he stood up abruptly. "I thought we were here to talk about music and maybe even play some. I think I have some guitars around the house."

"We're a little nervous," Paul admitted, "but we would love it."

Everyone was relieved after Elvis's outburst. The Colonel and Brian began talking in a corner, about management I presumed. George wandered into the family room in the middle of the house where we had a pool table and hit some balls. Some of the wives talked with Ringo. People were beginning to enjoy themselves. The maid brought in snacks, and in honor of our visitors, we stocked beer in the bar—only for this night. The Colonel asked me to show Brian the coffee table that converted into a roulette table. I removed the top section to reveal a complete roulette wheel with all the chips. Brian, Ringo, and the Colonel decided to play, and I was the bank. I wound up a few dollars ahead that night.

Meanwhile, Elvis, John, and Paul were playing guitars and singing in the den. The jam session—all rhythm and blues selections like Chuck Berry's "Roll Over Beethoven," "Promised Land," and "Maybellene," and Ray Charles's "What'd I Say"—lasted about forty-five minutes.

"When are you going to tour again?" John asked Elvis.

"I have too many film commitments," Elvis said. "Maybe after that."

"When are you going to come to England?" Paul wanted to know. "They love you there."

"Someday soon," was the vague answer.

It was getting late by now, and Elvis had an early call the next day. As the Beatles filed out the door, they invited Elvis and the guys to their house the next night.

"I'll let you know tomorrow," Elvis said. "It all depends on my shooting schedule." With that, everyone said goodnight. We had a great time, but no one has a single memento—not a single photo or an audiotape—of that historic meeting.

The next day, I called Malcolm to tell him that Elvis wouldn't be able to make it that night because he had a very early call the next day. Elvis had told me that he didn't feel like going. He said he was tired. His ego could have been the reason, but most likely it had something to do with his "no encore" policy. Elvis didn't do them. He always gave the audience the entire performance the first time out, holding back nothing for an encore. So the meeting with the Beatles was a kind of performance, and Elvis wouldn't do an encore.

Having met them, Elvis decided that the Beatles were terrific. He even recorded Beatles ballads like "Yesterday" and "Michelle." It was not until the group entered their psychedelic phase that Elvis changed his mind. Despite his own passion for exploring altered states of being and dimensions beyond the material, Elvis thought the music was horrible and the lyrics meaningless. The Beatles' music was influenced by the hippie culture and psychedelics. Elvis experimented with those drugs a bit, but his was a different mind-set, part New Age but mostly good ole boy.

So while the younger generation frolicked at be-ins and political rallies, life with Elvis Presley and the Memphis Mafia ran according to a well-worn routine. Being young and energetic, we all had a hard time adapting. Of all the Memphis Mafia, Jerry Schilling was probably the most restless and intelligent, and had the most difficulty adjusting to the monotony. Elvis had always known Jerry would have trouble living at our pace, and he could always tell when Jerry was growing bored. "You know what's going to be the hardest thing for you to do?" Elvis asked when he hired him. Jerry didn't know what he was talking about. "To do nothing," Elvis said. But he was also talking about himself. He understood Jerry's restless spirit because it mirrored his own. Later on, when Jerry told Elvis that he wanted to quit to study film editing full-time, Elvis's response was something along the lines of "You gotta do what you gotta do." Elvis wasn't the kind of person who said, "Oh, come on, stay. Please just stay. I need you." He made you think hard about leaving, because he was proud and wanted you to believe he could do without you. No matter how much he needed someone or became emotionally dependent, he couldn't admit it. "You want to go?" he'd say. "Go." Maintaining that facade was more important than his real feelings.

Elvis also had a hard time dealing with the restrictions his stardom imposed. I often wondered if the reason he changed houses in Hollywood so often was that he wanted a different view. We never went out in public except to cruise up and down the Sunset Strip, because everywhere he went, even all the way to Memphis, hordes of female fans followed. But only a few persistent ones ever became our friends.

The guys were always on the lookout for anything that would provide a break from the hours we logged in front of the television set. Unless Elvis was making a movie or visiting Las Vegas, we stayed in the house and tried to amuse ourselves, playing word games and waging mock wars. But there were times when those four walls, however luxurious or however many amusements we cooked up within them, closed in. We tried to find interesting diversions, but they always seemed to backfire on us.

At one point, Elvis bought a chimp he named Scatter, who had free rein in the house and was always dressed in little outfits. He was harmless and played with my small daughters, but he could be very destructive. One day, he discovered where the electrical equipment in the house was stored and pulled it all out. Another time, he decided to visit a formal dinner party at the house next door. He entered through the back door, his arms raised high, screaming and pulling up all the women's skirts. Another time, three or four of us were having breakfast in the kitchen when Scatter grabbed the leg of the housekeeper, who was doing the dishes. She howled and tried to shake him off, and Elvis was laughing so hard, he couldn't move. Finally, Alan Fortas, who was in charge of the animal, pulled Scatter off. We used to take Scatter to the studio, but we were told not to bring him on set because he made too much noise during takes. We locked him in the dressing room, but he got out one time and went into Samuel Goldwyn's office and tore it up. Goldwyn's assistant came back from lunch to find the office destroyed.

"Where did this monkey come from?" he demanded. He was told it belonged to Elvis, and Elvis was informed that Scatter was no longer welcome at the studio. So we sent Scatter to Memphis. But Scatter didn't last long because he was used to being with us. I think he died of a broken heart.

When we lived on Perugia Way, Elvis bought himself a gorgeous black-and-chrome Harley, a "fully dressed hog," which means it came with all the accessories, including saddlebags nearly large enough to accommodate Elvis's wardrobe. He decided it would be fun for all of us to have cycles, so he told Alan Fortas to call the Triumph dealership near the Samuel Goldwyn Studios on Santa Monica Boulevard and tell them we wanted ten 650 Triumph motorcycles. Alan called, explained who he was and what Elvis wanted.

"When does he want them?" the sales manager asked.

"Tonight," Alan replied. It was about 6:00 P.M.

The salesman laughed. "It's impossible," he said. "They're in crates. Only six motorcycles are uncrated, and it takes four days to assemble them."

Alan reported back to Elvis.

"If we can't have them tonight," Elvis said, "I don't want them." This was Elvis the big kid. He wanted his new toys and he wanted to play with them now! But he was a smart enough kid to know that most people went out of their way if he asked . . . or commanded.

Alan called the owner back.

"I'll have them there tonight," the owner promised.

At one o'clock in the morning, the owner himself drove up in a huge flatbed truck carrying ten fully assembled motorcycles.

Of course, most of us didn't know how to ride. That night, Elvis and Sonny jumped on two bikes and took a little spin around the neighborhood. The next day, Sonny taught me and the others. We started riding in a herd, like the pack in the Brando motorcycle flick, *The Wild Ones,* following a regular route around Bel Air and Beverly Glen. The Bel Air security patrol, a company owned by Howard Hughes, were our friends, and told us people were complaining that "Elvis's Angels" were disturbing the peace of the quiet Bel Air evenings. So we began riding quietly through Bel Air, no zooming, just gliding downhill, but that wasn't fun. Then Jerry Schilling and Sonny West had serious accidents, and that was the end of motorcycle racing in Hollywood for us.

Elaborate practical jokes also helped relieve the tedium. One of the funniest Elvis ever played was on Bill Reynolds, Debbie Reynolds's brother, who was Elvis's makeup man on *Charro!* Elvis learned that Bill was terrified of snakes, so he asked me to go to a pet store and buy a harmless snake. I went on my snake hunt and returned with a harmless gopher snake about three feet long. Elvis told me to hide with it in the small back bedroom of his trailer. He would ask Bill to come in to touch up his makeup and then he would excuse himself. That's when I was supposed to let the snake out into the main room. I got ready, and Elvis called Bill inside. "I'll be right back," Elvis told Bill, then exited the trailer, shutting the door and leaning his weight against it. I let the snake out, and it slithered straight toward Bill. Blood-chilling screams pierced the air as Bill struggled to open the door and escape. Elvis was laughing so hard he couldn't hold the door shut very long, and Bill burst from the trailer, screaming hysterically and pale as a ghost.

A few days later, Bill painted black shoe polish on a telephone receiver, then handed it to Elvis, saying he had a call from the Colonel. Elvis took the phone, but no one was there, so he just hung up. He walked around with a big black ring on his ear for thirty minutes, until someone finally told him. Elvis thought the joke was so funny that he pulled it several times himself, sometimes using binoculars. The chimp, the motorcycles, the clowning on the set, and even the affairs helped keep Elvis's mind off the nagging disappointment that he wasn't doing what he really wanted.

Some guys go to the factory. Elvis showed up at the studio. Making movies was his job, and as with any job, some days were better than others. I could always predict the two days that were the worst: the day he got the script and realized it was absolutely formulaic, a carbon copy of the last absurdity, and the day they shot the publicity stills. Elvis was always in a terrible mood on stills day. He had trouble standing in one place for very long anyway, and for stills, he had to sit on a bare stage for six or eight hours straight, changing outfits over and over, and smiling through it all as if he were having the time of his life. Aside from those two days, Elvis was usually in a good mood. And although he joked around between shots and complained about his scripts before the shoot, he took the business seriously. He was always on time and respectful and helpful to the director. Even during *Stay Away, Joe,* when a gay actor kept grabbing Elvis's crotch during their fight scenes, Elvis confined his fury to the trailer. "I'm going to kill that bastard if he grabs me one more time," Elvis snarled between takes. But he never did confront the actor. Elvis didn't want to embarrass him or upset the mood of the shoot. Once he was committed, he did his job with the utmost professionalism.

After the first few years of making movies, Elvis began going to bed at ten o'clock, so he'd be fresh for the camera in the morning. He always dieted a few weeks before and during the shoot. That was necessary because between films, we usually went back to Memphis to vegetate. We'd plant ourselves in front of the television set or play board games day and night while we chowed down on cheeseburgers and milkshakes. Elvis would shoot up from his normal weight of 170 to 200 pounds or so. We all ballooned out and dubbed ourselves "The Two Hundred-Plus Club."

Elvis understood that problems with scripts couldn't be resolved by consulting the director or rehearsing with his costars. He was usually one of the best actors in the movie, with the notable exception of *King Creole*. Supported by such fine actors as Walter Matthau and Jan Shepard, and directed by Michael Curtiz, Elvis's acting in that movie was nuanced and subtle.

He had great respect for Curtiz, who was almost as famous for his cruelty to actors as he was for the brilliance of his direction. Curtiz was furious when he learned he had to work with Elvis. By the time the movie was completed, Curtiz had nothing but compliments for him. The last day of shooting, Elvis approached Curtiz. "Mr. Curtiz, now I know what it's like to work with a great director," he said.

Elvis also liked Norman Taurog, the seasoned Hollywood veteran who had won an Academy Award in 1931 for *Skippy,* starring Jackie Cooper, and directed *G.I. Blues* and nine other Elvis vehicles. Elvis and Taurog became very close, and after Taurog retired, Elvis stopped by his house from time to time to visit. In 1969, Elvis drove a brand-new Cadillac Fleetwood to Taurog's home on Hillcrest Drive in Beverly Hills, while the guys followed in one of Elvis's Cadillacs. We all approached the front door together and Elvis rang the doorbell.

"Elvis, what are you doing here?" Mrs. Taurog asked in surprise. Normally, he called before a visit.

"We came by to show Mr. Taurog a new car I just bought," Elvis insisted. Elvis always addressed elders and people in positions of authority as "Mr."

"Come on in," Mrs. Taurog invited.

"Well, it's better if both of you come outside," he demurred.

She went back into the house and brought out her husband.

"Elvis, it's good to see you and the boys," Taurog enthused. "It's nice to know I'm still remembered in this town."

Elvis gave him a big hug. "I won't ever forget you," he said.

Then Elvis walked Taurog to where he'd parked the brand-new burgundy-and-black Cadillac.

"Well, what do you think of my new car?" Elvis asked.

Taurog said it was beautiful.

"Sit in the driver's seat," Elvis invited him.

After Taurog was comfortably settled, Elvis reached into his pocket and handed him the keys. "It's yours," Elvis said. "Just a little something for helping me get through those movies. I know it was just as hard for you to make those pictures as it was for me." The articulate director was at a loss for words. He got out of the car and hugged Elvis with tears in his eyes.

King Creole and his warm relationship with Taurog couldn't compensate for the depressing fact that Elvis's dreams of becoming a fine actor were being eroded by the sheer ridiculousness of the movies he was making. He told me he yearned for the chance to realize his acting potential. After a long day on the set, he began complaining bitterly about "those stupid movies." "Every two seconds, I've got to sing another song," he said. He never received anything from the studio but simple, formulaic scripts. Yet even after Elvis realized how horrendous they were, he was so naive that he never grasped the idea that all he had to do was have a heart-to-heart talk with the Colonel. I'm sure something could have been worked out. But he was a child of the South, raised to listen to his elders because they knew what they were doing. He "yes sirred" and "no sirred" movie executives and others in authority until the day he died. It was when he was alone with us that his frustration showed.

There were only a few times that he expressed his anger outside our circle. During a recording session for *Roustabout,* Elvis told the producer that he wanted the Jordanaires to sing backup for a tune he would sing in the movie as he rode a motorcycle down the highway.

"Where would the singers be?" the producer wanted to know.

"The same damn place as the band!" Elvis snapped back. He got his way that time. If he had protested more often, things could have been better.

In 1967, Elvis almost refused to make *Clambake.* He complained incessantly about the script from the moment he read it, telling the studio that he wasn't going to do any more of "those films." United Artists' top executives rushed over to Elvis's house with the Colonel. Elvis had been so angry for two days after getting the script that he had slipped, banging his head against the bathtub so he wouldn't have to show up on set. "This damn script," he told the Paramount executives. "The last time I was a race car driver. The time before that I was a speed boat driver. All the same stuff!" He told them he wanted to do serious movies. The problem was that he never followed through. After a while, he decided to forget about it and do what he was told. The studios wouldn't buy Elvis as a serious actor. If he didn't want to make the scripts they sent him, there would be no movies at all. By then, Elvis's movies weren't doing that well, and some of the studios were looking for ways to get out of their contracts with him. Elvis could have refused to do the movies, but I learned later that Vernon was telling Elvis to make them because they needed the money. Blame for the poor quality of the movies and Elvis's failure to fulfill his acting potential has been laid at the feet of Colonel Parker. But it's not a cut-and-dried issue. The Colonel has always maintained that he never read the scripts. When they came to his office from the studio, he forwarded them directly to Elvis. But perhaps he should have read them.

The mistake was made in the early sixties, when Elvis didn't get tough and refuse to do movies he didn't like. With hindsight, it seems that he and the Colonel should have handled Elvis's movie career differently, thinking less about money and more about establishing a long-range career as a serious movie actor.

the late sixties, the last of Elvis's Hollywood years, were a matter of grab the money and run. Elvis put more energy into our vacations. Hawaii was our family vacation spot, the closest we came to a normal life, and Elvis always took a huge group, never fewer than twelve people, including wives and girlfriends. I would leave a few days ahead to rent the presidential suite on the top floor of the Rainbow Towers at the Hilton Hawaiian Village Hotel and a house on a private beach. We would eat breakfast at the hotel together. Even Elvis got up early some days, appearing at the breakfast table in his "Hawaiian outfit," an aloha shirt with white cotton pants and a yachting cap. Everyone else wore shorts, which Elvis refused to wear because he thought his legs were too skinny. After breakfast, we would take the service elevator downstairs and drive to the private beach.

The first thing we did when we got to the beach was check out the surf. If the waves looked nice and choppy, we sent our driver to get boogie boards. Elvis stayed in the water, boogie boarding for five and six hours at a stretch, coming in only after the girls made his lunch. He would eat and then head straight back into the water amidst our loud and completely useless warnings about cramps. Of course, the guys had to stay in there with him. Elvis and Priscilla, in particular, had great times on those vacations.

Elvis also loved cold, snowy weather, and we spent many vacations in rented houses in Aspen and Vail, Colorado. He wasn't allowed to ski during his moviemaking days because of the risk of breaking a leg, so he took up snowmobiling with a passion. Of course, it wasn't enough just to rent snowmobiles. Elvis had to buy three, even if we were using them for just a week. He bought himself a Yamaha and two Johnsons, then gave them to Ron Pietrafeso, a good friend who still lives in Denver and has the Yamaha to this day.

Of all our vacation spots, our Palm Springs getaways—strictly boys only!—were the wildest. Priscilla unwittingly opened the way for that rule by complaining one weekend that she didn't feel like going to Palm Springs. That was all the excuse Elvis needed: She was never invited again. From then on, Elvis arrived home from a two- or three-month movie shoot, then announced to Priscilla that he had to get away for a rest. Of course, he just wanted to party in the large Spanish adobe house we rented from Jack Warner. It was the perfect party palace, built around a large swimming pool and made private by an eight-foot surrounding wall.

Palm Springs was the scene of one of the few times I saw Elvis drunk. We were filming outdoor shots for *Change of Habit* on the back lot of Universal Studios one bone-chilling Friday night, after which we planned to spend the weekend in Palm Springs. A crew member offered Elvis a drink of blackberry brandy to warm up. Elvis took a sip. He liked it and had a few more. As we left the studio, he told us to stop at a store to pick up a couple of bottles. Luckily, I was driving, because by the time we got to Palm Springs, Elvis was totally smashed. His date helped us get him into bed, where he promptly passed out.

A few hours later, I was awakened from a sound sleep by banging on my door. I jumped out of bed to find Elvis hanging on to the doorknob for dear life, his face a sickly gray-green. "Call a doctor," he murmured, "because I'm going to be really sick." No sooner did he get the last word out than he vomited, drenching me in partially digested blackberry brandy. He was sick the entire weekend. Needless to say, he never took another sip of blackberry brandy, and despite the damage done to me, I was glad Elvis got sick. If it weren't for the internal control mechanism that kicked in whenever he did drink, he would undoubtedly have become an alcoholic.

One day in Palm Springs, I casually mentioned that dune buggies looked like fun, so Elvis bought me a bright-green dune buggy with a Porsche engine. He bought himself a slick black one with a Volkswagen engine from Liberace. His looked better but mine was faster, and we loved racing around Palm Springs.

We decided to ride the sand dunes one night. It was against the law to drive over the dunes at night, but laws did not apply to Elvis. First, we cruised the dunes at a slow speed to check them out and count the number we'd have to jump. Then, amidst yelling and whooping, I took off. But I miscalculated and jumped one dune too many. I was already airborne when I noticed a huge boulder looming about ten feet ahead of me. I slammed on the brakes, but obviously they didn't work in midair: I smashed directly into it. My precious dune buggy's front end was completely destroyed. I got banged up a little when my mouth connected with the steering wheel and my teeth sliced through my bottom lip. Lots of blood ran, but it looked a lot worse than it was. Of course, Elvis and the rest of the guys were dying of laughter. The girl sitting next to me in the buggy didn't find it so amusing, but she was okay. I managed to drive out to the road, so the buggy could be towed the next day, and then I went to the hospital to have my lip stitched up.

In the sixties, Palm Springs jumped on the weekends with lots of folks out for a good time. We cruised the main street—we called it "trolling"—and with Elvis as our bait, always came back to the house with a few carloads of women. We talked, smoked grass, drank, went for late swims, and even had orgies. On some nights we swam nude, but not Elvis. He was too shy. One balmy night, Charlie, Red, Sonny, and I were playing in the pool with several girls we'd met earlier in the evening. Elvis was lying on a lounge chair with one of the girls, while everyone else was jumping into and out of the pool. He got up and slipped off to his room with the girl.

Red took off his bathing suit and started chasing girls. Before you knew it, bathing suits were flying out of the pool and we were frolicking nude in the water. Elvis heard all the laughing and came out of his bedroom door (which opened directly onto the pool area) to investigate. He stood poolside watching us, wearing only a towel wrapped around his waist.

"Come on in!" we yelled.

"Calm down, you guys are having too much fun," he said, laughing.

Then he realized that all the girls were nude. While Elvis was getting an eyeful, Red got out of the pool, snuck around, and yanked off his towel, then jumped back into the pool. For a split second, Elvis didn't know what to do. He stood there in shock, butt naked, before he finally recovered himself and leaped into the pool. When he got out, he wrapped a towel securely around his waist, returned to his room, and didn't emerge for the rest of the night.

Unlike the rest of us, Elvis didn't sleep with every girl he spent time with. He could enjoy girls for their personalities. Sally Struthers, who was playing in the hit TV sitcom *All in the Family*, wasn't Elvis's physical type. But she was a great girl, and they hit it off. Once she visited us in Palm Springs with a girlfriend named Robin, and Sally and Elvis spent the entire evening sitting at the piano and singing together. Sally had a very pretty alto singing voice, surprisingly low considering her high, squeaky speaking voice. It got late, so the girls stayed the night. I woke up the next morning to find Sally Struthers sleeping on the floor with a blanket and a pillow, her mass of blond curls pinned up in hair rollers.

Paradoxically, Palm Springs was also where Elvis indulged in his most extreme spiritual experiments. By the mid-sixties, his interest in religion and the occult had gone beyond late-night bull sessions, gazing at the heavens, and tours of the Memphis morgue, where he whipped off the sheets covering corpses just to hear his dates squeal. Elvis loved playing games like policeman, fireman, and spy, and now his favorite was "master instructing the multitudes." He'd gather his friends and whichever girls were around and read from the Bible and preach. One late night, about fourteen people were at the Palm Springs house. We'd all been smoking grass, laughing and talking, when Elvis turned the conversation to religion. He had smoked a lot of marijuana by then. He asked us to turn off the television and began preaching. Every time he made what he considered a key point, he waved a cane he was using as his staff, then paused to gaze portentously at us before picking up the thread of his theme. At one point, he looked at the Bible he was holding, then exclaimed, "You gotta hear this!" One of the guys groaned under his breath, "Oh, no, not again!" But Elvis was oblivious, pacing the room as he read aloud:

"'Verily I say onto you, except ye be converted and become as little children, ye shall not enter into the kingdom of Heaven. Whosoever therefore shall humble himself as this little child, the same is the greatest in the kingdom of Heaven. And whoso shall receive one such little child in my name receiveth me.'"

Elvis interrupted himself. "Jesus! This is unbelievable. Listen! 'But whoso shall offend one of these little ones which believe in me, it were better for him that a millstone were hanged about his neck, and that he were drowned in the depth of the sea!'" At this point, Elvis leaped onto the coffee table. He pointed the cane skyward and still clutching the Bible, improvised: "And Jesus said, 'Woe ye motherfuckers!' " With that, we all fell out laughing, including Elvis, once he'd realized what he'd said. Everyone was rolling on the floor. Someone lit up another joint and that was the end of Bible class for that night.

Another time when we were all high, we paid a visit to the Palm Springs jail at the invitation of one of our police officer friends, Dick Grob, who later came to work for us as a bodyguard. It happened that all the inmates at the time were locked up for marijuana offenses. And it seemed as if they could tell we were high, because they were grinning and flashing us the peace sign as we passed by the cells. We were becoming a bit paranoid, but Elvis thought the situation was hysterically funny. "Don't pay attention," he kept telling Pat, who was especially worried. "Just keep walking." In his own eyes, he could do no wrong. We got along well with the officers in Palm Springs, partly because Elvis donated large sums to them. During our heaviest gun period, around 1968, the force even allowed us to use the police firing range any time we wanted. Elvis bought guns for everyone, including the girls, whom he taught to shoot, and we spent many a night on the range, blasting away. He especially liked the .44 magnum, the Dirty Harry gun with the eight-inch barrel.

Elvis had begun to smoke marijuana in the late sixties at our suggestion. We hoped it would help him sleep and he wouldn't need the pills, which he was beginning to use regularly. But marijuana didn't alleviate his insomnia and he soon became bored with it.

Elvis even experimented with LSD. In fact, the closest Pat and Elvis ever came to making love together was one night in Palm Springs when they split a tab of LSD at 3:00 A.M. and made out on a lounge chair by the pool. He was a great kisser, Pat pronounced the next day, really wet and soft. Elvis considered his few LSD sessions part of his spiritual quest, an attempt to jam open "the doors of perception." I wouldn't go near the stuff, but Larry Geller, Elvis's occasional hairstylist and on-the-road guru, did. We had met Larry in May 1964, through Sal Orfice, who worked with Larry at Jay Sebring's famous Hollywood hair salon. Sebring, along with coffee heiress Abigail Folger, actress Sharon Tate, and others, later died tragically at the hands of the Manson family. Tall, dark, and good-looking, Larry was married, had kids, and fooled around with other women, just like the rest of us. When Larry cut and styled Elvis's hair, they would discuss mysticism and the occult.

Larry introduced Elvis to the Self-Realization Fellowship, a worldwide yoga organization based in Southern California. The organization had been formed by Parmahansa Yogananda, and after his death, the leadership was passed to his assistant, an American woman named Diamata. Elvis learned that Diamata lived in a house on Mount Washington that served as the center's headquarters, and he asked me to arrange our visit. We arrived at a huge complex with men who looked like monks strolling about and were ushered into Diamata's office, where an attractive, middle-aged white woman wearing a sari sat behind a desk. We talked with her for hours. Elvis signed us up and gave the organization five thousand dollars. It was a very impressive experience, but only Larry and Elvis really got into it. Soon afterward, Larry guided Elvis's first LSD trip with six or seven others at the Perugia Way house. The point wasn't to get high but to gain greater self-knowledge and enlightenment. Elvis had been very taken with an LSD primer written by Timothy Leary, the former Harvard professor, so everyone who was to take acid had to read Leary's book first. Sonny West would stay straight in case someone had a bad trip and needed help.

"We took the LSD with the idea of having a spiritual awakening," Jerry Schilling said. "This was supposed to be a mystical time, but mostly we laughed. I remember Elvis, who was looking great then, sitting in a chair. Suddenly, he began to look to me like a little fat boy whose feet couldn't even reach the floor. Some time later, we were moving into a different room, and I veered off from the group into a big walk-in closet right off the master bathroom. Elvis and I could hear each other laughing, and that set off one of those contagious laughing jags. But we were babes in the woods compared to what was going on at that time."

Elvis's experiments with recreational drugs were short-lived and harmless, but he was beginning to abuse prescription drugs. Like most addicts, Elvis refused to believe he had a problem, and his denial was aided by the fact that doctors were giving him the drugs by prescription. Everyone around Elvis knew when he was high, but then again, most of us were stoned, too! I remember once when we were sitting by the pool and Elvis announced to Pat that he was on the wagon.

"Elvis, you're stoned," she said.

"I am not," he insisted.

Just then Jerry Schilling walked by. "Jerry," Elvis called out, "Patricia says I'm loaded. Tell her I'm not loaded."

"Yeah, sure," Jerry answered, indulging him. "You're not loaded." Any other comment would have been futile.

"I would never get involved in something like that," Elvis said many times, referring to the Beatles' advocacy of a diet of psychedelics. "Okay, I've taken uppers and sleeping pills, and I've smoked a few joints, but I would never be that outrageous. I want too much to be in control."

All those years we were carrying on in Hollywood, Las Vegas, Palm Springs, and on various movie locations, Priscilla was waiting in Memphis for Elvis's visits. She had graduated high school in 1964, after living there one year, but Elvis didn't want her to work, so she filled the empty hours shopping and talking to Minnie Mae. Elvis expected the same devotion in his future wife that he'd received from Gladys, despite the fact that he rarely spent time alone with Priscilla anymore. When they were together, Elvis treated her with tenderness and love, but otherwise she was left to her own devices.

At fourteen, Priscilla had been timid and quiet, but she slowly gained confidence and started to pick up some of Elvis's cocky ways, even treating him to Memphis Mafia–style barbs. Elvis's plan of molding himself an ideal, compliant wife—an unrealistic goal at best—was in jeopardy. His little girl was growing up. For her part, Priscilla knew deep down that Elvis had other women but didn't want to admit it to herself. Yet she hunted for signs of his unfaithfulness. She snooped through his makeup kit, searching for notes from other women. Whenever she approached Elvis with hard evidence, he would go on the offensive. "Don't you trust me?" Elvis always asked her, initially playing it hurt and indignant. "Don't pay attention to what you read in the papers," he warned. "Oh, those are superimposed," he scoffed whenever she showed him photographs picturing him with other girls. If she pressed the issue, he exploded. Overpowered, she was forced to back down. Nevertheless, Priscilla couldn't stop checking up on him. Sometimes she tried to disguise her voice and called the Hollywood house. "Hey, boys! Any parties tonight?"

Sonny answered the phone one time. "Yeah, big party tonight," he said. "Elvis is getting a haircut right now. Come over after nine!" That really got to her.

One time, years later, when we were in Las Vegas playing the Hilton, Jo Smith, Billy's wife, and Priscilla drove from Los Angeles to Palm Springs on their own. There, they discovered notes in the mailbox left for us by various girls. One read, "Dear Sonny, I had a great time last weekend," and was signed "Lizard Tongue." There were a few others—luckily, none to me. Priscilla immediately called Vegas, and I answered the phone.

"I've got to talk to Elvis right now," she said.

"About what?" I asked. "He's getting ready to go on stage. Is it really important?"

"I have to talk to him right now!" Priscilla insisted.

Elvis got on the line, and Priscilla told him what she'd found. "I'm in Palm Springs," she said, "and I've got all these notes from women you guys have been out with."

Elvis took his usual tactic: a strong offensive.

"I'm getting ready to go on stage," he said in exasperated tones. "There's two thousand people out there waiting for me! I'm supposed to be out there, smiling and happy. What the hell are you doing calling me at this time? Those notes are all bullshit. Tear them up and throw them away! They don't mean a thing! It's just fans trying to cause trouble." He hung up without saying goodbye.

Another night, Jo and Priscilla drove down from Los Angeles to Palm Springs where we were supposedly resting. They parked on a dark street across from the house and watched the parade of women inside the house as they moved back and forth past the open windows. Then they drove to a pay phone and Jo called the house, trying to pretend she was one of our local girlfriends.

"I heard there's a party there tonight," she said. "Can we come over?" But Billy answered the phone and immediately recognized his wife's southern-inflected voice.

"Jo! What are you doing calling here?" he asked.

"Oh, I'm just kidding around," she said nervously.

The girls hung up and drove straight back to Los Angeles. They were so frightened of provoking our anger that they never said a word about it. In fact, it was only recently that Priscilla told me that story.

We kept our women sheltered from the outside world, partly because of how the public behaved whenever they spotted Elvis. They would literally elbow and push Priscilla out of the way to get to him. But we also kept them isolated because that way, we had better control. Priscilla once brought a friend home from her dance class. After the friend left, Elvis told Priscilla that the moment she'd left the room, the girl had made a play for him. He could have said that to keep Priscilla from making friends from outside the clan. For my part, I told Joan all about the other guys' extramarital exploits, and I'm sure Elvis told Priscilla about the rest of us. So Joan thought every husband cheated except hers, and Priscilla thought all the guys were unfaithful but Elvis. Except for Jo and Priscilla, none of the women voiced suspicions to each other because the Memphis Mafia and their women were a clan. Any individual dissenter automatically posed a threat to the integrity of the entire group. The girls barely talked among themselves, because no one wanted to be the troublemaker.

Once, in Vegas, we were watching a show with our wives. Joan thought it would be funny if she sent me a note saying "Dear Joe, I'm the girl you met in blah blah," just to see what I would do. She excused herself and gave the note to a bellhop in the lobby, telling him to ring the bell in five minutes. When the bellhop rang and announced he had a message for Joe Esposito, Sonny went to get the note and bring it back to our table. But he didn't give it to me, and Joan realized something was up.

"Sonny, didn't the bellhop give you a note for Joe?" she asked.

"Yes," Sonny said, coolly enough.

"Then why didn't you give it to him?" Joan wanted to know.

Sonny didn't answer right away, and Joan became furious.

"No one can even play a joke around here!" she complained. "This is ridiculous!" She stood up and stalked away from the table. Elvis hit the ceiling. I went after Joan and told her to apologize to Elvis for causing trouble. Joan thought she'd been playing a joke, but to us, it was serious. We were that paranoid and that ruthless, protecting each other because we were cheating so much. "Never, ever admit it," Elvis always told us. "The girl can be there, right in front of her eyes, but never admit it."

Another time, Joan decided to fly to Tahoe to pay me a surprise visit. Elvis had a housekeeper named Henrietta who came to my house once a week whenever he was out of town. She noticed Joan packing and asked where she was going. "I feel I have to see Joe," Joan told her. When the coast was clear, Henrietta called Tahoe to warn us. Everyone, including Elvis, got rid of their girlfriends, except for Sonny, who was in bed with a girl and just locked his door. Poor Joan had no idea why everyone was so cold to her that weekend.

Elvis was a devout follower of the old double standard. And it was convenient for the rest of us to fall in with his logic.

By 1967, Priscilla had been living with Elvis—after a fashion— for five years. She was twenty-one, certainly old enough to become a wife. Elvis and Priscilla had been talking about getting married for over a year, discussing when to do it and how it would affect his career. It was time for him to get married, and he knew it. He had been with Priscilla since she was barely sixteen, and there had to have been pressure from her family.

According to the Colonel, Elvis telephoned him in Palm Springs. "Priscilla and I want to get married," he announced.

"That's fine," the Colonel replied.

"I want to get married in Vegas," Elvis said. "Would you set it up?"

The Colonel called Milton Prell, our friend who owned the Aladdin Hotel. Then he asked Marty Lacker and me to meet with him and Elvis to make arrangements. At about 4:00 A.M. on May 1, 1967, Elvis, Priscilla, George Klein, Joan, and I snuck out the back of the Palm Springs house to avoid the fans and press, some of whom seemed to have gotten wind of the marriage plans. We climbed over a small wall and into a waiting car that took us to the Palm Springs airport. There we boarded a private Lear jet owned by Frank Sinatra and flew to Las Vegas, while Marty and the rest of the wedding party took a larger plane. At the Las Vegas airport, another car was waiting to take us to the courthouse to fill out papers for the marriage license. I paid the fifteen-dollar fee because Elvis wasn't carrying money. Then we went to the Aladdin so Elvis and Priscilla could rest before the wedding.

The ceremony, performed by Judge David Zenoff, a justice of the Nevada supreme court, took place at ten the next morning in Milton Prell's apartment in the hotel. The guests included Milton and his family, the Colonel and his wife, Marie, Colonel Beaulieu and his wife, their son Don, George Klein, Billy and Jo Smith, Patsy Presley Gambil and her husband, Gee Gee, and Vernon and Dee Presley. Priscilla's sister Michelle was the maid of honor; my wife Joan was the matron of honor; Marty and I were co–best men.

At the time Elvis decided to marry Priscilla, Marty was the flavor of the month. Elvis was like that. His moods changed and he was into different people at different times. There were periods when Elvis couldn't seem to get enough time with a particular person. Then, without any apparent reason, his interest would shift toward someone else. I was on the interest list more often than not, whereas Elvis and Marty had a love-hate relationship. After he'd asked Marty to be best man, he soured on him and asked me to be best man. That really upset Marty.

"Joe, you be the best man," he said with a martyred air.

"No," I said, "let's both be the best man." That worked out fine. The ceremony was over in a few moments. I handed Elvis the three-karat diamond wedding ring and he slipped it on Priscilla's finger. Afterward, we had a huge reception with a five-foot-tall wedding cake. Then Elvis and Priscilla held a press conference, and the news

This is the house at Goethestrasse 14 in Bad Nauheim that Elvis rented while he was in the Army. It is where I met Elvis in 1959, and where he met Priscilla Beaulieu.

I took this picture of Elvis on September 10, 1960, at his home at 525 Perugia Way in Bel Air, California. He was working out with Red and Sonny West in the backyard. (© Boulder City Productions)

Elvis, me, and Sonny West in 1960, sitting around between takes on the set of *Flaming Star* at the Conejo Movie Ranch in Thousand Oaks, California.

Juliet Prowse, Elvis, Pat Boone, and Sonny West on the set of *Wild in the Country* (1961). Juliet had costarred with Elvis in *G.I. Blues* earlier that year, and Pat, who was good friends with Elvis, stopped by the set to say hello.

Tuesday Weld and me on the set of *Wild in the Country* at the 20th Century Fox studios in Beverly Hills. Elvis and Tuesday had an affair during the making of that movie.

Santa Claus (Colonel Parker) and Elvis on the set of *Wild in the Country* (1961). The Colonel liked to play Santa during the holidays, and often went to children's hospitals to give out gifts.

Elvis and me in 1962 on the set of *It Happened at the World's Fair* on location in Seattle. I made my acting debut in this film as a carnival man.

On the set of *Fun in Acapulco* in February 1963. *(From left to right)* Colonel Parker (dressed as a Mexican general from Acapulco), Marie Parker, Charlie O'Curran (who staged the musical numbers), and Elvis.

Elvis and me, his best man, preparing for his wedding at the Aladdin Hotel in Las Vegas, May 1, 1967.

The Graceland wedding reception thrown by Elvis and Priscilla for all his relatives and friends who didn't attend the wedding in Las Vegas. *(From left to right)* Frank Esposito, Josephine Esposito, Elvis and Priscilla, Joan Esposito, and myself.

Elvis practicing karate with Red West in Bel Air. Elvis is going for a thumb to Red's eye. Only kidding.

Elvis elbowing Red West in the back. These karate practices would go on for hours.

Colonel Parker's office on the Paramount lot. *(From left to right)* Colonel Parker, me, Alan Fortas, Tom Disken (at the typewriter), Grelun Landon (who worked for RCA), and Jim O'Brien, the Colonel's secretary.

July 1967. Elvis and Priscilla at the Hillcrest house, preparing to go out to the Luau Restaurant in Beverly Hills, one of Elvis's favorite places to eat.

On the set of *Speedway* in 1968. *(From left to right, standing)* Jerry Schilling, Marty Lacker, Larry Jost (soundman on the film), Elvis, Don Sutton (rookie with the Dodgers), Richard Davis, and George Klein and me *(in the front)*. Larry Jost brought Don Sutton over to meet Elvis.

Debbie Esposito holding Lisa Marie Presley in her room at the Hillcrest house in May 1968.

Elvis on the set of *Live a Little, Love a Little* with director Norman Taurog. Taurog, who worked with Elvis on nine of his films, is showing Elvis how to throw a punch in the scene.

On vacation in Hawaii in 1968. Marvin Gambil,
Lamar Fike, Tom Jones, Elvis, me, and Charlie
Hodge *(in the front)*. Elvis and Tom, who was performing in Hawaii, were friends, and Elvis invited him
to spend the day with the Memphis Mafia.

May 23, 1968, at the USS *Arizona* Memorial in
Hawaii. *(From left to right)* Marvin (Gee Gee) Gambil, Patsy Presley Gambil (Elvis's first cousin),
Priscilla, Elvis, Joan Esposito, and me. Elvis did a
charity show in 1961 to raise money to build the
memorial.

Joan Esposito and Priscilla Presley in 1970. They were very close friends.

At the Houston Astrodome on February 27, 1970, Elvis is waving goodbye to his audience of 60,000 people, the largest crowd he had played up to that date. *(From left to right)* Sonny West, Red West, me, Vernon Presley, and Elvis. (Joe Tunzi)

Elvis met Hollywood starlet Barbara Leigh in Las Vegas in 1970. They dated for about two years. (Barbara Leigh)

Elvis and Priscilla at the Las Vegas International Hotel. This is my favorite picture of Elvis and Priscilla because they look so great together.

Sheila Ryan. I introduced her to Elvis in Las Vegas in 1972. They dated on and off for about two years. She later married actor James Caan. (Sheila Ryan Caan)

Elvis and Patti Parry in 1973. (Patti Parry)

September 7, 1974, at the Regency Hotel in Denver. Elvis with Denver police officers Robert Cantwell and Ron Pietrafeso. One of Elvis's great passions was collecting law enforcement uniforms and badges. Here he is wearing the uniform of Denver Police Captain Jerry Kennedy. (Robert Cantwell)

Elvis and Linda Thompson on the *Lisa Marie* in 1976. (Jeanne Lemay)

Mindi Miller, actress and model. Elvis and Mindi met in March 1975 and dated through November 1976. (Mindi Miller)

Elvis and Ginger Alden in Hawaii. Elvis met Ginger, who looks much like his mother, in November 1976. This was Elvis's last vacation before he died.

(From left to right) Jerry Schilling, Frank Dileo (Michael Jackson's manager at the time), me, and Colonel Parker having dinner at Stellini's Restaurant in Beverly Hills in 1986.

was flashed around world. They changed their clothes and we all flew back to Palm Springs where we enjoyed a group honeymoon for three or four days, beginning that night with a wonderful home-cooked wedding dinner. Elvis was in a rare romantic mood. That afternoon, he had gone out to the garden to pluck a rose for Priscilla, which he set next to her place on the table. He even carried her across the threshold. If Elvis was initially reluctant to get married, on his wedding day, he couldn't stop grinning. We were all happy, except for Red West, who was wounded deeply because he hadn't been included in the wedding party. Red and all the guys were in Vegas for the wedding, but the Colonel said there was only room for the family.

"Well, damn it," Red said, "if I can't go to the damn wedding, then I shouldn't even be here." Some of the other boys were upset too. Red stayed in his room and didn't even attend the reception. He and Elvis discussed it later, in Los Angeles, but of course, Elvis blamed Red's exclusion on the Colonel.

A few weeks after the wedding, we had another reception in Memphis for the rest of family. Then Elvis and Priscilla had another honeymoon on the Circle G, the ranch he'd bought shortly before their marriage.

The Circle G era started when Elvis bought Priscilla a horse for Christmas in 1966. Elvis asked Jerry Schilling to locate horse ranches around Memphis, and he had Graceland's maintenance man prepare the stables out back. Then Elvis and Jerry took off to see what the ranches had to offer. In a few hours, they returned with a beautiful quarter horse named Domino, solid black except for one white sock. Jerry held the horse while Elvis went into the house to bring Priscilla out. He led her out the front door, right up to Domino, with his hand covering her eyes. When he took his hand away, she was looking straight at this gorgeous animal.

"Where did he come from?" Priscilla gasped.

"I bought him for you," Elvis said, very pleased with her surprise and delight. "He's your Christmas present."

Priscilla went crazy, hugging and kissing Elvis.

"I've got to ride him right now!" she said. The horse was already saddled and bridled, so Priscilla jumped on and took off for the pastures. She rode Domino every day she was at Graceland.

Elvis decided he didn't want Priscilla to ride alone, so he asked

Jerry if it would be okay to buy a horse for his wife, Sandy, another animal lover. That started the ball rolling. Then Elvis rode Domino a few times.

"I need a horse for myself," he told Jerry. "I want a golden palomino. Call around and see if anyone has one for sale." Jerry located a palomino stallion at a ranch not far from Graceland. His name, Rising Sun, was a good selling point, and he was a beauty. The moment Elvis set eyes on him, this was the one. Now Graceland housed three horses, and Elvis was having so much fun that he wanted everyone to share his enjoyment. He bought horses and equipment for all the guys and their wives, if they wanted one. We all worked on the stables, cleaning them out and painting the stalls. Elvis was beginning to fancy himself as a rancher, so he had to dress like one. We went to a western clothier and Elvis bought us all outfits: jeans, cowboy boots, sheepskin jackets, and of course, western hats and ranchers' gloves. Before we knew it, the horse population, now at sixteen, had outgrown Graceland's eight stalls.

A few months past Christmas, Elvis and Priscilla were driving with Alan Fortas around Horn Lake, Mississippi, about fourteen miles from Graceland. They spotted a large ranch for sale, 160 acres with a large herd of Santa Gertrudis cattle. The property included a three-acre lake traversed by a white bridge. Next to it stood a twenty-foot-tall white cross that, for some reason, the cattle clustered around every evening. Scattered nearby were three barns, plenty of room for the horses. The ranch house was about one hundred years old, but it had been completely renovated to look like a home featured in a decorating magazine. Elvis asked Alan to go inside and find out what the owners wanted for the property. Alan came back a few minutes later.

"They want $485,000, and that includes the cattle," Alan reported.

"Let's go home and talk to Daddy," Elvis said.

They drove straight to Vernon's house.

"Daddy, I found the perfect ranch," Elvis said. "I want to buy it." He described the place and told him the price.

"Now, wait a minute, son," Vernon said. "That sounds like too much money to me. Do we have to buy the cattle with it?"

"I want the cattle," Elvis protested, his mind already spinning visions of himself as a rancher. "What's a ranch without cattle?"

The next morning, Vernon drove to the ranch to see the owner, Jack Adams. They struck a deal, and Vernon went to his bank to borrow the money. Elvis was now a full-fledged rancher, the proud owner of a herd of cattle and sixteen horses. He named his new place the Circle G, and bought pickup trucks for all the guys. Vernon was tearing his hair out. Then Elvis decided we all should live with him on the ranch, so he bought six extremely large trailers. Of course, he wanted them delivered the very next day. He wasn't aware that he needed permits from the city and he had to pour cement pads, not to mention get hookups for water, electricity, and sewage. So Elvis cast himself in the role of ranch foreman. He no longer looked like a famous singer and movie star. Wearing a cowboy hat and sheepskin jacket and sitting tall in the saddle, he was a dead ringer for the Marlboro man.

Every morning he saddled Rising Sun and rode out to issue instructions to the contractor on how to do things and where everything should go. Only one trailer was placed near the main house, the one designated for Alan Fortas—who was supposed to be in charge of the ranch—and his wife. Finally, everything was ready. We moved into our trailers, Elvis had all the horses shipped over, and we settled into ranch living. Of course, Elvis was so tickled by the notion of living in a trailer on his honeymoon that he asked Alan to move into the main house. Lisa Marie was conceived in that trailer.

When he tired of living in the trailer and moved back into the house, he and Priscilla saddled their horses every morning and rode out back to join us for a cup of coffee. On weekends, we threw giant barbecues. The wives prepared all the food, except for the meat, which I cooked on an open grill. We had great times.

For a year and a half after the marriage, between making movies we headed straight for the Circle G. Elvis felt very comfortable in his own little ranch world and usually hated to be torn from it.

During that time, Richard Cole, Led Zeppelin's road manager and a friend of Jerry Schilling's and mine, was also handling Eric Clapton's tour. Clapton was a big Elvis fan. He was scheduled to do a "touch-and-go" performance at the Mid South Coliseum in Memphis, so Richard called Jerry at the ranch. Richard wanted to fly into Memphis with Eric the night before his show so Eric could meet Elvis. If Eric couldn't get together with Elvis, they would come in the day of the concert, do the touch-and-go, and be consoled by saving hotel costs. Jerry knew Elvis wouldn't want to meet anyone. "Richard, you know he doesn't have anybody come up," Jerry told his friend. Elvis hadn't had a hit record in a while. He'd been busy making movies and he wasn't listening to the radio. Jerry knew Elvis had no idea how big Eric Clapton was. "The only thing I can tell you," Jerry offered, "is that if we go out to a movie that night, I'll ask Elvis if he'll meet Eric there." The chances of that happening were good because Elvis was on a movie streak, renting the Memphian six or seven nights a week. Jerry told Elvis about the call.

A few weeks later, Jerry mentioned again that Richard Cole and Eric Clapton were coming in. Of course, Elvis didn't remember.

"Well, Richard is doing this tour with Eric Clapton and he's flying in," Jerry explained once more. Elvis didn't answer, just shot him one of those "I don't believe you're saying this" looks.

"Elvis," Jerry pleaded, "if we go to a movie, would you do me a favor? Before or after the movie would you say hello to the guy?"

"All right, fine," Elvis agreed grudgingly.

The night Clapton was supposed to meet Elvis at the movie theater, Jerry rode into town with Elvis at the wheel of a Camaro pickup. He was wearing his cowboy hat and, because it was winter, his sheepskin ranchhand coat. On the way, Jerry nervously reminded Elvis of his promise.

"Elvis, remember Eric Clapton, the guy I was telling you about? He'll be coming here to be introduced to you."

"Fine," Elvis said.

When our pickup truck procession pulled up in back of the movie theater, two limousines were waiting.

"Who in the fuck is Eric Clapton?" Elvis growled.

"Oh, God," Jerry thought. Once again, he explained the visit to Elvis, emphasizing that Clapton was doing a big concert the next night. But Elvis was angry. The theater manager had already let in Eric, his girlfriend Patty Harrison, Richard Cole, and a couple of guys who worked on their tour. Jerry made the introductions. Elvis was as nice as he could be, and spent several minutes in pleasant conversation with Clapton. Then Elvis said, "We might as well start the show. Help yourselves to whatever you want." Eric and his party took their seats.

"That Eric Clapton is really a nice guy," Elvis remarked.

Elvis was the same when he was at Graceland. He wanted nothing to do with show business and refused to meet anyone, no matter how big a star. James Brown, who was an Elvis fan and for whom Elvis had tremendous respect, called every time he flew into Memphis on a Lear jet decorated with paintings of his gold records. Brown knew Alan Fortas, Richard Davis (who worked with us for a short time), and a couple of the other guys, but Elvis never took his calls. The reason had nothing to do with lack of respect on Elvis's part. That's just how adamant he was about not meeting anyone.

In Hollywood, he welcomed visitors, but he almost never went out in public. One night, however, he made an exception. We went to The Trip, a club on La Cienega Boulevard next to the old Hollywood Playboy Club, because Elvis wanted to see Jackie Wilson, a big star at the time, known as "Mr. Entertainment" for his amazing voice and even more astounding performing ability. Elvis admired Wilson tremendously and had been deeply influenced by his style. The Trip barely held two hundred people, but James Brown was also in the audience that night, as were the Rolling Stones. It was the Stones' first or second visit to Los Angeles, so we weren't really aware of them. But Elvis knew James Brown had called Graceland many times, so he walked over to his table and introduced himself.

"Why is it that whenever I call you, you're always asleep?" Brown asked. That was the entire conversation. Elvis kind of smiled, said goodbye, and walked back to us.

"Boy, that was strange," he said. Brown's comment was understandable from his point of view, but Elvis needed that time away from the business. He thought that by not seeing anyone, by being impartial, he could see to it that no one felt slighted. In later years, Brown and Elvis did get together and became good friends.

Elvis and Wilson got along terrifically from their first meeting, and after Wilson's show, Elvis invited him to the studio for a few days while he was shooting a movie. They talked a lot during Elvis's breaks, particularly about Wilson's ambition to act in films. The problem was that Jackie Wilson's management company, which was rumored to be associated with the Mafia, had its singer booked solid all year, mostly in its own clubs. Wilson never had three months free to do a film. Elvis identified with his dilemma. Like Elvis, Jackie was good-looking and intelligent, and the talent he longed to express was being wasted.

On February 1, 1968, toward the end of our ranching period, Lisa Marie was born. Priscilla was slim for the entire nine months and did anything she wanted. In fact, she went horseback riding the week before she gave birth. Just before Lisa Marie's arrival, Nancy Sinatra, Elvis's close friend, gave Priscilla a lovely baby shower. I was in California when Priscilla went into labor, and I got a phone call saying she was on the way to the hospital. "Tell her to hold on until I get there!" I said, only half-joking. I caught the next plane out of Los Angeles, and Jerry Schilling picked me up at the airport. We headed straight for the hospital. She gave birth immediately after I arrived.

Charlie told me that when Priscilla began feeling pains, she came downstairs. "Elvis, I've got to go to the hospital!" she said. Elvis and Charlie ran to get the car. As she was waiting on the front steps, her water burst. Panicked, the men bundled her in the car and promptly drove to the wrong hospital, Memphis Methodist instead of Memphis Baptist.

Elvis was thrilled with his baby girl. He loved babies and played with my kids all the time. Debbie, my daughter, was the first baby in our group. Elvis and whichever girl he was seeing often took Debbie up to his bedroom and played with her for an hour or two. The children were always around; it was never "keep the kids away." They were part of our family. Elvis was just a big baby himself. He even used baby language, giving his girlfriends names like "Satinin," the pet name he used for his mother and Priscilla. Priscilla called Elvis "Nungin," Gladys's name for her son, a mangled abbreviation of "Young one."

Elvis showered the tiny female replica of himself with lavish, often inappropriate gifts. For her second birthday, he gave Lisa a diamond ring and a mink coat. She and my kids spent most of their early years together. If one had a birthday, all three were there. At a very early age, Lisa knew who she was—the daughter of Elvis

Presley. She knew people were always watching her and behaved appropriately in public. At age four or five, she even started bopping out orders.

"If you don't do what I want, I'll tell my dad," she'd threaten every so often in her sweet, piping voice.

"Okay," we replied. "Tell him." She never did.

The birth of his daughter was a welcome bright spot in a life that was growing increasingly dull. As the decade drew to a close, Elvis counted the days until his movie contract ran out. He was itching for the challenge of live performance. In January 1968, the Colonel hit on the idea of doing a televised Christmas special. "Let's do it!" Elvis agreed happily. The Colonel negotiated a package deal with NBC for the show and another movie, *Change of Habit.* Work on "Elvis," the comeback special, started that June.

The Colonel proposed a Christmas show for Elvis's comeback in order to establish a precedent for an annual television event. But NBC wanted a one-time special that would showcase Elvis as the archetypal guitar man and reprise the highlights of his career. The Colonel was adamant, so the director, Steve Binder, went behind his back to Elvis. At first, Elvis was apprehensive about Steve and the others. They were strangers, telling him what to do. But gradually they won him over to their idea. The Colonel was furious. He confronted Binder, and long, heated discussions ensued between the Colonel, NBC, and RCA. In the end, Binder's concept prevailed.

"Who do you want for Elvis's guest stars?" the network asked the Colonel.

No one," he replied. "Elvis is the star."

The Colonel didn't have to consult Elvis to know he didn't want to share the spotlight that night. The network wanted Elvis to don a white engineer's coat and do a commercial for the sponsor, Singer Sewing Machines.

"Well, let me talk to Elvis about it," the Colonel said. He didn't even bother mentioning the commercial to Elvis. Two days later, NBC approached the Colonel again.

"We have to know," they urged.

"Okay," the Colonel improvised. "We'll do the commercial for half a million."

"Half a million!" they echoed in shock.

"That's right," the Colonel replied evenly. "And I don't know if I can persuade him to do it!"

The network offered fifty thousand dollars.

"I'm afraid you just can't afford Elvis," the Colonel said. This was the Colonel's usual tactic whenever he didn't want Elvis to do something. He never turned down a deal. He simply stated Elvis's price. If the party couldn't meet it, it was their problem.

Elvis was eager to perform live, but he was also terrified. He had never been comfortable before television cameras, and this was the first time the weight of a TV show rested entirely on his shoulders. Not only would the cameras focus on him almost exclusively, he would be facing his first live audience in eight years. Yet after the grind of the movies, Elvis was more than willing to take on a challenge like this. He was in his early thirties, one of the best-looking times of his life, and he was champing at the bit to do what he knew best.

The special gave Elvis all he craved and more. The producers presented Elvis with a selection of excellent material, and he ran with it, choosing musicians and songs with care. Elvis worked hard, listening attentively to Binder's ideas and coming up with his own, such as the improvised session where he sits on the stage cradling his guitar, joking and reminiscing with his musicians, and occasionally breaking into a few bars of his favorite songs.

Two days together backstage in the showbiz world equals two years of real-life friendship. Elvis loved the easy camaraderie and intimacy that develops rapidly during long, intense hours of rehearsal. He enjoyed hanging out with the musicians and dancers—show business gypsies—and he visited the cast of the innovative hit comedy show *Laugh-In,* which was shooting nearby. The rehearsals were charged with a heady sense of expectancy. The show was headed for the small screen, but everyone involved sensed something big and important was in the making.

We shot what was eventually edited down to seventy-four minutes of show time in three hectic days, working such long hours that Elvis and I camped out on rollaway beds in his dressing room. The night before the show, Elvis was so keyed up he couldn't sleep. At the last minute, while he was in makeup, he panicked. "I've changed my mind," he told Binder. "I don't want to go out there. What if I freeze and have nothing to say?" Steve and I calmed him down, and the rest is history. Elvis walked onstage into the intense glare of the television lights. The cameras rolled, the audience was screaming deliriously, and it all came back.

The show opens with a closeup on Elvis, shockingly handsome, a rock 'n' roll god in black leather. As he launches into the scorching anthem "Trouble," his lip curls into its signature sexual sneer, as he stares down the camera as if at a woman he's just tossed onto his bed. Despite a few hokey musical arrangements and female dancers so slathered with makeup they look like drag queens, the show presents classic Elvis at his peak. He eats up the tiny square stage set in what looks like a churning sea of transported females, and swings through a fast-chugging synopsis of his career. His voice sounds amazingly strong and flexible, and he looks happy. You can almost see him thinking, "Thank God I'm finally home!"

Relaxed, funny, charming, and even informative, Elvis clearly had the most fun in the improvised sessions where Charlie Hodge provides the perfect foil. At one point, Charlie suddenly excuses himself and leans toward Elvis to pluck a microscopic piece of tissue lint from his cheek, then solemnly presents the bit to a swooning fan in the first row. As I watched Elvis during those tapings, I was overcome with awe. It was hard to reconcile that super-presence with my buddy, the guy I chased girls, cleaned out barns, and played football with. I truly understood then that Elvis's life purpose was to sing for the world. "Elvis" was a major turning point in his career. The show aired on December 3, 1968, capturing the highest ratings for that year. Afterward, Elvis told me something I would hear him say many times again: that if he lost his voice, he'd rather not be on this earth.

After the New Year, Elvis went into a Memphis recording studio to lay down a huge reserve of tracks, a total of thirty-five songs recorded in two sessions. RCA assigned Felton Jarvis to produce. A year younger than Elvis, Felton was a charmer with a great sense of humor and a big Elvis fan whose favorite party trick was doing Elvis impersonations. He brought in good songs and had strong ideas, and would help Elvis produce his records and oversee the sound on concert tours until his death. Among the songs recorded in those sessions were sentimental heart-tuggers like "Mama Liked the Roses," "The Fair's Moving On," "Don't Cry Daddy," "You'll Think of Me," and one I talked him into doing, the Mac Davis–penned "In the Ghetto." Classic Elvis tracks also resulted: "Suspicious Minds," "Stranger in My Own Home Town," "After Loving You," "Kentucky Rain," "Long, Black Limousine," and a cover of the Beatles' "Hey Jude." That first session with Jarvis was the most commercial recording Elvis had done since 1960. Very little in between—musically or on film—had given Elvis as much creative satisfaction.

chapter 7

las vegas:
the comeback

SOON after the comeback special aired, the Colonel called me to set up a meeting at Elvis's house. He wanted to discuss an offer from a new Las Vegas hotel that was under construction. The International was designed to dwarf every other Vegas gambling palace. The pool, the casino, and the showroom would be the grandest and the largest the desert town had ever known. Naturally, the International wanted to inaugurate its spectacular showroom with the greatest star they could find. They wanted Elvis to do two engagements a year of four weeks each, two shows nightly. If he signed a five-year contract with the hotel exclusively, it would pay him five million dollars, all his expenses, and the cost of the band.

"What do you think?" the Colonel asked. He knew Elvis was reluctant to play Vegas again. He had played the town many years earlier, in 1956, and gone over like a lead balloon. When Elvis hesitated, the Colonel reminded him that things were different now. He was coming off the triumph of "Elvis," and in the thirteen years that had elapsed since that disastrous debut, he had captivated millions of new fans, plus his original fans had grown older and more sophisticated. Why not play Vegas? He liked the town, and we had had some pretty wild times there. He could do those two shows a night and party the rest of the time.

The Colonel has been accused of selling out Elvis in Las Vegas by taking money under the table for the contract in order to wipe out his own gambling debt. But the Colonel did not start gambling until after we began working Vegas, and he negotiated what must be considered a great financial deal for those days, the most lucrative any artist had ever received for playing Vegas. Other top stars at the time were pulling in about sixty thousand per week. The contract was completed over lunch at the Flamingo Hotel with Alex Shoofey.

As Alex and the Colonel worked out their deal, the Colonel scribbled important points on the white tablecloth, including a rider stating that if Alex Shoofey were to leave the hotel, the contract would be renegotiated. As it happened, in 1971, Kirk Kerkorian, the owner of both the Flamingo and the International, sold the hotels to Baron Hilton, of the Hilton Hotel Company. Shoofey retired, and Henry Lewin became the new president of what was renamed the Las Vegas Hilton. The Colonel had saved the tablecloth from the lunch with Shoofey, and he and Lewin made a new contract.

Shoofey wanted Elvis to be the International's debut act, but the Colonel refused. He knew that the performer who opens a new showroom endures all kinds of sound and lighting problems, and he was happy to let someone else inaugurate the showroom. Barbra Streisand opened the International instead, and sure enough, she suffered a series of technical glitches.

On July 31, 1969, Elvis performed his first official live concert in eight years. He traded in the black leather jacket and pants of the comeback special for elaborate two-piece stage suits patterned after karate outfits and designed by Bill Belew, who had done the wardrobe for the special. Elvis liked the suits and had them made in different colors. They worked fine for the first couple of days as he gradually accustomed himself to being back onstage. Then he started to incorporate karate moves into the show. One night, he crouched down very low on his left leg and kicked out his right.

Suddenly, we all heard an ominous ripping sound. The pants had split up the rear seam. Elvis must have felt a cold draft, since he rarely wore underwear. He jumped up immediately, interrupting his rendition of "Suspicious Minds." His face was bright red as he shielded his butt with his hand. "You have to excuse me for a few moments, folks," he said, managing to sound amused. "But I just ripped the seat out of my pants." The audience laughed and applauded as Elvis backed off stage. One of the guys ran down to the dressing room and got another pair of pants, and we stood around him to form a shield while Elvis changed right in the wings. He was back onstage in less than a minute. After that, Elvis started wearing jumpsuits; they can't drop down in the crotch.

Countless celebrities—Sammy Davis Jr., Wayne Newton, George Hamilton, Juliet Prowse, Charo, Xavier Cugat—were invited to opening night. Everyone who was playing Vegas came, if they didn't have to be onstage. Some only stayed for part of the show because they had to leave for their own performances. Many stars came backstage afterward to congratulate Elvis and eat from the lavish buffet. Cary Grant was so touched by Elvis's performance that he actually had tears in his eyes. Sammy gave Elvis a big hug and told him how great he was. Their enthusiasm made Elvis incredibly happy.

During that first engagement, backstage was always filled with celebrities. One night the singer Shirley Bassey showed up. She pursued Elvis heatedly, gazing longingly into his eyes and caressing him with long, talonlike red fingernails. Elvis kept ducking out of the room and moving around. Finally, he called me to one side.

"Listen, man," he said, "in about five minutes, come in and tell me we have to meet the Colonel in the suite." Another time, Debbie Reynolds came back and talked so much no one else could get a word in. Elvis kept casting meaningful looks at us that translated as "Enough!" Other times, he reversed the role and held someone captive to his monologue, especially women he was interested in, such as Phyllis McGuire of the McGuire Sisters, a singing group. We met Phyllis and her sisters one night after their show at the Desert Inn. Phyllis was a beautiful blonde, a fascinating older woman who lived in Las Vegas. What made her even more intriguing to Elvis was her long-time association with the mobster

Sam Giancana. The night after they met, Elvis saw Phyllis after the show. I don't know if they had a romantic relationship, but they were together for long periods behind closed doors.

Elvis broke all the attendance records for that first engagement: He grossed more than a million dollars in twenty-eight days for the International's showroom alone, not including the revenue he helped bring to the gambling tables. Elvis was amazed at the crowd's enthusiasm and hysteria. He just grinned and shook his head, mystified. One afternoon during that engagement, Elvis led Pat through the empty showroom and onto the vast stage. "It was awesome and frightening," she says, even though all she could see were rows of tables flanked by empty seats.

"This is what I have to do every night," Elvis told her. He wanted her to understand that his job wasn't easy. Being a superstar meant that he had to fill that room night after night. Elvis didn't like to show it, but he had his insecurities. That's where the Colonel's skills made the difference.

The Colonel worked every angle imaginable to promote those shows, including some no one had ever thought to work before. Billboards, newspaper advertisements, radio commercials, and a massive, highly organized merchandising campaign were all orchestrated by the Colonel himself. "Elvis, you're the star," he always said. "I'm the manager. All I can do is let everyone know you're here." For a solid month before each date, Elvis's name and image were emblazoned on over two hundred Vegas-area billboards. As Elvis's engagement grew near, the hotel was blanketed with Elvis posters. Television and radio spots aired every fifteen minutes.

"If you don't do any business, don't ever blame me," the Colonel said, "because the gophers in the desert know you're here! Believe me, everybody in town will know Elvis Presley is coming, but you're the only one who can bring them in." Just like the Colonel's offices on the studio lots, the Vegas office doubled as a shrine to his star. Every inch of wall and ceiling space was covered with Elvis posters, and samples of every item in the considerable battery of Elvis merchandise were on display.

A recent television movie about Elvis and the Colonel includes a fictitious scene in which the Colonel forces a distraught Vernon Presley to sign a merchandising contract over his son's coffin. In fact, that contract was written and signed many years before Elvis's death. According to its terms, Elvis and Vernon received $750 a month salary, plus 50 percent of the profits. A month after Elvis died, the Colonel turned over his latest share of the merchandising profits to Vernon, $133,000.

In the Hollywood days, the Colonel handed out *Tickle Me* feathers and hats to publicize Elvis's movie. If he was invited to a party for Bob Hope or another celebrity, he arranged to have an Elvis calendar slipped under each dinner plate. The Colonel and Elvis once attended a banquet for two thousand thrown by United Artists. The dinner had nothing to do with Elvis, but the Colonel managed to get a handbill advertising Elvis's new movie to each guest. When he was on the first Los Angeles–New York round-trip commercial jet flight, every passenger on the star-studded trip found a picture of Elvis on his or her seat. The list goes on and on.

Rogers and Cowan, the well-known public relations firm, once approached the Colonel about signing Elvis as a client.

"How much do you guys pay?" the Colonel asked.

"What do you mean?" they asked.

The Colonel explained: "Elvis is worth twenty-five thousand bucks just to use his name."

Rogers and Cowan had to laugh; the Colonel had a point. He continued to do the job himself, saving Elvis and himself many thousands of dollars.

Although some people think so, Elvis and the Colonel did not have a father-son relationship. Even when we were all together in Las Vegas, the Colonel and his crew rarely socialized with Elvis and the Memphis Mafia. We lived in two different worlds. The Colonel was much older and liked to go to bed early. He wouldn't have enjoyed hanging out with us. They were there for each other, but they were on two different wavelengths. The Colonel was a businessman and not very comfortable in the entertainer's party world. Once in a while we had dinner together to talk business and kid around. But otherwise, there was little socializing. I became their middleman because I was easily located, whereas Elvis wasn't always available. If he said "Do not disturb," that was it. You didn't disturb him for anyone, except in a dire emergency. So the Colonel naturally fell into the habit of asking me to relay messages. Elvis and the Colonel respected each other.

When it came to an important business decision, the two of them withdrew into a room alone and hashed it out together. The Colonel was forced to speak for Elvis many times because Elvis hated interviews, so it often appeared that the Colonel exercised more control than he actually did. Despite his complaints, Elvis always reserved the final decision. If he followed the Colonel's advice more often than he should have, it was because he preferred that someone else take responsibility in case a decision turned out to be wrong. The bottom line is that Elvis would never have been as popular as he was without the Colonel's brilliant management. Nor would the Colonel have had so much success with anyone else.

A few days before Elvis opened in Vegas, the Sweet Inspirations—a female quartet renowned for their background vocals with Aretha Franklin, Wilson Pickett, and the other R&B legends on Atlantic Records' roster—started singing backup with him. Elvis had heard their hit song, "Sweet Inspiration," on the radio and asked the Colonel's assistant Tom Diskin to call their agent. They made a deal stipulating that whenever the group wasn't working with Elvis, they could do their own shows. But over the years, they always dropped what they were doing whenever he called. Sylvia Shenwell, Estelle Brown, Cissy Houston (Whitney Houston's mother), and a stunning young woman named Myrna Smith, whose angelic features were crowned by a fluffy Afro, sang with Elvis until he died. When Cissy Houston left the group, she was replaced by Ann Williams, who left after a few months, turning the quartet into a trio. Myrna became Jerry Schilling's girlfriend, and after Elvis's death, Jerry's wife.

The four women were sitting on the edge of the International's main stage when Elvis walked in for their first rehearsal wearing a beautifully tailored cocoa-brown suit and sporting a carefully cultivated tan. "He looked absolutely impeccable," said Myrna. "He was the most gorgeous man I'd ever laid eyes on. Cissy swooned and almost fainted when he came over and introduced himself, as if we wouldn't know who Elvis was."

After those initial rehearsals, the Inspirations rehearsed with Elvis only when a new song was added to the show. Elvis gave the Sweet Inspirations some latitude to sing background parts they devised, but he edited out what he didn't like or thought was inappropriate for his concerts. Despite his swiveling hips and bumps and grinds, Elvis shied away from overly suggestive movements or background vocals in Vegas: If the Inspirations sounded too R&B, he asked them to tone it down or remove elements. Even though Elvis liked R&B and had always leaned toward a gospel-tinged sound, he knew exactly what he wanted for his own show.

Like the recording sessions, rehearsals were enlivened by Elvis's lighthearted joking. I taped a Las Vegas rehearsal that took place on July 24, 1970. Elvis was in a great mood that day. He sailed through a smooth, straightforward rendition of "I Can't Help Believin'," then clowned as he sang an uptempo treatment of the plaintive love ballad "Heart of Rome." Over the guitar's mandolinlike riffs, he interspersed falsetto trills, imitations of Barney Flintstone's "yabba dabba doo's," his impressions of coyote and wolf calls, owls hooting, and alley cat screeches, all of which were echoed by the giggling musicians. He laughed at his own antics in the middle of lyrics, then decided to amplify their meaning with sound effects, panting as if he were in heat when he sang of his lost love, making a bursting sound after a line about memories breaking apart, and mimicking the guitars and drums. After that display, Elvis threw himself completely into a pull-out-the-jams cover of Chuck Berry's classic rocker, "Johnny B. Goode." At the beginning of "Make the World Go Away" he seemed to take the song's fervent plea seriously as well. But midway, he looked at Charlie and cracked up, then, just as abruptly, dived back into the passion of the song. Afterward, he joked about his voice always cracking in the same spot. To make his point, he sang "make the world" loudly, exaggerating his voice cracking into a hoarse tenor. But Elvis was serious and working hard. He rapidly tossed off melodic lines from various songs to exercise his voice, then executed a smooth "and make the world go away" falsetto ending. Without a break, he slipped directly into a classic grinding blues, "Stranger in My Own Home Town," in which he sang improvised lewd lyrics beautifully, cracking himself up only once: "I'm goin' to go home to Memphis and drive that mother-f****** truck again/I'm going to go back to Memphis and drive that goddamn truck again/Yeah, ole Charlie, Joe, and Richard are goin' to starve to death/And Sonny'll be in the pen again/Yeah, that's why I'm like a stranger, like a stranger in my own home town/All them ****suckers stopped being friendly." The rehearsal wound up with a fast-chugging, bluesy take on the gospel classic "Muddy Waters."

Before she worked with him, Myrna hadn't been an Elvis fan. But after singing with him, she decided he had one of the best voices she'd ever heard. "I've known some singers who should be stars," Myrna said. "But they had too much voice to put on record. Elvis was fortunate in that they got just enough of him on vinyl so he could become as big as he was. But he had much more than that." The Sweet Inspirations had kept some pretty impressive company, but they were astounded by the enormous crowds that packed the room during that first month-long engagement, show after show, night after night. "When I first saw the size of the room," Myrna said, "I thought, 'Nobody can fill up this space for thirty days in a row.' That's when I realized what he was."

Certain black people were disturbed to learn that Myrna was singing with Elvis. A story was making the rounds at the time that Elvis had said all a black person could do for him was shine his shoes. Since then I've heard he said that about the Japanese, Chinese, and Polish people. "All I know is he treated me wonderfully," Myrna said. "I've worked with the Queen of Soul and with the King of Rock 'n' Roll, and Elvis was the most generous, caring person I've ever worked for. I had more fun with him onstage than anyone else I've ever worked with. He made you feel comfortable."

The Sweet Inspirations did more than sing background harmonies for Elvis. Almost from the first night they sang together, Elvis relied on the women for moral support. Whenever Elvis looked over to his left, he was checking the Sweet Inspirations because they fed him. If he didn't feel good, they made him feel good. If he didn't get the response he wanted from the audience, they gave it to him. Elvis often dropped by the Sweet Inspirations' dressing room after the shows. "He could really talk to us," Myrna said. "Not only about the show but if he did something we didn't like, we beat him up."

One night he came into their dressing room wearing a white suit. He thought they were going to say how gorgeous he looked.

That night he had taken off a ring and given it to a guy in the audience who was begging for it. "Give me a ring, give me a ring!" the guy kept saying, until Elvis finally did. "Elvis, close the door," Myrna said. Somebody tried to come into their dressing room, but she said, "No, no, nobody else can come in." Then they threw him on the floor, jumped on him, and pretended to beat the shit out of him. "And don't you ever do that again!" they warned. Elvis just laughed.

The Inspirations also forbade Elvis to bring guns to his dressing room. Elvis toted guns around with him wherever he went. During dinner between the two shows one time, Elvis asked Pat what she thought about that night's first performance.

"It wasn't great," she said. He pulled out a gun and held it to her head.

"Say that again," he warned her, then laughed.

That time it was a toy gun; other times, he used real guns for his mock threats, but he was always joking. He also liked knife tricks. "Patricia, stand here." he said another night. He performed a karate knife trick inches from her face.

"He didn't hurt me," Pat said, "but he could have. You got taken in . . . you just trusted him."

Elvis related to guns and knives like a kid playing tough guy. If he didn't like a television program, he shot out the set and then cracked up. Sometimes he used the glasses lined up at the bar in his suite for target practice. He thought that was hilarious too. Myrna says she will never forget a hair-raising spin around Memphis in his little yellow Ford Pantera. "He was a great driver but I knew he was trying to scare my ass off," she told me. "He thought it was funny." When they finally screeched to a stop in Graceland's driveway, Elvis completed the "shock treatment" by pulling out a gun and shooting out the dashboard as he castigated the car for not running right. "He thought that was funny, too," Myrna said.

In 1970, MGM shot a documentary of Elvis in Vegas. The Colonel made a deal for two documentaries: one to be shot in Vegas called, *Elvis—That's the Way It Is* and a later film called *Elvis on Tour.*

Elvis wasn't exactly thrilled to have a film crew trail him everywhere. Naturally, he was careful of what he said. Even though Dennis Sanders, the director, did a fine job capturing Elvis and the Memphis Mafia in their element, Elvis was still "on," not completely at ease as the film would have you believe. And it couldn't have been easy for the crew to follow us around. They encountered a lot of problems in the course of the project. For instance, whenever they shot audience reactions, they turned the house lights up and the audience froze. This annoyed Elvis, but it couldn't be helped. It took a lot of light in those days to film indoors. "We're trying to do a movie here for MGM, so don't let the cameras throw you," he tells the audience in one scene, "and I'll try not to throw the cameras."

In another scene, the filmmakers had talked Elvis into using the first cordless mike. Unfortunately, the mike keeps cutting out. Elvis is clearly annoyed, but he jokes about it, clutching a cluster of four cordless mikes like a bouquet of flowers and muttering, "You can't lose with four of these bastards." He tests each of them with a "hello," then chucks one offstage, muttering "sonuvabitch" under his breath. "Two out of four ain't bad," he finally concludes. Meanwhile, the Sweet Inspirations are laughing at him. "I'm going to bring in the Supremes tomorrow night with Mahalia Jackson singing lead," he threatens. Finally, he switches gears and croons "Love Me Tender," stooping every few bars to plant kisses on the swooning girls in the front row. Elvis seems untroubled and nonchalant, but when he came off stage, his frustration exploded all over us. He was going to tell "these damn filmmakers" that they couldn't shoot another frame. By the next day, the storm had blown over, and Elvis didn't utter a word of protest.

Despite a few rough spots, Vegas was a huge success and lots of fun for Elvis, and no one could match him for pulling in an audience, even such outstanding draws as Frank Sinatra and Dean Martin. The entire city celebrated when Elvis came to town because he brought so many people. Those people saw other shows, gambled, and spent their money. Articles in local papers often expressed amazement that one performer could do so much for the city. Planeloads of fans landed regularly in the Vegas airport from Europe and Japan when Elvis was playing. These people saved all year to accumulate a few thousand dollars for their summer vacation. They would attend several shows, fly to Memphis to visit Graceland, then travel to Tupelo, where Elvis spent his childhood.

Whenever Elvis played Vegas in the early seventies, he found time to see shows at other hotels. If the Clara Ward Gospel Singers were at the Frontier, Elvis was there for the entire engagement. One night a group of six or seven of us went to country singer and sausage king Jimmy Dean's show. As usual, we entered after the lights went out, so as not to distract the audience. Dean's microphone kept going in and out and giving feedback. Elvis rose from his seat, walked backstage to grab another mike from the soundman, then strolled on stage to hand it to a shocked Dean and strolled back off. The audience screamed and applauded wildly. Another time, we were all at a show and Elvis had to go to the bathroom badly. This time, he didn't want to get up and cause a commotion, so he took a tall empty glass and peed into it under our table.

Of course, a big part of Vegas' attraction was its gorgeous women. While Elvis was performing, or during the breaks between his shows, the guys scouted the audience, bars, and casinos. If Elvis spotted a pretty girl in the audience, he walked off stage. "See that girl in blue, fourth table from the right?" he would say to one of the guys. "Find out if she's with anyone. If not, bring her back." Red or Sonny located her in the audience and asked her, "You want to meet Elvis?" The answer was invariably a breathlessly squealed "Yes!" And the lucky lady was escorted backstage for an up-close dose of the Presley charm. We always came in three or four days before the show, when the town wasn't that busy and there weren't many women around except for the hookers. Once we arrived an entire week early. "Joe, we're going to have a party tonight," Elvis said. "Call down for a bunch of hookers." The guys were elated. They'd been dropping hints for quite some time, and Elvis had finally come through. We were so jaded by this point that it had become too much trouble to go out and look for women. Once Elvis started performing, there'd be no problem. The women would come to us in droves. As I reflect on our behavior today, I'm mortified. But the truth is that we often sent out for prostitutes, and everyone switched girls. Elvis was not as involved as the rest of us. "I'd rather watch," he would say. They weren't pure enough for him. Elvis romanticized sex, and paying by the hour grounded it all too well. Only on occasion would he disappear into his room with one.

We rarely saw daylight in Vegas. The ingenious hotels hung blackout drapes in the rooms to encourage guests to sleep all day and stay up all night gambling. We looked like zombies. But we had a fantastic time there, and all the shows sold out. Life was perfect.

After February 1970, we began preparing to tour. Elvis held rehearsals for the musicians and singers in RCA's recording studio on Sunset Boulevard in Hollywood. When they had been hired, they'd each received a complete set of Elvis's recordings so they could learn all the songs. Another set was kept at the rehearsal studio for reference, along with recordings by other artists Elvis liked. One of my jobs was to make a list of all the songs they rehearsed during those sessions. Elvis never came with a list ready; he suggested whatever song came to mind, and they all ran through it until he was satisfied with the results. Elvis was in total control, telling the singers and the musicians where to come in with what type of sound. I particularly remember his instructions to the drummer, Ronnie Tutt, "Ronnie, you have to keep an eye on me at all times," he said. "I want you to accent every move I make." Elvis was always open to suggestions from a band member or singer. He listened respectfully, then decided whether or not to follow it. During breaks, the group discussed the song lineup. "I want the introduction number to be like something from another world," Elvis said. "I love 'Also sprach Zarathustra' from *2001: A Space Odyssey*." Everyone liked that idea. Then Elvis wanted to segue into a tune that really rocked. He decided on "See See Rider," followed by some of his own records, such as "I Got a Woman," and "That's All Right." "We'll have a basic lineup," he said, "but I may change it anytime I feel like doing another song, so you guys have to be on your toes at all times." When we began playing live concerts, he'd occasionally call a change in song, but except for the first few months, Elvis rarely altered the established lineup. Instead, he periodically removed a song in order to insert a new one in its place.

"When do you want to introduce the band?" Charlie asked.

"After 'Suspicious Minds,' " Elvis decided. "I'll need a breather after that one." Following the introductions, Elvis performed his latest record release. "The show will always end with 'Can't Help Falling in Love,' " he announced. "That's my signature song."

The atmosphere for those initial touring rehearsals was relaxed, and, typically, as the night wore on, Elvis began changing the lyrics and clowning around. But everyone worked hard, and after a few nights, I had compiled a list of more than fifty songs.

Elvis planned the basic lineup he established in those few days of rehearsals—one he basically followed throughout his years on the road—on the basis of his feelings and on what he somehow knew the audience wanted to hear. After the dramatic introduction that would have been overwrought had it preceded anyone but Elvis, he came on fast and hard, toned down for a few ballads, surged back with strong vocals, and kept the energy going with a medley of his greatest hits: "Heart Break Hotel," "Teddy Bear," "Don't Be Cruel," "Blue Suede Shoes," "Hound Dog." He confided to me that he was tired of singing them, but he knew the fans had to hear those songs. He preferred the next phase of his show, when he seduced the ladies with swooning renditions of "You've Lost That Loving Feeling" and "Fever." The stage would darken for those songs, except for a warm, reddish spotlight that followed him as he stalked the edge of the stage, gazing directly into the faces of euphoric, screaming women. Then Elvis turned to stroll casually to the piano. Glen would move over on the bench while Elvis played and sang Roy Hamilton's hit, "Unchained Melody." Then he sang his closing number, "Can't Help Falling in Love," and that was it. Elvis would thank the by-now hysterical audience and exit the stage as they screamed their protest. "I like to leave them wanting more," he told me.

The shows were always simple. That red spotlight for "Fever" was one of only six lights we used for Elvis's show. And there were no special effects. Elvis didn't need much of a production: supported by the band and background singers, he was the real show.

Our first booking was at the Houston Astrodome, where Elvis was event number eight in the Houston Rodeo for two sold-out performances a day from February 27 to March 1. "Hey, Elvis, you're on right after the cows!" we kidded him. We had to lighten him up. The venue had a capacity of almost 60,000, the largest audience Elvis had ever played to, and he was nervous.

Kirk Kerkorian, the owner of the International Hotel, lent Elvis his private DC-9 jet to take us to Houston. The band flew by commercial airline. Red, Sonny, Jerry, Lamar, Charlie, Elvis, and I left Las Vegas on the afternoon of February 25 for a fun-filled three-hour flight. This was just before private planes became almost commonplace. Kerkorian's plane was divided into three rooms: a game room, a dining/conference room, and a bedroom. Elvis had never seen anything like it. When we landed, the Colonel was waiting at the airport, along with some of his Texan friends and a few thousand screaming fans held back by a tall fence. Elvis strolled over to sign autographs for twenty minutes or so, while the Memphis Mafia formed a protective barricade. Then we jumped into the limousines and headed to the Astroworld Hotel, accompanied by a police escort. We had police escorts everywhere we went for that date because Elvis was truly loved in Texas, going back to the early days when he played many small clubs throughout the state.

During that first time in Houston, we set the pattern for a routine we followed throughout Elvis's touring years. The limos pulled up to the rear of the hotel. We walked through the kitchen and went up to the suite via the service elevators. That became our usual mode of entry. Elvis never did get to see the lobbies of the many swank hotels where he stayed. His luxurious western-style suite overlooked the Astrodome. We sat around the dining room table and poured ourselves glasses of Mountain Valley water, which we always had waiting when he arrived. The windows were outfitted with blackout drapes so he could sleep during the day. If, for some reason, the drapes weren't installed, we covered the windows with some opaque material. Sonny disconnected the bell to the phone in Elvis's bedroom. I had rented a spare room for his ten four feet by three feet by two feet custom-made wardrobe cases. The hotel operators were instructed to route all calls for Elvis to that room. The fans would hear it ringing and think they'd reached Elvis. Sonny and Red set up security at the elevator on Elvis's floor with a list of people permitted entry. All this became standard procedure. A Lear jet brought Priscilla; Judy West, Sonny's wife; and my wife, Joan, to Houston. Then Red, Sonny, Jerry, and I rode over to the arena to look over the backstage setup and check its security. This was all new to us, and we were learning as we went along. After a few tours, everything fell into place and we ran things like a fine-tuned machine. Everyone knew his job and did it automatically. I simply told them when we were leaving for the show, and everything was taken care of.

Elvis usually ate about two hours before the show. That first night in Houston, our wives joined us for dinner. Talk at the table focused on the immense size of the Astrodome. Elvis began dressing thirty minutes before we had to leave for the arena. Then Red and Sonny led the way, with Elvis and me following, and the rest of the guys bringing up the rear. Each night we left the hotel, we used a different exit in order to avoid the crowds that had been tipped off to our plans by the hotel staff. We got a big kick at winning that cat-and-mouse game with the fans. About fifteen minutes before Elvis was due onstage, we reached the Arena, so he didn't have to linger backstage long enough to build up a severe case of nerves. The Astrodome's revolving stage was proportionately small, so before the show, Elvis, a few bodyguards, and I circled the stands in a jeep to give the audience a closer look. Elvis stood up, hanging onto the roll bar with a white-knuckled grip, while Sonny, Red, Jerry, and I sat in the back seat, awestruck. A ten-foot wall separated us from the stands and police held the people back, but quite a few fans tumbled over as they tried to get closer to Elvis.

The stands were approximately one hundred feet away from a stage that rotated back and forth. Elvis wasn't crazy about this setup, but the audience roared throughout his entire hour-long set. We climbed back into the jeep to circle the arena again before we left through the backstage area and returned to the hotel. After the last show, we flew back to Los Angeles with our wives, then left to continue the tour. That year, 1970, Elvis did one hundred thirty-seven shows. Over the next few years, the number of shows gradually increased. I never missed a single one of Elvis's live performances. In 1973, we peaked at one hundred sixty-eight shows, the most we ever did for one year. When we were on tour, we rarely took off a day: one show every night, and on weekends we did matinees. We'd finish the last show, go straight from the venue to the airport, and fly to the next city where we'd check into a hotel. The lobbies swarmed with women who'd been alerted to our arrival, so the guys went down to invite the prettiest ones to Elvis's suite. We always had more girls there than guys. We'd listen to music and talk, and if Elvis spotted someone he liked, he'd spend most of the evening talking to her. If there was no one special, he'd chat with a group of girls.

A few early engagements threatened to bring trouble. "Don't bring those black girls," a building manager warned Elvis.

"If they don't come, I don't come," Elvis replied. We all went, and no one ever tried that again. During a date in Mississippi, every time the Sweet Inspirations or the Stamps Gospel Quartet—who were white—stepped forward to sing their parts, people in the stands threw pennies. Elvis was incensed at what he interpreted as a flagrant display of racism. After the show, he called all the women to his room.

"We're flying out of here to Memphis 'cause these people are rude," Elvis said.

"No way," Myrna objected. They were scheduled to do another show. "Elvis, the reason they were throwing the pennies was not that we're black but that every time we stepped forward, they couldn't see you." Myrna was right. We stayed and Elvis had the stage set differently for the next show.

Running the concert tours required extra help. So Tom Hulett, a concert promoter, and Jerry Weintraub, a promoter and manager, joined forces to form Concerts West, the company that worked with the Colonel to book Elvis's tours. They met the Colonel through a mutual business friend, Steven Weiss, who was Jimi Hendrix's attorney. Weintraub and Hulett made an appointment with the Colonel in Las Vegas. They flew there and caught Elvis's show at the International. The morning after the show, they had a second meeting with the Colonel in his office. The Colonel struck a very tough deal.

"I want one million dollars up front," he said.

"Okay, you got a deal," Jerry replied, and he stuck out his hand to shake on it.

But the Colonel's right hand stayed by his side. "We don't have a deal until I see a cashier's check for the million," he said. "I want it here by noon tomorrow."

"We'll see you tomorrow," Tom promised.

Somehow, they came up with the money. After seeing Elvis perform live, Jerry and Tom were confident of their investment. There's virtually no risk in promoting such giants as the Beatles, Bruce Springsteen, the Rolling Stones, or Elvis Presley. The risk is in promoting middle-level acts.

The Colonel had already set up one concert in Phoenix, Arizona. He dictated the rest of the cities: St. Louis, Missouri; Detroit, Michigan; Mobile, Alabama; and Miami, Florida. But when Jerry and Tom looked at a map, they realized that the Colonel's routing was nearly impossible if you considered all the heavy sound equipment that would have to be moved. When the Colonel and Elvis had last toured it was a different era: Artists played with whatever public address system was already set up in the venue. They used the same PA system through which a sports arena announced baseball scores. Even the Beatles played through venue PAs when they first came to the United States. When Elvis did that first Las Vegas International engagement, we used two small Shure speakers laid sideways for Elvis's monitors—the kind of equipment you find in a music business executive's office today—and Elvis and the band played through the house sound system.

Tom Hulett, who was already actively involved in promoting major tours, routinely hired a sound company in Seattle, Washington, called Clare Brothers Sound, still one of the biggest outfits today. St. Louis was the first show in which Concerts West was involved. Not knowing any better, Hulett automatically hired Clare Brothers Sound for the date—a ten-thousand-seat venue called Kiel Arena. Meanwhile, we were on our way to St. Louis from our first stop of the tour in Arizona, where two nights earlier, we sold out the fifteen-thousand-seat Phoenix Coliseum using the house sound system. We met Hulett and Weintraub in St. Louis.

The afternoon of the show, Tom Diskin, the Colonel's assistant, walked into the arena just as band leader Joe Guercio's orchestra risers were being laid down. Then stagehands began wheeling in huge public address boxes. Diskin was irate, but finally agreed to try the system for one night if Hulett and Weintraub took the responsibility of telling Elvis about it themselves. If Elvis didn't like the sound system, they would have to cut it off. Roy and

Gene Clare, the system's inventors, witnessed the scene. Roy agreed to be on the monitor system onstage. Gene would be in the audience, checking the sound from there.

Hulett and Weintraub were waiting in the dressing room when Elvis and the guys got off the elevator. Suddenly, George Klein shouted out, "Tom!" He had met Tom Hulett about two months earlier in Memphis, when Tom was touring with Creedence Clearwater. Tom hurriedly told Elvis that he'd brought in a sound system and all the rock acts used them these days. Then he and Weintraub beat a hasty retreat. "How the hell do you know that guy?" Elvis asked George. George told him that Tom toured with Creedence and Jimi Hendrix, adding that with this promoter, Elvis had the best.

The show began. Tom Hulett was standing in the wings onstage left with Roy Clare. Elvis began singing, and his eyes widened. For the first time in his life, he heard himself as he was singing onstage. "We're going to have one great show tonight!" Elvis promised the audience. He never admitted that he liked the system, but from that point on, Jerry Weintraub and Tom Hulett were okay, and Elvis used the basic Clare Brothers PA, with monitors on himself, the band leader, Joe Guercio; the singers; and the band.

Such present-day commonplaces as contract riders, renting an outside PA system, and providing hamburgers and Cokes backstage for the performers were innovations for that time. Most concert promoters of that era were local disc jockeys, so radio stations were promoting shows in the big cities. There was a need for a new breed of professional promoter who could handle a star of Elvis's magnitude. The Colonel and Concerts West initiated many of the changes that became today's conventions.

Being the dictatorial force that he was, the Colonel needed a buffer between himself and the facilities. Concerts West filled that need, softening the demands the Colonel made on Elvis's behalf. Tom Hulett had established relationships with major venue managers all over the country. Whenever they got a call from Tom Hulett or Jerry Weintraub, they knew it was about a major show. No artist before or since has ever toured like Elvis. As concert promotion became a full-fledged business and amphitheaters opened up, the venues began to promote concerts themselves, and promoters sprang up in every town like weeds. After Elvis died and Led Zeppelin lost their drummer, Concerts West left the business. What could possibly follow promoting concerts for Elvis and Led Zeppelin?

Watching Tom Hulett and the Colonel book a tour was like watching a pair of master jugglers performing in the circus's center ring. Hulett flew down from his Concerts West offices in Seattle to the Colonel's office at MGM. After the Colonel conferred with Elvis and me, he and Tom sat across from each other, routing a tour with a map. Then they went to work on a bank of phones, playing what Tom called "building games." He'd start calling the buildings. "Are you open on such and such date?" he would ask the building manager in Greensboro or Roanoke. "If you aren't open, don't worry about it. We'll just play Raleigh." That shook the hell out of the manager. All of a sudden, the date they wanted was open because a boxing match or a wrestling event suddenly had been canceled.

The Colonel and Tom Hulett loved "good cop–bad cop," with Tom usually taking playing good cop. "Look, what kind of rent are we paying?" he would ask, let's say, Jim Ohsust, the building manager in Greensboro, North Carolina, while the Colonel listened on the extension. The percentage was cut down right from the start. This was Elvis, after all.

"Jim, I think maybe I can get you an Elvis date," Tom would then say. "But you have to give us two dates in case we sell out one quick. I don't want to go to the Colonel with just one date. You have to make me a great deal, so I can go to him with it. And you have to agree to hold a press conference if he wants you to."

"Tom!" the Colonel would hiss as he covered the mouth of the receiver. "Tell him we have to be able to go on sale this weekend."

"Can you get all the news there?" Tom would ask Ohsust. "You and the mayor. Whatever you've got to get, get it."

"Yeah, just tell the Colonel whatever he needs," Jim would agree. Those press conferences reaped ten or twenty grand worth of publicity before the Colonel and Concerts West even bought the first radio spot. Sometimes Tom told the manager, "Okay, it's Monday, can you make this conference Friday?" But the Colonel often changed his mind. "Have him announce it tonight," he would whisper to Tom. "Have him start accepting mail tomorrow."

Tom would hang up and call the manager back five minutes later, pretending that he'd just talked on the phone to the Colonel.

Then he'd ask the manager to push up the press conference.

Even compared to the high fees today's stars command, Elvis's deals have yet to be paralleled. If a building was getting 10, 12 percent of the gate, Concerts West and the Colonel demanded a cutoff point at three thousand or five thousand dollars. That way they paid the equivalent of 2, 3, or 4 percent. But the Colonel and Concerts West knew the buildings were making plenty of money with parking, hot dogs, popcorn, and drinks. Everyone ended up with a good deal. Even the city wound up with tax revenue. Elvis paid less for the rental of his facilities than any artist in the history of this business, and that saving went directly into his and the Colonel's pockets. Of course, there were expenses: We were a big show with a huge entourage, and we now traveled by airplane.

Everyone involved received a bonus at the end of each tour. That was the Colonel's idea. The bonuses were figured into the tour expenses and taken out before the split between Elvis and the Colonel.

"They did a good job," the Colonel told Elvis after the first tour. "We can write it off. We make a lot of money." Elvis agreed. After the second tour, the Colonel suggested bonuses again.

"Well, Daddy don't think we should do it," Elvis said.

"Let's have Vernon at the top of the bonus list," the Colonel suggested. Vernon was put down for the highest bonus, twenty-five hundred dollars. When Elvis showed his father the list, Vernon said, "I think that's a good idea."

The Colonel promoted Elvis out of instinct. During Elvis's first tour in 1969, Tom Hulett, the Colonel, and RCA's representatives, George Parkhill and Pat Kellerher, were driving to the building in Cleveland where Elvis was to perform that night. About a block away, they spotted a bootlegger on a street corner selling Elvis albums for five dollars apiece.

"Colonel! He's selling records!" Tom yelled, ready to leap out of the limo and collar the guy.

"Keep going," the Colonel told the driver. Then he turned to Tom. "You don't see no one out here selling Paul Anka tapes and records, do you? If you're not hot, you got no bootleggers. Just be happy we got 'em. It means we're hot."

George Parkhill explained that with the advent of tape cassettes, retailers were returning vinyl albums to RCA. The warehouses were full, so the bootleggers were probably buying the albums for two dollars apiece. He and the Colonel knew that the bootleggers were a healthy part of the Elvis moneymaking machine.

The Colonel toured with us from 1969 to 1974. Elvis, the guys, and I stayed on one floor of the hotel. The band stayed two or three floors below, and the Colonel and his crew were on another floor. The separation was necessary. The band members partied all night, and Elvis wanted quiet. By now the band included lead guitarist James Burton from Shreveport, Louisiana, a studio musician renowned for inimitable licks, nothing showy, but so smooth and fluid he made it look easy. Ronnie Tutt was hired after Elvis auditioned countless drummers, because he said Ronnie was the only one who watched every move Elvis made instead of doing his own thing. Jerry Scheff was the bassman. Elvis liked to introduce Scheff and Tutt as Teff and Schutt, making a pun of their names that sounded like "tough shit." Glen Hardin, the keyboard player, was a steady drinker. Whenever he wasn't onstage, he wandered around with a tall glass of bourbon permanently affixed to his hand. No matter how drunk he got, if Glen had to be up at six in the morning, he was there, even if he'd just gotten to bed at five. Rhythm guitarist John Wilkerson was the quietest. After shows, he disappeared into his room with a bucket of ice, and you didn't see him again until the next day. Of course, the Stamps Quartet, led by six-foot-four-inch, basso-voiced J. D. Sumner, were the worst carousers. J. D. was good-looking in a rugged sort of way, and when he wasn't singing about Heaven, he was following the Lord's advice to "go forth and multiply," chasing anything female on two legs.

Naturally, Elvis wanted to be quartered far from all the shenanigans, although when he didn't want to sleep, it was okay to make noise. But if he wanted an early night, everyone had to shut up. I didn't mind. A main part of my job was to make sure the guys fell in line with whatever Elvis wanted. When it was party time, we partied. When Elvis wanted to rest, we took the party elsewhere.

For the last few years of touring, the Colonel didn't travel with us. He was always one town ahead of us. We'd get off the plane at some town's airport, and there would be the Colonel, waiting to greet us. "Hello, everything's all set," he'd say. Then he'd board his plane and go to the next date. Everywhere we went, he was one step ahead, making sure everything was organized, the concert was being publicized, and arranging for people to meet us at the airport. Many times we arrived in a city to find the mayor standing on the runway a few yards from a crowd of screaming fans, waiting to hand Elvis a key to the city. The newspapers were always there, of course, taking pictures. We never needed a publicist.

The Memphis Mafia had become Elvis's de facto security team for those tours. Elvis adopted the Secret Service's strategy of having everyone in the unit wear the same color jacket, so we could always spot each other in a crowd. When Elvis came off stage, I was usually the first to grab him. We were joined by the other guys and moved swiftly out of the building before the audience knew Elvis was gone. I never did get to hear the announcer tell the crowd that was screaming for more, "Ladies and gentlemen, Elvis has left the building." We honed our security to the point where police departments were impressed. "You guys are so much better organized than us," they marveled. "It's amazing what you can do." We had to be good. Protecting Elvis was becoming more and more difficult.

One night in August 1970, during our second Las Vegas engagement, I had just fallen asleep when my private phone rang. It could have been only one of three people: the Colonel, Elvis, or my wife, Joan. It was about six in the morning, and I thought it was probably Elvis or the Colonel. But it was Joan.

"Joe, I just got a strange phone call," she said, sounding very agitated. "This man wouldn't give me his name, but he said he had to get hold of you, that it was very important. He said he tried to reach you at the hotel but the operators said you had a 'Do not disturb' on your line."

"What did he want?" I asked her.

"He told me that he had important information about a man who is driving to Vegas to kill Elvis. He said he would give you the man's name for fifty thousand dollars."

"What did you tell him?"

"I told him I would try to reach you," she answered. The man had said he would call again in an hour.

I told Joan I would call her back, then immediately dialed the number of Elvis's lawyer, Ed Hookstratten. I told him the story and he called the FBI. They called my wife and told her they would send agents to our apartment. They arrived in less than thirty minutes and connected a tape recorder to our phone. Meanwhile, I called the Colonel in his room and told him what had happened. He asked me to keep him informed.

The man called again and asked Joan if she had reached me. The FBI had instructed her to say she couldn't reach me, that I was out of the hotel. She asked him to call back later and said that she would keep trying. He said he would give her just thirty more minutes. The FBI suspected the man was just trying to hustle a quick fifty thousand, and he never did call back. We decided he was frightened off. The FBI stayed at my apartment until noon and showed Joan how to operate the tape recorder in case the man called again. This wasn't the first death threat we'd received that turned out to be nothing.

That afternoon, I picked up the mail at the hotel's front desk and took it back to my room to look it over. As I was wading through a mountain of fan letters, I found a large white envelope that hadn't come through the post. I opened it to discover a showroom menu with a picture of Elvis on it. Someone had drawn a gun pointed at Elvis's head and written in large letters "Die." I called hotel security and filled them in on the day's events. We contacted the FBI in Los Angeles and told them what I'd found. They sent two agents from the Vegas office, and we all met in the Colonel's office. The FBI said that we should consider the threat serious. Someone involved with the death threat was obviously here in Vegas. They took the envelope and menu to check for fingerprints.

Elvis woke at about three that afternoon. We waited until he finished breakfast to tell him what was going on and that the FBI wanted to talk to him. He seemed to take it in stride, and I called down to the Colonel's office to have the FBI come up. The FBI suggested to Elvis that he cancel his performances for a few days until they investigated further.

"I'm not canceling the show for that no-good bastard!" Elvis said. "I wouldn't give him the satisfaction of stopping me!" Then he turned to me. "Joe, call Ed Parker in Hawaii and Jerry Schilling in Los Angeles," he said. "Tell them I need them here. Then call Red in Memphis and tell him too. Make the arrangements to get them here." He was angry and becoming more so by the minute.

"What could I have done that someone would want to kill me?" he kept asking. "I try to make people happy with my music!"

That evening before the show, all the guys were armed and posted at various strategic spots. Some stood at the entrance with FBI guys, looking out for suspicious characters. Red and Sonny were stationed on opposite ends of the stage. Others roamed the showroom. We even had an ambulance parked right at the stage door. We could tell Elvis's mind wasn't fully on his performance because he moved about more than usual, but I don't think the audience suspected anything was wrong. We all sighed in relief after the show, but in two hours we had another one. Things were tense for the next few days, but we heard no more from the telephone caller or the letter writer.

Except for such occasional excitement, touring quickly became routine. What had first been so glamorous—traveling from city to city—eventually became tedious. Most of the time, all we saw were the backstages of arenas and hotel rooms. We were always on the move, so there wasn't time for anything else. It was hardest on Elvis. At least, we could steal a few moments for a walk outside, but fame kept him a virtual prisoner in his suite. Any diversion from the routine, no matter how trivial, was welcome.

We began the second tour of 1972 at Madison Square Garden in New York City. We flew from Memphis the night before the first show; the band and singers were already waiting in the hotel. That night, the Colonel had a brainstorm. Why not have Elvis do a live recording from the fabled Big Apple venue? RCA was hesitant about attempting such a complicated project on short notice, but the Colonel worked it out and the album was released only ten days after the concert. Elvis was always nervous about facing the notoriously tough New York audience. He calmed down by playing the piano we always had in his suites and harmonizing with the Stamps and the Sweet Inspirations on gospel favorites.

The media were pressuring him for a press conference, and Elvis finally caved in. The room was packed with reporters and Geraldo Rivera, a big Elvis fan, acted as M.C. Elvis sat at a long table, flanked by his father and me.

"Are you satisfied with the image you've established?" one reporter asked.

"Well, the image is one thing and the human being is another," Elvis observed.

"How close does the image come to the man himself?" the reporter pressed.

"It's very hard to live up to an image," Elvis commented obliquely.

When they attempted to get a fix on his political leanings, Elvis demurred. "I'm just an entertainer," he said. The press was surprisingly tactful, refraining from questions about his personal life.

We returned to the suite and Elvis retired to his bedroom to rest before the 8:00 P.M. show. By now, he adhered to a strict routine: At 6:00 P.M., dinner was delivered to the suite. Elvis came out of his room at 6:15 to eat and talk over that night's show. At 7:00 P.M., he went back to his bedroom to get ready. He brushed his teeth and gargled with warm salt water to prepare his throat, while one of the guys laid out a few costumes on his bed. Elvis finished with a few drops of eye wash, then he came out of the bathroom to get dressed, after which Charlie or Larry Geller was called in to do his hair, which took about fifteen minutes. After that it was time for Elvis to sort through his makeup case, picking out rings and necklaces for that night. By then it was eight o'clock, showtime. Comedian Jackie Kahane opened the show that night, struggling through twenty-five minutes of jokes while the stadium rang with loud demands for Elvis, who was due onstage at 9:00. I notified security, and we left for the venue, surrounded by police and hotel security. The hallways were lined with hotel employees, and Elvis shook hands as we went. Despite a police escort, the snarled Manhattan traffic held us up, and we finally arrived during intermission, eight minutes before Elvis was due onstage. To our surprise, George Harrison was waiting for us, but there was only time for quick hellos. I got Elvis into his dressing room, then set up a spot where George could view the show without being bothered. I ran onstage to see how it was laid out, so I could tell Elvis if he was entering from the right or left, and which way to exit at the end of the show. I returned to the dressing room. "Are you ready?" I asked.

"This time is as good as any," he replied, and I gave Tom Diskin, the Colonel's assistant, the high sign. He told the light man to bring down the house lights, and we waited in the dressing room until we heard the band begin "Also sprach Zarathustra," our cue to walk to the stage. I led the way to the steps with the guys surrounding us. We stopped at the foot of the steps, waiting until we heard Elvis's new opening song, "That's All Right." As we chorused "Good luck," he climbed up to the stage, and the guys then took their positions around it.

The crowd was on their feet, screaming; I'd never seen so many flash bulbs ignite at once. A huge wave of fans attempted to assault the stage, knocking over a few ushers in their progress. Elvis walked around, waving, then he approached the microphone to ask the crowd to be careful. He didn't want anyone to be hurt, he told them. He began singing, every once in a while flashing a big grin to me as I stood in the wings. He was having a ball. He gave out scarves to the fans and they threw gifts on stage: flowers, stuffed animals, notes. He sang twenty-one songs until "Can't Help Falling in Love," which the audience knew was his finale. They rushed the stage again to say goodbye, while the guys formed their end-of-the-show barricade. As usual, they let a few of the girls through, just to make it more exciting, as Elvis paced the edge of the stage and shook hands. When he was ready to leave, he nodded to me and walked over to the side where I was standing. Blinded by the stage lights, his hand holding my shoulder, he followed me down the stairs, through the backstage, and into the limo, where someone handed him a quart bottle of water and a towel to dry his face. We were out of the building and on the way back to the hotel before the audience stopped applauding.

During that night's post-show discussion, Elvis wore a huge smile on his face, a sure signal that he'd liked the show. If he hadn't, his look would have been concentrated and serious. That show was one of the few where Elvis had no complaints. He was so wired, he couldn't sleep that night. The band members and singers sat with him in the suite until 6:00 A.M., talking and singing "Bosom of Abraham," "Lead Me, Guide Me," "How Great Thou Art," and other favorites, while Elvis played the piano. He went to sleep at about seven in the morning. I knocked on his door at eleven; we had a 2:00 P.M. matinee. Breakfast with a pot of hot coffee was waiting, the TV was on, and the newspapers, full of rave reviews, were piled on the coffee table. If the reviews had been any less enthusiastic, they wouldn't have been there.

We did four shows in New York that time. Elton John came to the second show and watched another great performance from the same spot George Harrison occupied the night before. We left the city on June 12 to fly to the Midwest for a touch-and-go in Fort Wayne, Indiana. We drove to the hotel where Elvis changed into a stage costume, then headed for the Memorial Coliseum. He did his show and went straight back to the airport, where we flew to Chicago, followed an hour later by the show plane with the singers and the band. We were going to be in Chicago for six nights, so we stationed ourselves at the Conrad Hilton, and took advantage of the time to send out our clothes to be cleaned and even unpack our suitcases. We also squeezed in some monotony-relieving antics.

That first night, one of the band members had a few drinks too many and retired early to his room. Elvis suggested that we move a Coke machine in front of his door. We began yelling "Fire!" He jumped out of bed, opened his door, and ran straight into the Coke machine, much to our amusement. Then Elvis went to bed, but he stayed up reading. No one knew he was in town, so the lobby contained only the occasional businessman. No girls.

I got up early the next day to visit my family and returned in the afternoon, as Elvis was having breakfast. We left for the airport at five to fly to Evansville, Indiana, for an 8:00 P.M. show at Roberts Municipal Stadium. About five minutes into the show, Elvis told Charlie Hodge to ask the sound man to turn up the stage monitors. He couldn't hear himself sing. But every time the volume was increased, he'd get feedback. Elvis got angrier and angrier. In the limo on the way back to the airport, Elvis said, "Joe, tell Felton I want to see him after he gets to the hotel." Felton Jarvis was Elvis's record producer and supervisor for the sound engineers on the road. Elvis kept up his complaints all the way back to Chicago. But by the time Felton came up to the suite, Elvis had calmed down, realizing that some of these sports venues simply weren't constructed for the demands of music concerts. He asked me to call Kathy Westmoreland, one of his backup singers, to the room. They'd been having a little on-the-road affair. Kathy was a sweet young lady with a beautiful voice and she seemed to have a good effect on Elvis. They disappeared into his bedroom, and the rest of the guys started up a game of hearts that lasted the rest of the night.

The next day followed a similar routine. The only change of pace was that we took a limo, not a plane, to the Milwaukee Arena, about 120 miles from Chicago. Red, Elvis, and Charlie amused themselves singing oldies for the two-hour trip, and Elvis stayed in the Sweet Inspirations' dressing room until they had to go on stage. Luckily, the sound went off without any problems, or it would have been a long drive back. We returned at about one in the morning, and ate the meal I'd arranged to be waiting for us.

We did three shows in Chicago, one Friday night, and two on Saturday. By Friday, the lobby was buzzing with beautiful women. My entire family attended that night's show, and, as usual, Elvis took the time to welcome them. He even dedicated a song to them, "It's Now or Never," and presented my mother with a TLC necklace. After the show, Elvis was ready to meet girls, so the guys escorted about twenty women to the suite and we ordered drinks. Elvis selected a cute, twenty-five-year-old redhead with a bubbly personality for his special attentions. He enlisted Red to demonstrate karate. All the women were impressed; of course, no matter what he did, they were impressed. Soon after the demonstration, Elvis and his date disappeared into his room, while the rest of us partied a few more hours. At about 6:00 A.M., Elvis called my room to ask for a limo to take his date home and to make sure she had good tickets for the following night's show.

The next day, he had a matinee. I let him sleep as long as I could, but he was dragging his feet. Once he got onstage, the energy from the fans galvanized him and he came to life. He tried to rest before the evening show, staying in his room and reading. The rest of the guys took naps. The second show was even better than the first. Night shows were always better, because Elvis woke up after the sun set. When we returned to the hotel, the redhead called up from the lobby. Some of the girls from the night before and a few new ones came up to meet Elvis. He joined us for a short while; he was more interested in spending time with his new girl.

Meanwhile, that evening after performance, Red learned that Rick Stanley, Elvis's stepbrother, was getting stoned in a band member's room in the two-story motel where we were staying. Red and a few of the guys pounded on the door, yelling, "Open the door!

It's the police!" They heard muffled sounds of panic and confusion inside. Two minutes later, after the guys had flushed all their marijuana and pills down the toilet, the door opened. But Rick wasn't there. A few moments passed before Rick came off the elevator, wearing a "What's going on?" innocent look. The sight of him made us laugh all the harder. His arms were all scratched up, leaves were trapped in his hair from his quick exit out the second-floor window, and he was still stoned. We didn't tell Elvis about it because Rick would have been in serious trouble, but we laughed about that joke for a long time.

The next day, we flew to Fort Worth, Texas, for a show at the Tarrant County Convention Center. Elvis loved playing Texas because it boasts the greatest concentration of beautiful women in the world, and we had many friends there. Elvis had arranged to meet his girlfriend Susie, a beautiful schoolteacher from Dallas, whom he'd met in Vegas through our good friend, Billy Bob Harris. After the show, Billy Bob, Susie, and other women friends visited for about three hours, and Susie spent the night with Elvis. The next day, we flew to Wichita, Kansas, for another touch-and-go at the Henry Levitt Arena. We left that stage to set out for our last city on the tour—Tulsa, Oklahoma. We were all feeling pretty good. The tour was almost over, and Elvis planned to leave for Los Angeles directly after the show.

That night, we arrived at the arena earlier than usual, so Elvis could say goodbye to the tour members. He planned to go straight to the plane after he walked offstage. He shook hands and thanked everyone for a good job. It seemed to me that the band played a bit faster and the show's tempo picked up that night. We were all eager to get home. Elvis waved goodbye again, then jumped into a limo. On board the plane, he changed out of his wet stage clothes and joined us in the front sitting room for a snack. He'd really enjoyed this tour, he told us and couldn't wait for the next one. We landed in Los Angeles at midnight, Pacific time. Three limos and a small truck for the luggage took us to Elvis's house, where Priscilla and the other wives were waiting. We sorted out our luggage, loaded our individual cars, and went home. Until the next one.

Despite of our well-honed routine, almost from the first few dates on the road, our tours had the feel of traveling with a huge, sprawling family.

• • •

When Elvis was onstage, he liked to wing little asides to the Inspirations. One time in South Carolina, the joking got out of hand. Kathy Westmoreland, Elvis's solo backup singer, was already fuming because Elvis had recently cut off their brief fling. She complained to me that men in the audience were calling her room and making lewd remarks because Elvis wasn't introducing her correctly onstage. Instead of presenting her as the lady that she that was, Elvis was making an off-color joke. This had been going on for a few days before anyone thought to say anything to him. One night, before Elvis went on stage, Tom Diskin, the Colonel's assistant, asked Elvis to be kinder in his introduction of Kathy. It was the worst thing you could ever tell Elvis. Any time Elvis was *told* to do something, you could be certain he would do the opposite, particularly if the request sounded like a demand.

That night he introduced Kathy: "Kathy Westmoreland gives great head. Ask anybody in the band." She fled from the stage in tears. On a roll, Elvis introduced the Sweet Inspirations: "The Sweet Inspirations eat catfish," he said, an apparently innocuous remark but a mortal wound to any southerner. Two of the Inspirations stalked off the stage, leaving Myrna by herself. Realizing he had gone too far, Elvis removed a ten-thousand-dollar ring from his hand and attempted to put it on Myrna's finger. He couldn't say, "Myrna, I'm sorry," or "Girls, I'm sorry." To admit aloud he'd been wrong was too painful. Elvis's apologies took the form of gifts. But Myrna didn't want the ring and tried to give it back to him. After four or five minutes struggling onstage, she finally accepted it. After all, they were supposed to be doing a show.

On the flight to the next engagement, Myrna returned the ring. "Here, Elvis," she said. "I did what I did because it's my job. You don't have to pay me extra." The next night, Elvis tossed the ring into the audience. He was showing Myrna that he was hurt and that if he gave you a present, you had to accept it. Some fan got the ring, and Elvis bought Myrna a Cadillac Eldorado, which she kept.

Elvis was always giving his rings away. Sammy Davis Jr. was a wonderful audience for Elvis, always jumping up and down in his chair, applauding wildly and shouting encouragement. They were great friends. During a 1970 show in Las Vegas, Elvis took off the fifty-two-carat black star sapphire he wore on his middle finger and slipped it onto Sammy's finger.

That same year, we were flying back first class from a vacation in Hawaii. The stewardess told us that a singing group called the Young Americans was on board and that they were entertaining their fellow passengers in coach class. Elvis wanted to meet them. One of the group, a young African-American man, admired Elvis's ring with the three big diamonds.

"One of these days I'll be able to afford a ring like that," he told Elvis. That was all Elvis needed to hear; it was the perfect setup for a great shock treatment.

"You don't have to wait any longer," he said. He took off the ring and gave it to the astounded young man. A week later, I received a call from the Beverly Hills police department. The young man had gone to a jeweler to have the ring appraised and, because he was black, the police were called. "This boy said Elvis Presley gave him the ring," the police said. It was true, I told the police, and they let him go.

I'll never forget December 8, 1970. I was at home with my wife, Joan, and our two little girls. We'd just finished dinner and were watching television when there was a knock on the door. I asked who it was, and heard, "It's me."

Elvis, Jerry Schilling, and Priscilla were standing there, with big grins on their faces. Elvis was wearing his usual outfit, a silk print shirt and black slacks and his gold-framed sunglasses, even though it was dark outside.

"What are you guys doing here?" I asked.

"We've been riding around with a real estate person, looking at houses," Elvis said.

"What's wrong with your house?"

"I'm not looking for a house for me, dummy," Elvis teased. "Priscilla and I decided that it's time you and Joan had a house."

I was shocked, but managed to invite them in for a drink.

"Where's Joan?" Elvis wanted to know. I told him she was taking a shower.

"Well, tell her to get her wet ass out here," Elvis ordered.

He was having a great time. I ran to the bathroom and told Joan that Elvis and Priscilla were here and that they had found a house for us. She laughed, dismissing it as one of Elvis's jokes.

"I don't think so," I said. "He's serious. Get dressed."

I went back into the living room where Elvis was sitting with both my daughters on his lap. I couldn't hear what he was whispering to them, but they were giggling in delight. Joan came out in a few moments and hugged Elvis and Priscilla. She told Elvis he was crazy, and he laughed and agreed as we headed for the door.

"All right," he said, "let's take care of business! Joe, you follow us."

We followed Elvis's car to the house they'd picked out for us. We were disappointed and tried hard not to let Elvis know. But he could tell.

"This house doesn't have warmth," he told the real estate agent. "Let's go back to the office and see what else you have."

Joan told them what we wanted, and we went through the books until we found a likely prospect on Hillsboro Avenue in West Los Angeles. We piled back into our cars and drove over. By now it was about 8:30 P.M., but Elvis was determined to find us a new home if it took all night. This one was perfect. It was freshly painted and situated on a quiet, tree-lined street. All seven of us came inside, and the family was pretty cool even though no one had warned them that Elvis Presley was among the party. Elvis signed an autograph for one of the children, but only Joan was allowed in the master bedroom because the owner's wife was concerned for her husband, who was recuperating from a heart attack.

We loved the house. It had three bedrooms, two bathrooms, a den with a fireplace and bar, a formal dining room, a big kitchen, a large backyard, and a two-car garage. But we knew we couldn't afford the mortgage, even with Elvis paying the down payment.. We went outside to talk, and I thanked Elvis and Priscilla, but told them I would have to refuse it.

"Don't worry about it, Joe," he said. "I've got it all figured out. I'll give you a raise, and you'll afford it."

Joan and I hugged him. Again, we were at a loss for words. I wrote out a check for a ten-thousand-dollar payment, and Elvis signed it. The house cost forty-five thousand, and I wanted to bargain the owners down. But Elvis refused, saying that with the owner's heart attack, they needed the money. A few days later, he went to Memphis for Christmas, and I moved into the house with my family in January 1971.

That was a good example of the Presley shock treatment working in tandem with his exceptional generosity. But the stellar example has to be his impromptu visit with President Nixon. Less than two weeks before Christmas 1970, Vernon and Priscilla complained to Elvis about his spending. Furious, he stormed out of Graceland and went straight to the airport, where he bought a plane ticket for Los Angeles under an assumed name. At the time, Jerry Schilling was living in Los Angeles, learning film editing at Paramount studios and barely making the rent on his tiny Culver City apartment. At three o'clock that morning, his phone rang.

"Who is this?" Jerry asked.

"Me." It was Elvis.

"Where are you?" Jerry asked.

"I'm changing planes in Dallas," Elvis said. "I'm arriving on an American flight."

"What do you mean you're going to be on an American flight?" Since 1960, Elvis had never traveled without at least two people.

"I don't want anyone to know where I am," Elvis said. "Could you meet me at the airport? It's okay if you call the limo company. You can let Sir Gerald know," Elvis instructed. (He was referring to Gerald Peters, "Sir Gerald" to us, the English owner of London Towne Livery Service.) "Both of you come pick me up. Tell him not to say a word to anyone." Jerry was impressed. Whatever was happening, Elvis wasn't fooling around. Elvis gave him the flight number and arrival time, and Sir Gerald drove onto the runway right up to the plane.

All the passengers had disembarked when Elvis finally came down the steps. His face was swollen and dotted with red spots, his hair and sideburns were especially long, and he was wearing a black cape and carrying a carved wooden cane. Now Jerry was really concerned. "I had this penicillin reaction," Elvis explained. "And then I ate chocolate on the plane. I guess it brought the reaction back."

Jerry asked Gerald to call a doctor to Elvis's house. But then the stewardesses showed up. Elvis had promised to take them home.

"Elvis, we have a doctor waiting outside your house," Jerry pleaded. "It's 4:00 A.M.!"

"But, Jerry," Elvis said, "I promised these people."

They dropped each of the girls off at her apartment and then drove to Elvis's house on Hillcrest Drive. By the time they arrived, it was almost daybreak Sunday morning, and the doctor was waiting outside. He gave Elvis medication for the penicillin reaction and Elvis went to sleep. Jerry grabbed a few hours of rest, then got up, planning to talk with Elvis a bit and then go home. But Elvis had other plans.

"Jerry, I need to go to Washington," he announced.

"I can't go," Jerry said. "I have to be at the studio for my editing job."

"I'll get a private plane and have them fly you back," Elvis offered.

"That won't get me back any faster than a commercial plane," Jerry pointed out. "It's just going to cost more money."

"Okay," Elvis decided, "I'll go by myself."

That was not a good idea. The flight to Los Angeles had not been easy, because Elvis boarded the plane with one gun in his waistband and a smaller one tucked in his boot. A steward told Elvis he would take the guns and return them after they landed. Already worked up from the argument with Priscilla and Vernon, Elvis stomped off the plane. The pilot found out what happened, and got off the plane himself to personally ask Elvis to reboard—*with* his guns. Another instance where someone couldn't say no.

"You know what?" Jerry said after a few moments' consideration. "I'll go with you."

At this point, no one but Jerry knew where Elvis was—not me, not Priscilla, not Vernon, not the guys. And Jerry still had no idea why Elvis "needed" to go to Washington.

Elvis had left Graceland with no cash, only a credit card, so he wrote out a check for five hundred dollars from the checkbook he kept at the Hillcrest house. Jerry called Sir Gerald to pick them up. It was Sunday evening, but Sir Gerald persuaded someone at the Beverly Hilton Hotel to cash the check, and Jerry took charge of the money. Sir Gerald drove them right up to the plane, and Elvis and Jerry were preboarded three rows back in first class. Most of the passengers just walked by, but a few shook Elvis's hand and said hello. One young man, just back from service in Vietnam, became very excited.

"Are you going home for Christmas?" Elvis asked. He was.

Elvis nudged Jerry. "Where's that money?"

"What money?" Jerry said. "We've only got five hundred dollars."

"I need it," Elvis said. "I want to give it to this guy."

"Elvis," Jerry protested, "we won't have a penny! We're going to Washington, D.C.!" Elvis shot him that look, and Jerry handed over the five hundred dollars. Elvis gave it all to the serviceman.

After the plane was in the air, Elvis finally told Jerry that he planned to meet with President Nixon. But first, he said, he would visit John Finlator, head of the Federal Narcotics Bureau. Elvis had been collecting law enforcement badges for years. The first, a deputy sheriff's badge, was cajoled from a Memphis police officer. Gradually, Elvis worked his way up to a chief deputy's badge. Finally, he asked the Memphis sheriff for a sheriff's badge. The sheriff happened to be Jerry Schilling's brother, and there was only one sheriff's badge—his own. "You wouldn't want to run against me, would you?" Elvis asked. They reached a compromise. Elvis became the honorary sheriff and got his badge.

One night, Elvis, Priscilla, Charlie, Sonny, and I were having dinner at La Scala in Beverly Hills. Elvis rarely ate out, but the restaurant had given us a private room. Our party also included Ed Hookstratten, Elvis's attorney, and a private detective named John O'Grady. John was working for Elvis, gathering evidence for a paternity suit brought against Elvis by a Hollywood waitress named Pat Parker. The case never got to court, because the blood tests proved Elvis was not the father, and the girl never even had a date with Elvis. That night at La Scala, O'Grady introduced Elvis to a man named Paul Frees. Frees did voices for many animation films, for such characters as Ludwig Von Drake, Captain Crunch, and the Pillsbury Doughboy. He was also an adamant antidrug crusader who had been honored for his work with a badge from the Bureau of Narcotics and Dangerous Drugs. Frees showed the badge to Elvis. It is the ultimate law enforcement badge, recognized throughout the world. One of Elvis's fantasies had always been to be a spy, an undercover type. And ever since that night at La Scala, Elvis had been determined to get that badge for himself.

On the flight, Elvis composed a letter to President Nixon on American Airlines stationery, and he asked Jerry to proofread it. Jerry knew enough grammar to recognize that it was riddled with errors. But it was sincere and it was written by Elvis Presley, so Jerry thought it should be sent as it was. Elvis had written that he had a collection of law enforcement badges from Memphis, Denver, and other cities, and that he felt very fortunate to have done so well as a rock 'n' roll artist in America. He went on to write that he was very supportive of the White House. Many people confided information to him that they wouldn't reveal to others, he said, and he would be willing to pass along anything pertinent. He felt a particular responsibility, he told the president, because rock 'n' roll was getting pretty crazy. The irony in his writing this, while he was becoming more and more enmeshed in his own drug habit, was completely lost on him.

"It's fine," Jerry told Elvis. In his own way, he had known exactly what to say and how to say it. Elvis folded the letter, sealed it in an envelope, and scribbled "Confidential, For the President Only" on the outside.

They arrived in Washington just before daybreak, where a limo was waiting. By now Jerry had been up two nights running with barely any rest. But Elvis wanted to deliver the letter to the White House straight away.

"Let's go to the hotel first and check in," Jerry suggested.

"No, I want to go there now," Elvis insisted.

There he was, his swollen face framed by long jet-black hair and sideburns, wearing a voluminous black cape topped by an extremely high Nehru collar, carrying a large and elaborately carved cane, and getting out of a limo at the White House gates. A wary White House security man—who failed to recognize Elvis at first—was obviously trying to decide what to make of this apparition, while Jerry monitored the scene nervously from inside the car. Elvis just handed the guard the letter for the president and drove away.

Then he dropped Jerry off at the hotel to await the president's summons before going off to John Finlator's office at the Federal Narcotics Bureau building to get his badge. Jerry thought to himself, sure, the President is going to call. An hour later, the phone rang. "The president would like to meet Mr. Presley in twenty minutes," an official-sounding voice said. Jerry called Elvis at Finlator's office. Elvis didn't sound happy. Finlator had refused his request for a Federal Bureau of Narcotics badge.

"The president wants to meet with you in twenty minutes," Jerry said.

"Fine," Elvis replied, "because I'm not doing any good here. Wait for me in front of the hotel. I'll pick you up on the way to the White House."

By then, Jerry had convinced Elvis to allow him to return to his job in Los Angeles and to call Graceland. Sonny West was on his way to Washington from Memphis. Elvis's limousine was just pulling up in front of the hotel when Sonny came puffing up to the lobby. "Leave your luggage with the bellman. We're going to the White House," Jerry told him, and Sonny climbed into the limo.

When Elvis had stormed out of Graceland, he had taken along a commemorative World War I gun in a case from his collection at Graceland, which he intended to present to Nixon. At the White House, Sonny, Jerry, and Elvis were briefed according to regulations. Elvis was asked why he wanted to meet the president. To present him with the gun, he said.

Elvis was ushered into the Oval Office, and Sonny and Jerry were taken to a waiting room. After a few more questions, they were told that they couldn't join Elvis and the president. It's hard to say no to Elvis, Sonny and Jerry warned. Out of the question, the security men repeated. Anyway, it wasn't even their decision, because more Secret Service personnel would be required. About ten minutes later, the phone rang.

"The president wants to meet Elvis Presley's friends," someone said to the security man.

"You know what?" the astonished man said to Jerry and Sonny. "A lot of people come to meet the president, and they never think about their friends." That was another facet of Elvis's generosity. A big part of the thrill he received from his fame and extraordinary powers of persuasion was sharing the fruits with his friends.

Jerry and Sonny were led to the president's office, where Elvis was standing in the doorway, grinning hugely and inviting them in as casually as if he were standing at the entrance to Graceland. They peeked through the door and spotted Nixon seated at a desk at the far end of the office, signing papers. The scene is engraved in Jerry's memory: Elvis, poised at the door and obviously relishing his friends' amazement, offering a hearty invitation to "Come on in!" as President Nixon, framed by the fabled arch of the presidential office, signed official papers.

Elvis introduced Jerry and Sonny to the president, and they all had pictures taken. Nixon presented them with presidential key chains. "They've got wives too," Elvis said. So Nixon went back and got more. "I'm waiting for the badge," Elvis informed Sonny and Jerry. The situation had been resolved. It was simply a matter of going over Finlator's head.

When the badge arrived, Elvis noticed the written credentials were missing, so Nixon got on the phone again to Finlator. "We must get someone here to fingerprint Mr. Presley," Nixon told Finlator. "He wants the credentials that go with his badge." By now, the White House was buzzing. Word had spread that Elvis was on the premises, and everyone wanted to see him. They invited Elvis, Sonny, and Jerry on a tour. But as soon as the credentials arrived, Elvis had what he came for and he was ready to leave. "Let's just go back to the hotel," he said. Jerry flew to Los Angeles, and Elvis and Sonny returned to Memphis. The badge hangs on the wall of Graceland's trophy room today. But while he was alive, Elvis carried it on his person at all times. Every few months or so, the Federal Bureau of Narcotics telephoned him, as they do all holders of that badge, making sure it was intact and still in his possession. Elvis may have been a big kid, but he was big enough to get what he wanted. Even the president stopped everything for Elvis. He knew how to reach anyone, but he gave as much attention to the serviceman on the plane as he did to the president of the United States.

chapter 8
heartbreak hotel

in 1971, the unbelievable happened. Priscilla left Elvis. We were playing Vegas when I received a phone call one night from Elvis's attorney, Ed Hookstratten.

"Joe, I want to let you know something," he said without any preamble. "Priscilla is having an affair with her karate instructor, a guy named Mike Stone."

"No! It can't be!" I exclaimed.

"You'd better talk to Elvis," Hookstratten advised.

I hung up the receiver and gathered my thoughts. Elvis rarely, if ever, made love to Priscilla, but she had accepted the situation for so long, it was hard to imagine that she had actually taken a lover. When I had steadied my nerve, I phoned Elvis's room.

"I think we've got a problem here that we should talk about," I began tentatively. I was genuinely afraid to drop this piece of news on him, but I went ahead. "I got a phone call from Hook-stratten saying he knows Priscilla is having an affair."

"That's bullshit!" Elvis yelled in my ear. "What the hell is he doing sticking his nose in my business?"

The notion was inconceivable to him. Priscilla, *his* wife, having an affair? It didn't matter that he was with someone else that very night. I realized that I wasn't going to get through to him, so I dropped the subject.

Elvis never said anything to Priscilla, but a few months after Ed Hookstratten's call, Priscilla flew to Vegas to tell Elvis she was leaving him. She had fallen in love with someone else. Priscilla later told me that a look of shock came over his face. He didn't become angry, but tears sprang to his eyes.

"Who is it?" he asked. Priscilla refused to say. "I'm leaving," she repeated. "I don't feel as if we are married. It's over." She never told him who the man was.

Elvis came out of the room with his eyes blazing. "Priscilla's leaving me," he announced. For a moment, everyone was silent. We didn't know what to say. Finally, Red spoke up. "I know who the son of a bitch is," he said.

"Who?" Elvis demanded.

"Mike Stone."

Elvis was furious. He was the one who had introduced Mike to Priscilla and told her to take karate lessons from him. We first met Mike in Hawaii at a karate tournament sponsored by another karate champ, our friend Ed Parker. As the undefeated champion, Mike Stone was very famous, a good-looking man who was part Hawaiian, standing at least six feet tall, with deep-set eyes, an Afro hairstyle, and a body as hard as a rock. Elvis thought he was great. Two months later, while we were in Vegas, Phil Spector came backstage with Mike Stone as his bodyguard. Elvis recognized Mike, and they talked about karate.

"I'm living in L.A. now, and I've got this karate school," Stone told Elvis.

Priscilla was interested in karate, so Elvis said, "Hey, Priscilla. Karate school! Mike Stone! Great! Why don't you start taking lessons?" She did, and over the course of a year or so, she and Mike fell in love.

Elvis sat in that hotel hallway for over an hour. "She's leaving me," he kept repeating. "I'm losing her."

Afterward, he went to his room and called Pat to him. He cried on her shoulder.

"Yes, Priscilla left you," Pat told him, patting his back and trying to coax him into accepting some responsibility. "Why are you crying, Elvis? You can't blame her. You fooled around on her for years."

No one blamed Priscilla for leaving. She was young, beautiful, and neglected; now she'd found someone to really love her. She moved out of Elvis's house on February 23, 1972, the last day of his Las Vegas engagement.

In the months following the separation, blind rages swept over Elvis. He tore up rooms, shouting that he wanted Mike Stone dead. Every afternoon, he woke up with a look of pain on his face. We sat with him at the table while he ate breakfast and ranted on and on about Mike and Priscilla.

"That no good bitch! I gave her everything she wanted and this is how I'm treated!" He would rave for hours. We had to reorder his breakfast two or three times because it kept getting cold. This went on for months. The same thing every day.

One day, he called Red and Sonny into his bedroom.

"I want you to have Mike Stone killed," he said. "Call some people and get it done."

"Hey, E," they protested, "you can't do that. It's over, you can't do that." He was adamant, so they humored him. "Yeah, we'll work on it," one of the guys finally said. They left and came directly to my room.

"Forget about it," I advised. I knew that, in part, this was a show for our benefit, a way to prop up his injured ego.

"Did you get anything done?" Elvis asked Red from time to time.

"I'm making phone calls," he'd hedge. "I'm calling people. It's not that easy, you know."

Elvis tried to hide from us the fact that he was telephoning Priscilla frequently in the middle of the night, threatening to have Mike's legs broken and even to have him killed.

Priscilla tried to calm him. "Elvis, don't talk that way," she'd plead. "Think about it. What would happen if you really did something like that? What would your daughter think?" That would quiet him, but only temporarily. He was very, very upset. He kept after Red, all the while cursing Mike. He blamed the breakup of his marriage on everyone but himself. It was all Priscilla's and Mike's fault. Eventually, Red made some contacts.

"Okay," he told Elvis. "Ten thousand dollars and we get it done."

By then Elvis had cooled down a bit. "I'll let you know," he said. He never mentioned the matter again.

The divorce was a terrible blow to Elvis's ego, from which he never fully recovered. He couldn't believe that Priscilla had the effrontery to leave him. But deep down, he also knew that Mike Stone was a tough guy with plenty of self-respect, and a good man. On an even more profound level, Elvis knew he'd failed, and he didn't like the idea of being separated from Lisa. It pained him to realize that his little girl now came from a broken home.

Elvis was very proud to be a father, to be the head of a proper family. But he separated that aspect of his life from everything else. Marriage and fatherhood hadn't altered his behavior with other women in the slightest. He had continued to have his many affairs and one-night stands, juggling three or more women at a time. It never occurred to him that a real family man focuses entirely on his family. Elvis had a wife and a child, and he had his girlfriends. He was fulfilled.

As a ploy to discourage the competition, when Priscilla visited him on tour or in Vegas, she often left her clothes in Elvis's closet, hoping another girl would be tempted to take something. Evidence! But one of the guys always listed every item she left behind, even drawing a diagram of the order in which the clothes were placed. Then he hung them somewhere else. When Priscilla returned, they were right back in the closet, exactly as she'd left them. Elvis never admitted his infidelities. Instead, he turned in some of his finest. acting performances, and Priscilla always gave in.

So she tried to build a life for herself and found activities to occupy her time. She took a lot of photos of the baby and tried to keep Elvis involved in family life by sending him pictures. Lisa Marie was their strongest link, but it was clear that their marriage was in trouble. In 1970, we took a group vacation with our wives to Hawaii. Elvis and Priscilla and Joan and I shared a two-bedroom hut at the Coco Palms Hotel on the island of Kauai, where we'd

shot the wedding scene in *Blue Hawaii*. Late one night we over-
heard a heated argument through the thin wall separating our head-
boards. It was over his refusal to make love. "Ever since I had Lisa
you don't want to touch me anymore," Priscilla cried.

Elvis had a full-blown Madonna complex. "I don't like to make
love to somebody who's had a kid," he often told me. "I don't feel
comfortable doing it." We all knew about his complex before
Priscilla had the baby and wondered what would happen afterward.

Before Lisa's birth, they had shared a good sex life, spiced
with Elvis's tendencies toward voyeurism. When he purchased the
first home video camera in 1964, a Sony reel-to-reel, the guys had
asked him teasingly why he'd bought it. "I'm going to tape some
TV programs," he answered, shrugging us off. But he didn't fool
us. Elvis wouldn't have enjoyed today's hardcore pornographic
movies, but he loved to watch girls wrestling on a bed wearing
lacy white bras and panties—never totally nude. The panties had
to be white. He was particularly turned on by two girls together,
a relatively innocent fantasy. Elvis convinced Priscilla to perform
while he played video director. Though he appears in a couple of
shots, Elvis is always in his pajamas, never naked, as has been reported. I've seen many of the tapes, and they wouldn't even merit
an "R" rating in today's mainstream movies. Neither Priscilla nor
Elvis ever knew I saw them. The guys noticed the tapes lying
around, but Elvis always dismissed them as "just some stuff I
recorded off the television."

"Okay," I once challenged him. "Show us what you recorded."

"Nah, nah."

One day in 1971, I was in Elvis's house in California with one
of the guys. Elvis was far away, at home in Memphis. Four or five
big reels of three-quarter-inch tape and the tape machine were sitting there, right in front of us. "Well, shit, let's watch these tapes,"
we decided. But we couldn't find the power cord. Elvis had taken
it with him. We got into the car, drove to Sony headquarters, bought
another power cord, then turned around and headed back to the
house to watch those tapes.

Elvis usually kept those tapes locked up in a small blue Samsonite case, along with a big stack of Polaroids of Priscilla. She was
about eighteen at the time the tapes and pictures were taken, and
the shots were very sexy. Priscilla probably tried to get the tapes

and photographs from Elvis after their divorce, but he undoubt-edly told her they were destroyed. Priscilla has them now. I gave her the blue Samsonite case within minutes of her arrival at Grace-land the day after Elvis died.

Many women passed through Elvis's life, but only a few—Anita Wood, Priscilla, Ann-Margret, Linda Thompson, Sheila Ryan, and Barbara Leigh—really meant something to him. They were the "Lif-ers," as Pat Parry and Myrna Smith dubbed them, as opposed to the "Queens for a Day."

In certain ways, Elvis was a very unsophisticated man. He loved women, but he was not the super-suave stud everyone thought he was. No one could live up to that image. Elvis slept with a lot of women, especially in the early days, but he couldn't have slept with every girl he dated. While it's true that Elvis always had to have a woman around, part of that need for constant female companionship was his lifelong craving for mothering. Pat Parry knew this best. She was the one who made his breakfast, rubbed his back, cut up his meat, and listened to graphic and dramatic recitals of his physical ills, if there was no other woman around.

Toward the end of his marriage he had one of his major af-fairs, with the starlet Barbara Leigh. Barbara was exotically beau-tiful, incredibly sexy, sweet-natured, and fun, and like Elvis, she was a child of the South. In 1970, twenty-three-year-old Barbara was dating fifty-something Jim Aubrey, the president of MGM and Hollywood's most notorious Casanova. He was even rumored to be the model for the protagonist of Jackie Collins's steamy show-biz potboiler *The Stud.* MGM had produced the documentary *Elvis—That's the Way It Is,* so Aubrey took Barbara—who had been an Elvis fan since third grade—to Vegas to see Elvis's show. Back-stage, Aubrey headed for the bar, while Barbara sat at a table talk-ing with singer Rick Nelson and his wife, Chris.

A few minutes had passed when Barbara sensed that some-one was staring at her. She turned her head to the left and dis-covered Elvis sitting next to her, flashing the smile. I'd spotted Barbara in the audience the moment she walked in with Aubrey. She had a knockout body and an exquisite face, and her long, straight, dark hair was parted in the middle, accenting her Ameri-can Indian heritage, a hip thing in those days. Barbara was spe-cial, and I knew Elvis would love her. After the show, I rushed to the dressing room. "E," I said, "wait till you see this girl with Jim Aubrey. She's beautiful!" He changed his clothes in record time and came out to see for himself. Meanwhile, Aubrey was deep in conversation at the bar, oblivious to what was going on. He and Elvis were longtime competitors over women, and Aubrey was known around town as "the smiling cobra," a tough businessman and a masterful seducer. Elvis fancied himself the mongoose who could take that cobra down. Elvis muttered a request for "little darlin's" phone number; Barbara scribbled it on a scrap of paper and passed it to him under the table before Aubrey joined them.

After the show, Jim and Barbara flew back to Los Angeles and visited some friends at the beach. As Barbara pulled her Porsche up to her apartment building Sunday evening, she heard her telephone ringing. She leaped out of the car and ran inside, leaving her suitcase. It was Elvis. As they talked, Barbara undressed, changed into a robe, and lay down on the bed. "Why don't you come visit me?" Elvis asked. Barbara agreed to come. As she got up to close her windows, she saw a young man wearing a yarmulke standing outside, watching her. "Oh, my bag!" she cried. She got off the phone and ran out to her car. Her suitcase was gone and with it her only beautiful dress, a black Grecian design.

Barbara made up a story for Jim and flew that Tuesday to Las Vegas. "You can't come to the show," Charlie announced when he picked Barbara up at the airport. "Jim is here with Jo Anne Worley." Okay, Barbara thought, two are playing this game. Charlie brought Barbara directly to the twenty-ninth floor, to Elvis's pink suite—the one he used for girls—which was equipped with a huge pink bed and mirrored ceiling. After a few hours, Elvis joined her. He took one look at Barbara's dress and sent her out with one of the guys to Suzie Creamcheese, where she picked out four or five gowns.

Barbara was emotionally torn, excited over Elvis but hurt by Jim Aubrey's infidelity. Elvis attracted her, but she was really in love with Jim. They had planned a cruise that coming weekend, Labor Day. She decided to stand Aubrey up and stay with Elvis. Elvis was so proud of stealing Aubrey's girl that he bought a stuffed mongoose and cobra to commemorate the event. After they were alone that first night, Elvis gave Barbara a medallion of Jesus and a book entitled *The Impersonal Life* that he bought by the case in order to give away. Elvis loved long talks on spiritual and occult matters with beautiful, sympathetic women, and Barbara knew the Bible as well as he did.

For six months, they shared a highly romantic, physical relationship. Normally, Elvis just talked and maybe kissed on the first date, but that night he and Barbara made love. "He was a good lover," Barbara told me years later. "He was just natural, not technical, and he was really free. Above all, he was a great kisser. He liked certain little things, like white lace panties with a bit of pubic hair coming out the sides. He told me that was very important because when he was a young boy of thirteen or fourteen, he tumbled around with some girls in the yard and saw their white panties."

Barbara even visited Graceland while Priscilla was at her parents' home in New Jersey. Their rapport extended to such trivialities as the sweet, lemony iced tea Elvis loved to drink while he was in Memphis. Barbara remembered that tea from her childhood. They stayed in his bedroom for hours at a time, talking about religion, the South, and Gladys, subjects Elvis rarely broached with the guys.

"For some reason he related me to his mother," Barbara said. "I guess it was the dark hair and eyes. I remember he held me and said, 'My mom told me I would marry a brown-eyed girl, honey. You might be it.' Of course, he was still married to Priscilla, so I took all that as just talk. He adored his mother and he said his dad didn't treat her very well."

Elvis told more than one woman that she reminded him of his mother, but he had strong feelings for Barbara and appreciated her care in not leaving behind any incriminating items. She instinctively knew that if she wanted to come back, she must never get him into trouble.

Elvis loved to give his friends and girlfriends guns. He bought Barbara a fine collection: dueling pistols and Colts from the little gun shop he frequented in Palm Springs, and a small Beretta automatic from Mike McGregor, who lived in a trailer behind the property at Graceland and took care of Elvis's horses. I still have several guns Elvis gave me. Barbara, Elvis, and I were shopping at the Palm

Springs gun shop one day when a scruffy-looking man with a sad-looking wife and child were looking at a rifle. It was obvious that they had no money, so Elvis bought the rifle for them.

Besides jewelry and clothes, Elvis also bought Barbara a beautiful Mercedes, right after he bought one for Charlie Hodge. "I was sitting there thinking, 'I wish I had a Mercedes,' " Barbara said. "And he picked up on my thought. I thought that was so sweet of him. I picked license plates with the number 111-CPT, because Elvis had involved me in numerology and 111 added up to three, a good number."

Some of the guys thought Barbara was a gold digger, but she was one of my favorites. She saved up to buy Elvis a beautiful pharaoh's-head ring from a Beverly Hills shop because he was fascinated by Egypt. She also gave him a china statue of an owl because he loved owls. The guys were not always perceptive judges of character. When it came to women, their standards were completely superficial: How does she look? Will she jump into bed with me? They rated Elvis's girlfriends according to a peculiar and exacting standard. The more she assumed the burden of Elvis's care, the better they liked her because it meant less work for them. For her part, Barbara didn't appreciate the fact that the guys brought other women to meet Elvis, even when she was present. Those girls made plays for him all night, and Barbara complained to Elvis. She hated the pressure of having to compete. "It was exhausting," she said. "I had to be on twice as much."

I once had a very pretty girlfriend who secretly liked Elvis and decided that the best way to get to him, besides hooking up with me, was to undermine Barbara. "Oh, he's just using you," she kept telling Barbara one night. "You don't mean anything to him."

Later, when Barbara and Elvis were alone, he sensed her mood. Finally, in the middle of the night, she told Elvis what my girlfriend had said. Elvis called my room to announce he was coming.

"He dragged me down the hallway of this little hotel in Mobile, Alabama, at about three in the morning to confront her," Barbara said. "I was really embarrassed. 'What have I done?' I thought. I rushed to the bathroom to tell her I was sorry, and there she was, trying to glue on her eyelashes before Elvis saw her! He confronted her, and she backed down. That's when he wrote me a little note I still have today: 'I love you and I will always love you, the Panther.' "

Like all of Elvis's girls, Barbara saw him whenever she was summoned to join him—usually by me or one of the guys—either on the road or in Hollywood, Las Vegas, or Palm Springs. One day, I called Barbara to invite her to Palm Springs. Her best girlfriend happened to be there, a tall, beautiful blonde with catlike blue eyes named Jessica St. John. Jessica was crying on Barbara's shoulder over a recent breakup with a boyfriend, and they had just split a dose of mescaline to calm her down. In those days, that was considered a good idea.

I sent the plane to pick up both girls. The irony was that Jessica was a bigger Elvis fan than Barbara. She had been president of her high school Elvis Presley fan club and had even met him once in that capacity. To this day, Jessica still has her collection of rare Elvis forty-fives. By the time the girls walked into Elvis's living room, they were only slightly under the influence. "God, he looks different," Barbara thought to herself. She wasn't sure if it was Elvis or the hallucinogenic altering her vision. Then Elvis decided to practice karate, and Barbara realized why he had looked different when the wig he was wearing flew off his head. We all held our breath for a moment, then Elvis burst out laughing, and we all cracked up. He wasn't wearing the wig to conceal baldness. It was just another toy, like his handcuffs or his guns, or the big police flashlight he carried around.

That night Elvis gave Barbara the pills he usually gave his girls. She always took whatever he gave her, but this night she was afraid to mix anything with the mescaline. She hid the first pill under her pillow. But Elvis was watching as he handed her a second one, an amphetamine. She swallowed it and became very sick. I took her to a room at the back of the house to lie down. That was an opportunity for Jessica, who moved over to sit next to Elvis in "Barbara's" chair.

"Don't sit in that chair, that's Barbara's," Sonny warned abruptly. He wanted Jessica for himself.

"You can sit there, darlin'," Elvis said. "Barbara's not here." Jessica was certainly beautiful, but nothing happened between her and Elvis. She was too intellectual for him, a writer who later created a rock opera based on the life of Buddha called *The Prince.* Besides, she was a loyal friend to Barbara.

Elvis was very upset about Barbara's illness and blamed himself. He kept sending me into the room where she was resting to ask if she'd taken anything else, and she kept insisting that she hadn't. Barbara knew Elvis would be angry if he found out.

Barbara confided in me that she never allowed herself to fall completely in love with Elvis because she knew that in the end, she was just another girl. He had Priscilla.

"Had I known she would leave," Barbara told me, "I probably could have let myself go more, fallen in love, gone after him, and made myself available all the time. In those days, I was traveling around, doing films here and there, and juggling men the way Elvis juggled women."

Barbara was also still in love with Jim Aubrey. Then, late in 1971, toward the end of her relationship with Elvis, she and Steve McQueen costarred in *Junior Bonner*. For a brief period, Barbara was simultaneously dating Jim Aubrey, Elvis Presley, and Steve Mc-Queen!

"Steve referred to Elvis as 'that guitar guy,' putting him down as a hick who strummed a guitar," Barbara said. "Elvis called Steve 'that motorcycle hick.' They were both hicks, but I mean that in an affectionate way, because I'm a hick as well. Steve was great, but he was the kind of guy who burped and ate with his feet on the table, very natural. For a little while, we had the competition going between the three guys."

The spark began to fade for Elvis when, more and more, Barbara failed to respond to his summonses. He called her on the *Junior Bonner* location in Arizona and discovered she was living with Steve. Elvis was too proud to say anything directly to Barbara. He could never acknowledge that other people had their own lives. Then, a few months after the year-and-a-half affair with Barbara wound down, Priscilla left.

The breakup of his marriage plunged Elvis into a depression from which he would emerge only for brief periods. At first, he didn't meet anyone to replace Priscilla, and he was forced to look at himself in order to understand why the marriage had failed. But he was never able to admit the obvious: that his inability to be a real husband had cost him his marriage. It was easier to seek relief in metaphysical pursuits and drugs.

It was more pleasant to ponder the mysteries of communi-
cating God's will through music. It disturbed him to realize that
others didn't understand his belief. He complained that "Priscilla
never enjoyed meditation or spiritual readings with me." Elvis knew
I wasn't interested either, so we never discussed it much. But Larry
Geller and he talked for hours on end, trying to unravel the meaning of life. At Larry's suggestion, Elvis had astrological and nu-
merological charts drawn up, and he devoured books on those
subjects. Elvis read aloud to Jerry the interpretation of his number,
eight, from *Cheiro's Book of Numbers.*

> These people are invariably much misunderstood in their lives,
> and perhaps for this reason they feel intensely lonely at heart.
> They have deep and very intense natures, great strength of indi-
> viduality; they generally play some important role on life's stage,
> but usually one which is fatalistic, or as the instrument of Fate for
> others.
> If at all religious they go to extremes and are fanatic in their zeal.
> In any cause they take up, they attempt to carry it through in spite
> of all arguments or opposition, and in doing so they generally make
> bitter and relentless enemies.
> They often appear cold and undemonstrative, though in reality
> they have warm hearts towards the oppressed of all classes; but they
> hide their feelings and allow people to think just what they please.
> These number 8 people are either great successes or great fail-
> ures; there appears to be no happy medium in their case.
> If ambitious, they generally aim for public life or government re-
> sponsibility of some kind, and often hold very high positions in-
> volving great sacrifices on their part . . . .
> All persons who have the number 8 clearly associated with their
> lives feel that they are distinct and different from their fellows. At
> heart they are lonely; they are misunderstood, and they seldom reap
> the reward for the good they may do while they are living. After
> death, they are often extolled, their works praised, and lasting trib-
> utes offered to their memory.

Jerry was amazed to realize that the book described Elvis precisely.
Elvis reread his occult and science-fiction books, going over
favorites three or four times and memorizing much of the contents
so he could quote passages at will. He dog-eared page corners,

jotted notes in the margins, underlined passages, and scribbled the initials of the person with whom he wanted to discuss a particular point. He analyzed the Bible sentence by sentence to form his own interpretations, then preached to us on his findings. The word "Israel," he'd intone with great authority, really meant "is real." He'd pause dramatically, two fingers poised in a karate posture in the listener's face. "God's name is really 'hallowed,' " he'd say without the trace of a smile, "because it says hallowed be thy name." He got that one from Myrna, who heard it from her grandfather, a church deacon. Myrna thought that was hilarious, so she told Elvis. She didn't take the statement seriously, but Elvis did. He passed on Myrna's grandfather's little nugget of wisdom to anyone willing to listen.

Elvis believed fervently in reincarnation. Someone gave him a photograph of a statue in Rome and then placed it next to Elvis's photograph to highlight their identical profiles. Elvis thought about those two photographs long and hard. "Maybe I was here before," he concluded. So he looked for answers to the breakup of his marriage in past lifetimes instead of this one.

When my wife, Joan, was put in traction for a ruptured spinal disc, Elvis decided to heal her. He came with Priscilla and Jerry, and Jerry's wife at the time, Sandy, a lovely girl he'd met in Hawaii. Elvis placed a blue scarf over Joan and told us to form a circle and clasp one another's hands. Then he led us in prayer. I went along with it, because Elvis was so sincere and eager to help. Three weeks later, much earlier than the doctors predicted, she was greatly improved. Whether it was Elvis or the traction no one can say, but I know that Elvis put his heart into trying to help others. He hated to see anyone suffer. It was one of the reasons I loved him. Even if it was sometimes ridiculous, when you looked into his eyes as he preached or healed, all you saw was a sincere desire to help. Only those close to Elvis knew that part of him.

During his laying-on-of-hands period, he began calling the band and backup singers together to pray before each show. "Elvis really had something going there," said Myrna. "If I don't believe it, it comes across as insincere to me."

Myrna told me of an incident involving Sylvia Shenwell, one of the Sweet Inspirations. Sylvia had a pap test before she came to Vegas one time. As soon as she arrived at the hotel, her doctors called and told her to go directly to the hospital because the test showed evidence of cancer. Sylvia was hysterical. "After the show, Elvis came into our dressing room," said Myrna. "He put his hands on Sylvia's stomach and prayed for her. It was just the three of us and Elvis. He prayed sincerely for Sylvia, and he really believed he could heal her. I was touched by his prayer, and though I don't remember exactly what the words were, I know he was praying to God for a healing. We were all crying, including Elvis. When Sylvia went to the hospital the next day, there was no trace of cancer. As far as I'm concerned, she was healed."

Elvis spent months immersed in numerology, astrology, healing, and other occult subjects. But for equally long periods, he never mentioned them because he was into something else, such as guns. Elvis's spiritual pursuit was now shadowed by a desperate urgency. What he was really searching for was a sense of self. His spiritual quest intensified with his unhappiness, but so did his drug abuse.

The Christmas after Priscilla left, Elvis didn't feel up to facing relatives he barely saw during the year who were gathered for their holiday handout. He had presented his annual gifts of a thousand-dollar check each to fifty Memphis organizations and charities, and that would be it. He and Jerry stayed upstairs in Elvis's bedroom.

"I don't feel like going down there," he told Jerry. "Everybody's just waiting for their presents."

"Don't do it," Jerry said.

"We have to get Grandma and Daddy something," Elvis said. "Why don't you call Harry Levitch's and ask him to come over?" Levitch was a jeweler in Memphis.

"Jerry, I want to read your number to you," Elvis said after Harry had left. At the end of the *Book of Numbers'* description of the number six, Elvis read, "'Always have an emerald close to your skin.'" Then he presented Jerry with an emerald ring. No matter how depressed he got, he always got a kick from a good shock treatment.

Barbara Leigh saw Elvis one more time, a year or so into Linda Thompson's reign, which began in 1972. Barbara was shocked at the evidence of his decline. "When I was with him, from 1970 to 1971 or so, he was still gorgeous and thin," she said. "When Priscilla left, everything changed." Lisa, who was four years old, was visiting her father at the time. "I remember Lisa was combing the hair on a little doll's head that was stuck on a pole," Barbara said. "Elvis had a light system that flicked on and off to the stereo system, and his music was playing. Lisa was sitting on the floor as the lights danced to her father's music, combing the doll's head and singing along, not paying any attention to me or anyone else."

Barbara sensed that this might be the last time she would see Elvis. By now, he had a strong relationship with Linda, who was in Hawaii, though her clothes were in the closet. They spent the night reading spiritual books and going through his jewelry case. "He fell asleep on me," Barbara says. "I never heard from him again, and I wasn't surprised. That last night was like déjà vu, like the first time we were together, except we didn't make love, and we hadn't for a long time. He was bloated and he was taking a lot of pills. Because of the drugs and those silk pajamas he wore, he sweated a lot. He always kept the bedroom ice cold and he slept with cotton in his ears. He wet the cotton with his tongue and put it in his ears. To this day, I sleep with cotton in my ears."

When Elvis began his relationship with Linda Thompson, his depression over Priscilla lifted for a time. But even Linda's relentlessly upbeat personality and warm nurturance couldn't halt Elvis's downward spiral. Linda was a beautiful, willowy, brown-eyed blonde with a lively sense of humor and a fine intelligence, and she was that year's Miss Tennessee. George Klein, who was always on the lookout for local girls to bring to Elvis, had introduced them.

"Hey, Elvis," George said, "I've got a pretty girl you've got to meet."

"Oh, yeah? Bring her to the movie tonight," Elvis said. Linda and Elvis sat together in the theater, got acquainted, and began dating.

Linda was a great girl for Elvis, probably the best he ever had as far as giving him all the mothering he wanted. She was always smiling, cracking little jokes, and coddling Elvis out of his moods. They had a good relationship for more than four years. Linda traveled on the road with us a lot and was often in Las Vegas for Elvis's entire engagement. Even so, whenever Linda wasn't there, Elvis fooled around with other women. And if he saw someone else he liked, he made a lame excuse and sent Linda home. Linda was a sharp, observant girl, and she had to have figured things out. She had been a virgin when she met Elvis, and at first, they shared a good sex life. But as Elvis began taking more and more drugs and became increasingly unhealthy, his sex drive diminished and he was always tired. She never discussed this with me, but it wasn't hard to figure out. Linda was a vibrant, intelligent woman who was wasting her youth taking care of an unfaithful man who toured from one faceless city to the next, sleeping all day and staying up all night. "What kind of life is this?" she must have asked herself.

Elvis demanded absolute control in his relationships. That's why he preferred young, unworldly women. Maybe he was retaliating unconsciously for the rejections he had suffered from girls before he became a star. Or he could have been acting out what he'd modeled from his parents' relationship. Whatever his reasons, Elvis got away with it. For as long as I knew him, girls trooped into and out of his life, marching to his orders.

chapter 9

dr. strangelove

despite Elvis's strong relationship with Linda, after the loss of his wife and child, he became increasingly isolated and his drug use continued to escalate. Dr. George Nichopoulos had been with Elvis since early 1967, when George Klein recommended him to treat Elvis's saddle sores. Dr. Nick, as we called him, had become Elvis's close friend and family doctor. Now he found himself writing more and more prescriptions for sleeping pills and amphetamines. If he balked at the amount of medication Elvis demanded, Elvis usually convinced him that there was no problem, that he planned to quit the drugs soon. On the rare occasions when Dr. Nick said "no," Elvis got what he wanted from more compliant doctors. None of them knew how much Elvis was actually taking. To make things worse, our "Two-Hundred-Plus" club was no longer a joke; Elvis had begun to bloat into a caricature of himself, though he could still pull himself together when he had to.

In 1973, he taped "Elvis: Aloha from Hawaii," a television special beamed by satellite to approximately one billion people in forty countries. He looked terrific. Without a word to anyone, he had suddenly stopped the drugs and shed the bloat. Whenever he did that and returned to his old self, there wasn't a greater man and friend.

Elvis worked hard to get himself in shape for that special. No individual had ever rented a satellite before. Satellite news existed, but this would be the first time in history that a live performance would be beamed by satellite to television sets around the world. When the Colonel had conceived the idea, he didn't know if it could be done. He'd arranged a meeting with RCA at his office in the Las Vegas Hilton.

"Gentleman, I had a dream last night," he began. "I dreamed that an Elvis performance was beamed around the world by satellite. Would you be interested?"

The men looked at each other and nodded. "That sounds great, Colonel," they said. "We'll look into the costs and get back to you." A few days later, they confirmed. The Colonel recommended that the show be televised from Hawaii because the time zone would work for other countries. Also, Elvis liked Hawaii and he would be comfortable there. Simulcast satellite entertainment began with the Colonel.

Now the Colonel had to broach the idea to Elvis. He called my room to ask me to set up a meeting. I let Elvis know at breakfast and we fixed the meeting for 7:00 P.M. They had been talking alone in Elvis's bedroom for about forty-five minutes when I knocked on the door to let Elvis know it was time for his first show. Five minutes later, they both came out smiling.

"The Colonel's come up with a great idea," Elvis announced to the guys. "I'm going to be the first to do a live show telecast by satellite!" We congratulated them, and Elvis talked exclusively about the project for days. The challenge propelled him out of his depression and gave him the energy and hope he needed to cut off the drugs and get in shape.

On January 9, 1973, the day after his birthday, we arrived in Hawaii, where the production crew had been working for three weeks. The Colonel had a helicopter waiting to take Elvis, Red, and me to the Hilton Hawaiian Village. Camera crews taped our arrival, which became part of the special's opening scenes. Elvis signed autographs and accepted leis, beaming all the while. For the two days he rehearsed, Elvis maintained his buoyant mood and confidence that the show would be great. The evening of his performance, Elvis was in his suite with Charlie, Red, and me.

"Well, I'm going to lie down and rest before the show," he said.

"But, E," I protested, "we've got to give Mr. Pasetta [the director] the song lineup."

"You guys make up the lineup and give it to him," Elvis said. "I'll just go by that. Wake me up in two hours before we leave for the show."

We did it, proud that he had so much trust in us. The show was beamed by the Intelsat IV communications satellite on January 14, 1973, at 12:30 A.M. (Honolulu time) to Japan, South Korea, South Vietnam, Thailand, Australia, New Zealand, and the Philippines. Even people from Communist China saw it. The United States viewed the special on April 4, 1973. It was a huge success and another first for Elvis. He was distracted from his pain for a while, but all too soon, the charge of his triumph dissipated, and he was back on the drugs.

In 1973, Tom Hulett toured Japan with the Moody Blues. "Hey, Tom, Elvis heard you were in Japan," Lamar told him when he got back. "He wants to talk to you about it."

Tom knew better than to discuss Japan with Elvis without the Colonel's knowledge. He was not going to play big shot with Elvis Presley and get fired the next day by the Colonel. Jerry Weintraub, Tom, and the Colonel had already met in Las Vegas with Japanese publisher Tots Nabagema, who had promoted the Beatles and was the biggest concert promoter in his country.

"Colonel, Lamar says Elvis wants to ask me a couple of things about Japan," Tom began.

"Well, talk to him," the Colonel said. "But we ain't going. What are you going to do? Have a press conference over there? You can't. speak Japanese. You trust that Japanese guy?"

"Yeah," Tom said.

"How well do you know him?" the Colonel wanted to know. Nothing was said about visas, but the Colonel would never mention Elvis's drug problem, even to Tom Hulett. Tom went backstage to see Elvis. Of course, he couldn't be direct. He let it drop casually that he was just back from Japan.

"Man, they've got a billboard of you over there on the main

street, the Ginza, five or six stories high!" he told Elvis.

Elvis laughed. "How was it?" he asked.

"Very different," Tom answered truthfully.

Elvis was intrigued, and Tots would have met whatever reasonable price the Colonel named, but the Budacan, the biggest building in Japan at the time, held only twelve thousand seats. The Tokyo Dome had not been built yet, so we would have had to play at least thirty dates to satisfy the country. Today, such superstars as Michael Jackson can play ten shows at the Tokyo Dome and then come home. Playing Japan was feasible, but unprofitable. Elvis could play as much as he wanted in America, and it was tough enough touring with him here. If we had to tell him he couldn't get a hamburger, forget it. Those considerations, compounded with the problem of bringing Elvis's drugs and guns through Customs, made playing outside the United States a bad idea.

"Why should we travel six thousand miles to play for ten thousand people when we can travel six hundred miles and do the same thing?" the Colonel argued. According to Colonel Parker's logic, touring abroad didn't make sense.

"He'd have to have a press conference at the airport when he lands and it would be a nightmare," the Colonel went on. "There's no way to secure the place properly." He listed many factors weighing against the tour. But the bottom line was that the Colonel wasn't going to take Elvis to a foreign country knowing that he would take along his drugs and guns.

Todd Slaughter, the head of England's largest fan club, once approached the Colonel in the office of Artie Newman, one of the Hilton casino bosses.

"I just asked Elvis when he's going to England," Slaughter told the Colonel.

"Todd, you told me that last year," the Colonel reminded him..

"But he just said that you won't let him go," Todd argued.

"You go back to wherever you were talking with him, and tell him I'm right here. Ask him when he wants to go," the Colonel said with a long-suffering, martyred look.

Some time later, Elvis sent a message to the Colonel: He'd heard that the Osmond Brothers' plane and their persons had been checked for drugs during a tour outside the States. "I don't want to go over there at all unless I can take my guns," he told the Colonel. "I don't care about going."

Many rumors have sprung up because of Elvis's refusal to tour outside the United States, including the charge that the Colonel is an illegal alien. But the reasons had to do with Elvis alone. In fact, he did play outside the country once, in 1957, in Vancouver, British Columbia. In order to re-enter America, the Colonel had to show U.S. Immigration officials an Army discharge and social security card. While I was with Elvis, we never went to Canada. Even if the Colonel was an illegal alien, he could have set up a big Canadian tour and sent Tom Hulett, Tom Diskin, and others to run it. We could have done Vancouver very easily when we played Seattle and Portland. The reason we never did was that we didn't need to and it was inconvenient. Whenever the Seattle Coliseum was available, the Vancouver building was usually booked with a hockey game. It was the only facility in the city, so it was full 365 days a year. When you're trying to route one, two, and three buildings, it's not worth juggling to find a single empty space. That's why we played the South and the Midwest so much. Down there, if the city building wasn't available, there was a college facility or some other building. The West had fewer venues. The situation with Toronto was similar. Before each date in Buffalo, we opened an outlet across the border to sell tickets in Toronto. We probably sold five thousand to ten thousand seats in Canada for every Buffalo show we did.

The "illegal alien" rumor about the Colonel apparently originated with two Dutch journalists who telephoned the Colonel in Las Vegas in the early seventies.

"We want to do a nice story, Colonel," they said. "Give us three or four hours."

"I don't do interviews," he told them.

"If you don't give us an interview," they threatened, "you won't be very happy with what we're going to say." The Colonel decided it was easier to talk with them. But they preferred a sensational story to the plain truth. Since then, many other writers have been more than happy to rewrite that story.

The Colonel's title was honorary, but when a southern governor makes you an honorary colonel, it's significant. Colonel Tom

Parker was born in the Netherlands and never claimed to be a real Army colonel, but he did serve in the United States Army for four years.

Although Elvis had nothing to do with the rumor, he didn't discourage it. The Colonel was a convenient excuse for not touring abroad.

In the beginning, touring was great: the romance of the road, the roar of the crowds, criss-crossing the country in private planes. But slowly, as with making movies, the novelty and glamour faded for Elvis. The present and the future seemed to offer little, so the past and its ties became his focus. Loyalty became a key theme.

"Man, loyalty is the most important thing in life," he said on the many occasions he refused to meet some bigwig backstage. "You don't get that from stars and politicians; you get it from your fans." But there were still those times when Elvis shook off his funk and returned to his clear-eyed, life-loving self. One of those occasions involved a rare violation of the Colonel's and Elvis's "no outsiders backstage" rule.

In May 1974, Led Zeppelin came to Los Angeles to announce the formation of Swan Song Records, their own label, at the same time that Elvis was scheduled to play the Felt Forum there. Tom Hulett, who also worked on Led Zeppelin's tours, got a call from Richard Cole, their road manager.

"Tom, the guys want to know if there's any chance to meet him," Cole said. "They'll stay over just to say 'hi' for two seconds." Tom wanted to help out, but he didn't have the nerve to ask the Colonel. Two days before Elvis's show, he took a gamble and walked into Elvis's room at the hotel across the street from the Forum.

"Elvis, the biggest band—*not* solo artist—in the world, wants to see you at the Forum," Tom said.

Elvis gave him that eloquent look.

Then Tom named the band: Led Zeppelin. Rick and David Stanley, who were hanging out with their stepbrother, leaped to their feet. Led Zeppelin! For these kids, Led Zeppelin was the penultimate thrill. Elvis registered his stepbrothers' excitement and gave Tom the okay.

Tom called Claire Rothman, the Forum's manager. "Claire," he said, "Zeppelin's coming to the Elvis show. I don't want an uproar, but I want them to have seats. After the show, as Elvis leaves the building, I'm going to be walking them backstage and across the street. Tell your security guards they're okay."

Everyone in Led Zeppelin was a diehard Elvis fan, especially Jimmy Page and Robert Plant. Plant was a walking encyclopedia on Elvis's early R&B recordings. When Zeppelin did their sound checks, Robert often said, "Here's one, Tom," and sang an old R&B or blues number from a Sun album Tom had never even heard. The night of the scheduled meeting, Rick and David were nearly hysterical with excitement. They'd bought up all the Zeppelin albums they could find for autographs. After Elvis and the guys arrived at the Forum, David and Rick kept yelling every few minutes, "Are they here yet? Are they here?" Elvis realized they were not just another band. This wasn't Olivia Newton-John coming to say "hi." Two-thirds through his performance, Elvis broke another precedent. "I understand we've got a really big band in the audience," he said. "Where's Led Zeppelin?" The group stood up, and the audience went crazy. We had to put security around the group for the rest of the show.

After the show, Tom walked the band past the barricade of autograph seekers, through the back door, across the street, and into the elevator of the hotel. They waited in Elvis's suite for fifteen or twenty minutes, while Rick and David clutched their Zeppelin albums. Everyone was keyed up, waiting for the big meeting. Vernon was there, and Peter Grant, Zeppelin's manager, was impressed at meeting Vernon, Elvis's father!

Finally, Elvis made his entrance. He was his old self, full of energy, suntanned and suave in a Hawaiian shirt, slacks, and a sports jacket. The guys were dumbstruck. Tom introduced them: "Elvis, I'd like you to meet Jimmy Page . . . ." Elvis and Robert Plant settled into a conversation about Elvis's music. Everyone relaxed because Elvis was comfortable.

I remember David asking Tom, "Can I ask for an autograph?"

"Sure," he said. "Jimmy, Robert, come here and give the kids an autograph."

Then Jimmy Page turned to Tom. "Tom!" he whispered. "Can I get an autograph from Elvis?" Richard Cole found paper and pens in a drawer.

"Elvis, can you make mine to Maureen [his wife]?" Plant asked.

After an hour or so, I nodded to Tom, signaling that it was time to break up the party, although Page lingered a while longer. "This could be a five-minute meeting," Tom had warned the band beforehand. "Elvis doesn't like to meet anyone." The band was halfway down the hotel hallway when Elvis poked his head out the door. "Hey, guys!" he called out, and began singing "Treat Me Like a Fool." Robert Plant turned around and grinned. Right on cue and without breaking stride, he sang the second line, "Treat Me Mean and Cruel"; and then they finished the chorus together, "But Love Me."

Elvis was in great form that night, but those moments were becoming increasingly rare and his behavior more erratic. Despite the huge income he brought in from Vegas and touring, he was spending money faster than he earned it, especially when he was under the influence, which was becoming most of the time.

In January 1975, Elvis decided to buy his own airplane. He was often displeased with the planes we chartered and had read in the newspaper that the Boeing 707 jetliner belonging to Robert Vesco, the fugitive financier, was for sale. Vesco had used it to flee the United States in 1972, taking with him millions of stolen dollars. The plane was stolen back from him and flown to the United States and was now being sold. Elvis asked Vernon to see about buying it. Vernon made a deal and left a check for seventy-five thousand dollars as a deposit. But when we inspected it, we discovered that the plane was in terrible condition, its wiring rotted and its radio equipment unusable. It would cost a fortune to rebuild. Elvis told Vernon to forget about it, but they were unable to recover the deposit.

Lamar and I located some airplane agents. We met with one who kept his planes in Tucson, Arizona. It was amazing—at least two hundred planes stored in the middle of the Arizona desert because the dry weather kept the metal and wiring from corroding. We viewed at least thirty planes before we found an 880 Convair, a four-engine jet designed to hold one hundred passengers that had been owned by Delta Airlines. The price was right: $250,000. We called Elvis from a pay phone.

"Tell the agent I'll take it," he said.

"Elvis, don't you think you should see it first?"

"I know what a large four-engine jet looks like. Have him take pictures and send them to you. Give him Daddy's phone number and he'll make arrangements for the financing."

After the deal was completed, we had the plane flown down to Fort Worth, Texas, where, at a cost of approximately $450,000, it was customized to Elvis's specifications. That was Elvis's first look at it, and he told the designers what he wanted. All the equipment in the flight compartment was replaced. The original seats were ripped out to make room for a master bedroom, an office, a conference room, a dining room, and the lounge, where we spent most of our time. Elvis had it painted blue and white—Graceland's colors, with the Memphis Mafia logo, TCB, on the tail. Though he named his plane the *Lisa Marie,* air controllers all over the country referred to it as *Hound Dog One.* Soon after he bought the *Lisa Marie,* Elvis bought another smaller plane, the *Jet Star,* just so he could fly back and forth to Fort Worth and check on the process of his larger jet's customization!

Not long afterward, Elvis was listening to Jerry Weintraub tell the Colonel and others that his client John Denver had just given him a brand-new Rolls-Royce convertible for his birthday. Elvis would not be outdone. He decided to buy the Colonel an airplane. He asked me to find a G-1, a beautiful twelve-passenger corporate prop jet. We were touring the East Coast, so I called around and found one in the Southeast for six hundred thousand dollars. I asked the salespeople to show it to Elvis, and they flew it up the next day. When they telephoned from the airport, Elvis called the Colonel and invited him for a little ride to see something. We drove out to the airport where the plane was waiting, and Elvis took the Colonel aboard "this new plane I'm thinking of buying." The Colonel said it was very nice, a beautiful airplane. Then Elvis told him that it was his birthday present.

The Colonel was stunned. He thanked Elvis, and there was a lot of hugging, but the Colonel didn't know how to react to the gift. We looked the plane over again, and the sellers told us all about it. It was gorgeous, one of the best private planes available. Then the Colonel returned with his party to the hotel.

"Okay, Joe," Elvis said. "Let's buy it."

"Let's see if we can get it cheaper," I suggested.

"No, let's just buy it," Elvis insisted. He was high, of course. I told Elvis I had to call his father to take care of the financing, and we headed back to the hotel.

That night, the Colonel called me. "Why did Elvis buy me that plane?" he asked. "It was a nice thought, but I don't want to own an airplane. They're expensive. You have to have a crew on payroll all the time, and upkeep and insurance are high. All I want is to rent one. I use it, then I'm through with it." Apparently, the Colonel talked privately to Vernon, and they worked it out so that Elvis never did buy it. I'm sure that made Vernon happy. Elvis was very upset that the Colonel refused his present, but he never said anything to him about it.

The Circle G ranch in Mississippi, the mobile homes and trucks for everyone, the *Lisa Marie,* the *Jet Star,* hundreds of thousands of dollars' worth of jewelry and cars, and, of course, Uncle Sam's share were all making a huge dent even in Elvis's considerable income. He needed money fast. RCA had already put in a $2.5 million offer for Elvis's publishing company, and he wanted to accept. But the sale also meant a loss of possible future revenue for the Colonel, who split the publishing profits with Elvis fifty-fifty. The Colonel went to him with the papers but advised him not to take the offer. He found Elvis sitting by the pool at his Los Angeles house. It was one of Elvis's "bad," that is, drugged-out days.

"I need the money, Colonel," he said.

"I know you do," the Colonel said. "But you don't need it that badly. We could play more dates. I don't want to give up my future royalties because you need money. We're going to have to hold off for a price of $5 million for you to get the $2.5 million you want, and it still won't be a good deal."

The matter was left at that. Then Vernon telephoned to report that Elvis was angry because the Colonel didn't want to make the deal with RCA.

"We have a lot of problems, Colonel," Vernon argued. "You got these deals which are great, and you made a lot of money for 50 percent." They sold the publishing rights to RCA.

The deal wasn't all that bad for the time, but if Elvis had kept the publishing company for another six or eight years, its value would have tripled.

Obviously, Elvis's problem wasn't money: It was drugs. In my opinion, that problem originated in his lifelong struggle with insomnia. Even when I first knew Elvis in the Army, he had difficulty sleeping. He'd snatch a few hours of sleep, wake up, then try to go back to sleep. He wasn't taking sleeping pills then, but he did tell me that ever since he'd become rich and famous, he was afraid to go to sleep because when he woke up in the morning, it would all vanish, like a dream. Elvis had another sleeping problem. The Army distributed amphetamines to soldiers in the field and on maneuvers to keep them awake. When Elvis was discharged, someone presented him with a farewell gift—a box of twelve amphetamine bottles, about twelve hundred pills of pure speed. Naturally, the drug made it even more difficult to sleep, so Elvis consulted a doctor, who prescribed sleeping pills for him. Since he was taking sleeping pills at night, he was a bit groggy in the morning. So he took even more speed to wake up. That's when the vicious cycle started. Elvis just needed more and more. Now Elvis's "slim and sober" periods were rare.

He was out of control. One night, during a "good" phase, Elvis publicly denied a rumor that he was addicted to heroin. "If I ever find the individual who said those things about me," he declared self-righteously from the Las Vegas Hilton stage, "I'll pull his goddamn tongue out by the roots." But not long after, his drug abuse almost cost him his contract with the hotel.

We'd become friendly with the maître d' from the hotel's Italian restaurant. He used to come up to the suite to cook for Elvis and hang out with us. The hotel fired the maître d', and he complained to Elvis. Elvis, champion of the underdog, became incensed over the matter, and that night he did a terrible show. The next night, the incident was still on his mind. He stopped singing to tell the audience about the hotel's unfair treatment of the maître d' and to condemn the management and the hotel's owner, Baron Hilton. Elvis all but forgot about his performance. He certainly didn't remember his audience, because he did only a few songs and spent the rest of the time joking with a table of four in the front row. At least three hundred people walked out that night and demanded their money back. Backstage, we all sensed a looming disaster. I told him that three hundred people had left.

"What are you talking about?" Elvis yelled. "People were loving the show!"

"Elvis, the people you could *see* were loving the show," Jerry pointed out. "That was one table down in front. Anytime a star of your stature plays to one table, sure, they're going to love it."

Henry Lewin, the hotel president, met with the Colonel. Obviously, he was not happy with Elvis's behavior.

"Colonel, you better have a talk with Elvis," he said. The Colonel agreed. He called me and said he'd be up to see Elvis in a little while. I could tell he was upset because of his tone and because he didn't *ask* if he could come up, he told me.

"Elvis, the Colonel is coming up," I told Elvis.

"What does he want now?" he asked wearily.

In a few moments, we heard a knock on the door. Sonny opened it, and the Colonel charged through like a mad bull. He didn't say a word to any of us.

"Elvis, can we talk in private?" he asked.

Elvis rose in silence from the couch and walked into his bedroom. The Colonel followed, but they didn't close the door.

"Elvis, you made a big mistake tonight," the Colonel said. "The management is paying you good money to perform here, not to tell them how to run their hotel."

Elvis was silent.

"If you have a problem pertaining to the hotel, you should come to me," the Colonel continued, as Elvis fumed in silence.

"I don't need you to solve all my problems," Elvis suddenly exploded.

"You do when it comes to your contracts. It's my business too," the Colonel pointed out.

"I don't need you, I can handle my own business," Elvis retorted. "Why don't you just leave?"

We were sitting at the bar, stunned by what we were hearing.

"Very good," the Colonel said. "I'll leave. We'll draw up the papers and break this deal. You pay me off what you owe me, and we'll go our separate ways, okay?"

"Fine," Elvis shouted. "Get the hell out!"

The Colonel stormed out of the bedroom and left the suite without a word to us. Then Elvis came out.

"Well, I just fired the Colonel," he announced with a show of bravado.

We were silent for a moment, then one of the guys asked, "What happened?"

"He was trying to tell me what I could and couldn't do. No one can run my life!"

This wasn't Elvis talking; it was the drugs. "I'm going to bed, I'm tired," he finally said, and disappeared into his room. The Colonel must have gone straight to his office, where he dictated to Jim O'Brien the contents of release papers. He had to have stayed up all night working on them, because the next afternoon, Elvis received a thick package with all the legal forms.

"To hell with the old man," Elvis said after leafing through them. "We'll find someone better. We'll do something."

But I could see through his act. Elvis hadn't expected something like this to happen, at least not so quickly. I think he was hoping that when he woke up that morning, it would have all gone away. Now he had no choice but to pretend he didn't care. Anything was better than swallowing his pride and admitting he'd been wrong. Elvis passed the papers to Vernon, who didn't say much. I guess he also hoped it would just blow over. The feud lasted several weeks. They didn't speak for the last few shows of the engagement, which improved following the argument. They still hadn't exchanged a word when we left town. Elvis began considering candidates to take the Colonel's place. He thought of Jerry Weintraub, who was an accomplished manager. But Jerry was leaning more toward movie producing and concert promotion. Anyway, Jerry never could have handled Elvis. Tom Hulett, Weintraub's partner in Concerts West, was very understanding, and we got along well with him. We had him come up to the suite to talk to Elvis. But Hulett was smart enough to know that it was just a blowup. "I don't know anyone as good as the Colonel," he told Elvis. "Forget deals and all that. This guy is behind you and he protects you. You've got a very unique situation, and boy, I wouldn't want to come between you. If there was ever a situation where an accident happened or it was a health thing, that's different. But, Elvis, you're better off with what you're doing."

Elvis met Tom's nervous demurrals with silence. He knew Tom was right. Colonel Parker had been writing his own book. There were no precedents for his managerial style. Elvis had the best, and he had to consider what their relationship was worth.

Elvis finally cooled down and realized that we'd better call the Colonel. The two of them talked, and everything was fine from then on.

The Colonel was a great manager for Elvis Presley, and for

every fault, there were nine great things he did for his artist. Who knows what their partnership might have accomplished if Elvis had practiced a healthier lifestyle? Or if Elvis had assumed responsibility for more creative decisions, like the time Barbra Streisand offered him a costarring movie role.

In 1974, she presented Elvis with the kind of part he always claimed he'd dreamed of. It was just the challenge that could have propelled him out of his slump, but by now, he was too demoralized to take advantage of it. Streisand and her boyfriend, Jon Peters, a famous Beverly Hills hairdresser at the time, came backstage at the Las Vegas Hilton. About three months earlier, Elvis had visited backstage after her show at Caesar's Palace.

With him that night were Linda Thompson, British singer Tom Jones, Jerry Schilling, me, and a very drunk Charlie Hodge. Tom, Charlie, and Elvis demonstrated a little karate until an overly aggressive Charlie was rewarded with a bloody nose. Then Elvis proceeded to offer Barbra "constructive" criticism on her show. Her hand movements were obscuring her face, he told her. It was a sincere but tactless effort to help make her show even greater. Barbra just stood there; she didn't utter a word. Now she was returning the visit. It was very crowded that night with band members and friends, and Elvis was his old charming self. He gave Barbra a big hug and met Peters.

"Elvis, can we go someplace where we can talk in private?" she asked. "I have something I would like to tell you about." I suggested the room next to his dressing room, where Elvis rested between shows. Elvis asked Jerry and me to come in with them. Barbra and Jon sat on the two chairs, Elvis on the bed, and Jerry and I sat on the floor. I ordered some food.

Barbra explained the purpose of her visit.

"Elvis, I bought the rights to the Judy Garland movie *A Star Is Born*," she said. "I'm going to remake it, and I thought you might be interested in starring in it with me." Elvis hadn't been interested in making movies for a long time, but Barbra explained the entire story. Two hours later, he was hooked.

"I'll have to think about it. The Colonel will get back to you," he told her before she left. But to the guys he was more enthusiastic. "I'm going to do it!" he vowed.

Jerry thought the film was a good idea, but he pointed out that

Jon Peters, her boyfriend, was going to produce it. The guy was just a hairdresser, and besides, he would make sure the movie showcased Streisand, not Elvis.

"Barbra and I will do what we want anyway," Elvis countered.

"Yeah, but the two of you are strong personalities and you'll clash," Jerry said. Elvis became angry, so Jerry dropped the matter. According to the Colonel, Elvis called him the next night.

"I thought I would do it," Elvis said. "But, Colonel, you think I'm going to take orders from that hairdresser?" He had been furious when Jerry said it, but as suggestible as Elvis was, Jerry's argument had gotten to him.

"I've got news for you," the Colonel said. "I guarantee that they'll turn the contract down because I'm going to request that you get top billing."

A few days later, the Colonel reported back to Elvis. He'd asked for top billing. "That took care of that," the Colonel said. Streisand and Peters never even responded to his offer. The Colonel had made one of his offers that was impossible to accept. At the time, we figured that Barbra never intended to use Elvis anyway, that she was really getting back at him for the incident that had taken place at Caesar's. But now I think she and Peters had come up with an inspired casting choice, and that the role might have been the one to showcase Elvis's talent. He himself mentioned that it could be an opportunity parallel to Frank Sinatra's performance in *From Here to Eternity*. On the other hand, I can't imagine Elvis and Streisand lasting one week on set together. For a while, all Elvis talked about was that movie. Then it was over with and we never heard another word about it. It was the same thing we'd gone through with so many other enthusiasms.

Whenever Elvis caught a clear glimpse of himself and realized what he was doing, he became so depressed he had to take more pills to feel better. But if his drug abuse was pointed out, however circumspectly, Elvis refused to listen. "I can stop any time," he always said. By now, drugs regulated his life. He took them to sleep, to wake up, and to perform, insisting all the while that he didn't have a problem. He was particularly fond of pain medication, which deadens both emotional and physical pain, but eventually also deadens the entire system. He also took a lot of amphetamine and B$_{12}$ injections.

"One night at Tahoe, he came into our dressing room," Myrna Smith told me. "The three of us were sitting there. 'Sylvia, Estelle,' he said, 'come here.' He took them into the small dressing room of his backstage suite and pulled down his pants to show them his butt. 'Have you ever seen anything like this?' he asked. His butt was mottled with bruises." He would tell doctors he had pain in various parts of his body in order to get the shots, but he was usually lying. One of those doctors worked for a Las Vegas hotel and gave Elvis virtually all he wanted. We called him "Flash" because he dashed backstage to inject Elvis with uppers before the show. Immediately afterward, this silent, skeletally thin man in his fifties reappeared just as quickly to administer downers. For a brief time, Elvis even dabbled in illegal hard drugs. One day, I discovered that despite his professed concern for his stepbrother's drug habit, Elvis had sent Rick to Nashville to buy cocaine.

"I want to see you," I told Rick when he returned. I hustled him into a private corner of Graceland. "Give me that bottle," I said.

"I can't," he whined. "Elvis will be mad." I grabbed the bottle and took it into the kitchen, where I emptied out the coke and substituted ground-up Aspirin. Then I sent Rick upstairs where Elvis was waiting for the coke with his cousin Billy Smith. Billy later told me he couldn't understand why his nose burned so much. That was one rare occasion when I was able to protect Elvis from himself.

Even the Memphis Mafia occasionally tried to intercept drug shipments from various doctors. One night, Red accidentally broke a delivery boy's toe. He threatened to break the kid's body if he didn't quit delivering to Elvis, but Elvis heard about it. He called Red, Sonny, and me into his bedroom. "I need it," Elvis finally said to us with a piteous look. If anyone pushed too hard, Elvis's stock response was, "If you don't like it, there's the door! Get the hell out of here! I don't need you." He was manipulating us and we let him. "God, I'm going to straighten my life out but I need this right now," he would intone fervently, his blue eyes wide and sincere. And we believed him!

Elvis would walk into a pharmacy, shop for toothpaste, shampoo, and the like, and then casually strike up a conversation with the pharmacist. He was very knowledgeable about prescription drugs because he owned a well-thumbed *Physician's Desk Reference* and knew what each drug could do and which combinations were safe. But it often suited his purpose to play dumb. Flashing that smile, he would approach the prescription counter.

"Someone told me about this drug here," he would begin, awkward as a country boy and acting as if only this smart man behind the counter could help poor ole Elvis. "I have a slight problem with pain. I can't take codeine because it upsets my stomach and I've got a toothache." He knew exactly what symptoms would get him the particular drug he wanted.

"Here, take a couple of these," the pharmacist invariably offered, eager to assist Elvis Presley, who seemed a sweet, kind of bashful guy, after all.

"Well, why don't you give me a dozen," Elvis would then suggest mildly, as if the thought had just struck him. "I'm getting ready to go on the road. I'll be gone for a month and may need them." The flattered pharmacist would hand over a few dozen. Elvis pulled this stunt many times.

Elvis was using a variation of the same charm that still turned women to mush. Women fell in love with him because he was so needy, like a little boy. It made them feel special to be so important to such a desirable superstar. I remember one night he came downstairs, nodding out from the drugs. "Patricia, rub my back," he said in baby talk. His father was sitting there, just looking at him. "I don't feel good, Patricia," Elvis moaned. As she rubbed his back, his father kept asking, "What's wrong with him?" We all knew he was stoned, but I just said, "He doesn't feel good." He was like a little baby boy with women: "Cut my toenails, my feet hurt." He made them feel as if they were the single person he trusted, the only one who could make him feel good.

Dr. Nick has been blamed for Elvis's drug habit. While it's true that he could have said "no" more often, he was also the only doctor who tried to get Elvis off drugs. I was present many times when Dr. Nick tried to talk to Elvis about "the problem." He substituted placebos for pills, tried to get Elvis to see a psychiatrist, and even introduced him to racquetball in an attempt to make him active again. True, he did write large numbers of prescriptions, but he also knew Elvis distributed many of them to his friends. He filled prescriptions for Elvis in other people's names, perhaps because he didn't want to keep calling in Elvis's name. Dr. Nick reasoned that if he was fired, Elvis would get whatever he wanted from someone else anyway. Then no one would be monitoring his drug intake. If he gave him most of what he wanted and cut the dosage by substituting placebos, he felt that he was buying time until he could convince Elvis to take a cure. Dr. Nick often ordered us to empty out the capsules and fill them with powdered sugar. Surprisingly, Elvis never realized what we'd done.

When Elvis was hospitalized in 1973 for a medical complaint, Dr. Nick called in two psychiatric experts in drug addiction, and told Elvis they were regular doctors. They tried to ease Elvis off drugs gradually and get him into a hospital for detoxification and rehabilitation, but Elvis caught on and immediately checked himself out.

During another hospital stay ordered by Dr. Nick in 1974, Elvis played his hand more craftily. Jerry was coming downstairs from his room at Graceland late one morning, when Delta, Elvis's aunt, stopped him.

"Jerry, Sonny is supposed to take this bag to Elvis at the hospital, but I don't know when he's going to get his fat ass out of bed. Would you mind taking it up there?" Jerry agreed. He figured the bag contained food and fresh pajamas, the usual bundle, but he noticed that on top of the bag was a small brown package that had been mailed to Graceland without a return address. Sonny was waking up as Jerry was about to leave, so Jerry asked him what was in the package. Sonny said he didn't know, and Jerry was able to decipher a Las Vegas postmark. Jerry opened it and found a powerful pain medication. He knew exactly who had sent it.

Elvis had been doing very well during this hospital stay. He had been seeing a psychiatrist and things were looking bright. He'd even learned that the doctor was not really a liver specialist but a psychiatrist, and accepted it. Jerry showed the package to Dr. Nick. "I can't get any help from Elvis's other doctors," Dr. Nick complained dejectedly when he saw it. He sent a sample to a lab to make sure what it was, and Jerry took the package into Elvis's room, where I was visiting along with some of the other guys.

"Will everyone please excuse me?" Elvis asked politely. "I have to talk to Jerry."

At this point, he'd been in the hospital for twelve drug-free days.

"Elvis, I opened this package as a security precaution because I didn't know who it was from," said Jerry, who was pretty fast on his feet. But Elvis was even faster. "Jerry, I had everyone leave here because Daddy has a prostate problem," he said. "I got him this medication. Just put it in the medicine cabinet."

Every day, Jerry checked to see if the medication was still there. It sat there undisturbed for four or five days. Elvis was a packrat; he often hoarded medication. But Dr. Nick was impressed. Finally, after a week had passed, Dr. Nick went into the bathroom and came out holding the bottle, pretending he'd never seen it before.

"Elvis, what's this?" he asked.

"I don't know," Elvis said with an innocent look. "It must have been left there by the last patient. Throw it away."

We were hopeful that time. Elvis had convinced us that he really wanted to beat his habit. But he relapsed once again, and became even worse.

During the last few years, there were several times that we almost lost Elvis because he had taken too many downers. Those incidents were thoroughly quashed, and no one outside his intimate circle ever heard a word. Once, in Las Vegas, Elvis just about stopped breathing. Luckily, Linda Thompson was with him. At about 4:00 A.M., she couldn't rouse him from a comatose sleep. I had taken my usual two sleeping pills and was sound asleep myself in my bedroom in Elvis's thirtieth-floor Hilton suite when the phone rang.

"Joe," Linda cried, "Elvis is having a hard time breathing and I can't wake him. You'd better call the doctor." I leaped out of bed and got on the phone to the hotel doctor. I told him about Elvis's condition and he said he was on his way. I threw on some clothes and ran into Elvis's room. Linda was waiting at the door, a look of concern clouding her lovely face. Elvis was sprawled out on his back in the king-sized bed, wearing dark blue pajamas with the top unbuttoned. I put my ear near to his mouth and could barely detect the sound of his breathing. I couldn't tell if I was hearing my heart pumping or his lungs working. We tried to rouse him, but it was no use. The doctor arrived. He gave Elvis two shots, then put a catheter in his penis to remove excess fluid from his body. After a few tense moments, Elvis finally began breathing more deeply.

"I guess the shots are working," I whispered to Linda. I don't know why I whispered. A herd of elephants could have tap-danced in front of Elvis's bed and he wouldn't have heard a thing. We heaved a sigh of relief.

"Just let him rest and he'll be fine," the doctor said. "Joe, I'll call you later to see how he's doing." I hugged Linda and told her I would be in my room if she needed me. We never told anyone about the incident.

That was the only time I was involved, but according to Linda and other girls, there were many close calls. She and Elvis broke up about a year before he died. I've often wondered in the years since if her vigilant care could have saved Elvis one more time.

Linda nursed Elvis when he attempted a two-week sleep diet. The idea was to give him enough medication to keep him asleep for two weeks. He would wake only long enough to drink a special diet drink. It was a ridiculous idea because you could never give Elvis enough medication to keep him asleep for even one night. About halfway through the diet, Jerry paid Elvis a visit at the doctor's home where Elvis was staying. Jerry found Elvis lying in bed, still fat. The doctor was nowhere to be seen. Not long after Jerry returned to his hotel, Elvis called.

"Jerry, I need help. I'm on the floor and my legs won't work," he said. Linda couldn't lift Elvis by herself, and the doctor still hadn't shown up. Linda agreed with Jerry that the diet was dangerous, but Elvis insisted that he knew what he was doing. She threw in the towel, and another girlfriend, Sheila Ryan, was called in.

Sheila, a blond Irish beauty with delicate, cherubic features, was another "Lifer" whose term overlapped Linda Thompson's. Linda was still Elvis's official girlfriend, so he kept his affair with Sheila secret. Sheila performed her share of rescue efforts, removing food from Elvis's mouth after he'd fallen asleep while eating, and even diapering him at night when drugs put him into a sleep so sound he couldn't wake to go to the bathroom. During her turn babysitting Elvis's sleep diet, he came down with pneumonia because he wasn't moving.

"Who are you?" the doctor kept yelling, trying to determine if Elvis was coherent. "Who are you? Who are you?"

"Dr. Strangelove," Elvis finally muttered. At least his sense of humor had not deserted him.

Of course, it wasn't like that in the beginning of their romance. Elvis and Sheila got together in 1972 in Vegas after I met her through the singer James Darren, our close mutual friend, and brought her backstage. Elvis was still changing in the smaller dressing room. When he came out, he glanced at me, got a look at Sheila, and they made eye contact. He looked back at me and smiled. Of course, he couldn't pay too much attention to Sheila because Linda was right next to him. So he talked to everyone else. At one point, Elvis plucked a grape from a huge fruit basket and winged it at me from across the room. It hit Sheila smack in the middle of her forehead. He knew what he was doing. He used it as an excuse to come over and apologize so I could introduce them. Sheila stayed just long enough for her departure to be noticed. The next day, Elvis fabricated an excuse and sent Linda to Memphis. I couldn't reach Sheila for three days, because she was moving and didn't have a new telephone number. By the time I finally reached her, Elvis was even more anxious to see her. She showed up that night wearing her favorite man-tailored plaid slacks and a shirt, not Elvis's style at all. After the first show, I brought her up to Elvis's penthouse suite. She was sitting at the small bar when Elvis and the guys came in. Elvis hugged her. "The first thing we have to do," he said, "is get you out of those pants." He called Suzy Creamcheese to bring up several racks of women's clothes and boxes of shoes. Sheila modeled all the outfits for Elvis, and he selected six slinky and expensive dresses featuring her sexy rear end. After everyone else had left, they hugged and kissed, then lay down on the bed. Elvis fell asleep, expecting Sheila to sleep beside him. She dozed off, but when she awoke early the next morning, she left. Elvis was still sleeping.

"Where in the hell are you?" I asked when I called her that afternoon. "Jesus Christ, Elvis is having a fit. He wakes up in the morning and you're not here." Then Elvis got on the line.

"I don't like to wake up in the morning and have you not here," he pouted.

"Oh, all right," Sheila said. She grabbed some things and came back. Later, she confessed to me that she did that on purpose. She knew this wouldn't be a one-night stand, but she didn't want to be taken for granted.

Three or four dates later, Sheila and Elvis finally made love. But he was no longer the healthy young man he'd been with Barbara Leigh and Linda Thompson. "It was really sort of sweet," Sheila told me. "More than anything, he liked to make out with clothes on. Actually, I did too. It was great fun, very teenagerish." They spent the five remaining days of Elvis's engagement together. Before he left, Elvis bought Sheila a blue Camaro with a white vinyl top because he didn't like her 1959 red Volvo. Months later, Sheila wrecked the Camaro, so he bought her another car. I had to coach Sheila on how to act excited at her gift: She was so insecure that she hadn't known how to react when he'd given her the Camaro.

Eventually, as with all of Elvis's women, the romance waned, and the relationship came to be based on care and friendship, involving nightly rituals such as "Who has the medicine kit?" and other duties of a Lifer. Sometimes Sheila lied to Elvis to keep him from taking more pills. "I already gave you the kit," she would say, trusting that he was so stoned he wouldn't remember.

Sheila hated when Elvis took Valium injections to help him rest. As soon as they took effect, he would grin sloppily and drawl, "Baby . . . come here." Sheila was exhausted from touring and taking care of him, and sex was the last thing on her mind. No one was taking care of her.

The drugs made it difficult for Elvis to get and maintain an erection and to have an orgasm during intercourse, so he would masturbate instead. "At that time, I thought it was very perverse," Sheila said, "and I was very confused.

"It's funny to me when people say he was a sex symbol. I wonder, are we talking about the same person? Elvis wasn't about sex for me. He was about innocence and being a kid. The look that everyone died over, that twinkle in his eye, that charisma, that personality never happened as a prelude to sex, it happened in conversation. He'd be saying how cute I looked, flirting in a very innocent way. That was only the little boy in him."

During a date in Indiana, Sheila came close to collapse. "I've got to get out of here," she told me. "I need a couple of days to rest." Elvis wouldn't have accepted that, so we told him Sheila had lumps that had to be examined. When Sheila got back to Vegas, she actually had her breasts mammogramed in case Elvis checked. I remember the day I drove Sheila to Palm Springs after she and Elvis hadn't seen each other for a while.

"Now Sheila, this is supposed to be a surprise," I said. "I know it's absurd. You won't be surprised, but just act surprised, okay?" She was resting on the living room couch when Elvis burst into the room and leaped onto the coffee table. She didn't have to act surprised. He weighed about 240 pounds, the heaviest he'd ever been. The last time Sheila had seen Elvis, he was slim and handsome. She was horrified, and tried to hide it. But when she saw him again a few weeks later, the pounds had magically melted away.

"It's this constant frustration that I can't make him well," Sheila told me. "Am I going to be able to do it and feel like I had a big part in it?" The need to get him well was almost a sickness.

"He's my mission," Sheila said. "The funny thing is he goes away again and I see him a couple of weeks later, slim and healthy. 'How did it happen?' I'd wonder. 'I wasn't there.'" Being with Elvis was fast becoming a girlfriend's nightmare. The real Elvis was charming, giving, witty, gifted, and tender-hearted. But we were seeing less and less of the real Elvis and more and more of a drugged-out stranger.

One day in Vegas, Elvis was stoned and in a foul mood. We were watching the Stamps Gospel Quartet sing in a local charity show that was being broadcast from the Frontier Hotel. Elvis decided to call up the Frontier.

"I'll give you five thousand dollars if the Stamps Quartet jumps in the swimming pool right now," he told the host.

"Elvis is on the phone," the host announced gleefully to the television audience and the Stamps. "He told me if the Stamps Quartet jumps in the pool, right now, he'll give us five thousand." Being crazy guys themselves, they jumped in the pool. Elvis thought that was hilarious. Then he decided that he wanted to go over there and run the show. He was completely drugged out, and looked terrible. I was not about to let him make a fool of himself on television.

"Elvis, you can't go," I said.

"Have the car meet me at the side door," he ordered.

"I'm not going to do that," I insisted.

"Get them on the phone," he shouted.

"Elvis, you can't go," I repeated. "Forget it." We argued, with Sheila and the guys supporting me. Elvis picked up a large glass ashtray from the bar. "Goddamnit, if you don't call the goddamn limousine right now, I'm going to hit you with this ashtray," he said. It was the first time he'd ever threatened me with violence.

"You mean you're really going to hit me?" I asked, astonished. Elvis stopped in his tracks. He put down the ashtray, and without saying a word, went into his room and shut the door. Sheila, who had witnessed the scene, was crying, and I had tears in my eyes. When he woke the next day, it was as if nothing had happened. No one mentioned the incident.

Toward the end of their eighteen-month relationship, Sheila felt only relief at the knowledge that Elvis could bring in a second team, another woman. "I need to see my family in Chicago," she told Elvis one night. "I can live with being number two to another girl." She held up a bottle of pills. "But I can't be number two to these."

Not long after, Elvis wanted Sheila to come to New York where he was scheduled to perform. But she had met the man who would become her husband, actor James Caan. I knew they had fallen in love, so Sheila and I concocted a story to get Elvis through the tour. We told him she had an ear infection.

"Get the Lear jet," Elvis ordered.

"It flies too high," I said. "It would hurt her ears."

"Get her a low-flying plane, then," he said.

"Elvis, it has to go over mountains!" I explained. I asked Dr. Cantor to cover for us because I knew Elvis would want him to examine her. Then we couldn't locate Sheila for weeks. Finally she told James she had to go home and face the situation. That night, the phone rang at five in the morning.

"How are you doing? Where have you been?" Elvis wanted to know.

Sheila made excuses about being busy and unwell.

"Will you come home?" he asked plaintively.

Sheila had visited Memphis twice; it was hardly her home.

"What do you mean, home?" she asked. She'd never confronted him about Linda, and now Linda was the excuse Sheila needed.

But Linda had also had enough. She had been the main girl-friend for four and a half years, the one who took care of Elvis the most. She was tired of his cheating and of ministering to him night after night in his room. "I'm going to go see some of the people in the band," Linda began saying after spending several hours vege-tating with him in front of the television. If Elvis minded, he didn't show it. He'd just nod, keeping his gaze fixed on the screen. Finally, she had an affair with David Briggs, the piano player. We knew about it, but we understood. It was inevitable that their relationship would end. Linda had hoped something would divert Elvis from his col-lision course. She had tried to help him as best she could, but he wouldn't listen.

"Linda's gone," Elvis told Sheila. "This is your home. Come. You've got your horse." He went on to list all the belongings Sheila supposedly had at "home."

"I need a few days, I'll call you," was her answer. She'd never refused Elvis before, so he knew right then that it was over. There was no need to be explicit or to tell him she'd fallen in love with someone else. "It was very sad," Sheila said. "The first time he of-fered me the whole picture, I didn't want it."

There seemed to be nothing Linda, Sheila, Jerry, I, or anyone else who loved him could do. But there were some people who encouraged his drug use because when he was out of it, he didn't bother them with things to do. I actually overheard one of the guys say, "Shit, I like Elvis better when he's stoned. He gives more away." Elvis suspected certain people's motives but hated confrontation. A few friends who didn't realize how far gone Elvis actually was tried to interest him in new projects. But it was hard to tell whether they were motivated to help Elvis or to capitalize on his drug-addled state.

Near the end of 1975, Bruce Lee's *Enter the Dragon* made a huge splash. It inspired Elvis's final dream: to produce and star in a karate movie. He asked Rick Husky, his fraternity "big brother," who had become a good friend and was now a successful Holly-wood writer, to come to his Los Angeles house for a meeting. They talked in the den with Ed Parker, Elvis's friend and sometime se-curity force member who was a karate champion from Hawaii. Ed started talking about how he was going to whip Elvis into shape, and Rick presented a story idea for an action film. But Elvis was drugged, really out of it, and Ed Parker kept butting in and domi-nating the conversation. Finally, Rick asked Ed to excuse him so he could talk to Elvis about the project. He advised Elvis to look upon the project as an opportunity to write an acting role for him-self and that karate should be a part of the movie, not the focus. Ed got his back up, and the discussion went downhill from there.

After that meeting, the project changed from a vehicle for Elvis to a documentary featuring Parker and other karate experts, with Elvis acting as executive producer and perhaps supplying voiceover narration. Elvis drew up a contract in which all participants in the project would receive a certain number of points (a percentage) of future profits. But when he added up the points, he realized the total exceeded 100 percent. Not only that: Nothing was left for him! He called on the Colonel for help. The Colonel didn't want any-thing to do with the project, which he felt was shaky, but to help Elvis out, he made up a rough contract. Elvis also wanted to give Parker and another man thirty thousand dollars to start filming in Europe. The Colonel rarely interfered in his star's personal finan-cial business, but he advised against it, and Elvis promised he wouldn't give them the money. The very next day, he did just that. The Colonel found out when he received a call from a hotel in Las Vegas, asking if it was okay for Parker to cash Elvis's check for thirty thousand dollars. Needless to say, the thirty thousand was wasted, and the film was never made.

All that's left of that project is a treatment for a projected screenplay written in Elvis's hand, with additional notes by Linda Thompson. Elvis could have been a great actor, but the likelihood of his ever becoming a great director or producer was slim to nonexistent. He would have had to learn film technique and busi-ness, about which he knew little. Who knows, though? Maybe he could have done it.

I felt sorry for Elvis, and at the same time, I hated him for be-ing drugged and out of control and wasting his wonderful gifts. Yet I loved the guy because I knew who he really was and I prayed the real Elvis would return. Talking to him did no good, and it was frustrating because I didn't know what else to do about it. Putting him into a rehab center would have jeopardized his career. Besides, he refused to go. Only Vernon could have forced him, but Vernon was too intimidated by his son to insist. Many nights, I lay awake hoping that the next day would be the one when Elvis would come to his senses and clean up his act. We'd all seen him suddenly stop drugs, so there was always that hope that one day he would clean up for good. Then my own sleeping pills would kick in and I'd be out like a light. You had to be there to understand why we all put up with it. I certainly didn't go to work for Elvis and immediately start covering his drug habit from the world. For many years, everything was fine, and we had as normal a life as was possible given Elvis's celebrity. His drug abuse was a slow, gradual process that pulled you in as well. Before you knew it, even the craziness at the end seemed almost normal.

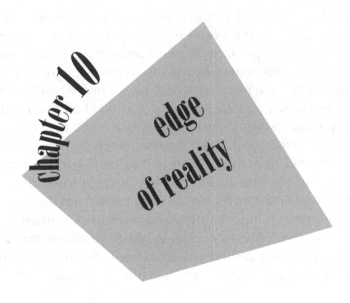

chapter 10

edge of reality

by late 1975, Linda and Sheila were gone, but Elvis's love life was far from over. He always kept backups. In March of that year, as Linda and Sheila were bowing out of his life, Elvis had begun seeing actress/model Mindi Miller. She was not as close to Elvis as Sheila or Linda, but she stayed with him for approximately six months.

The dark-haired twenty-four-year-old beauty had been working as a model in Rome, Italy, when she visited Hollywood for two weeks in order to close her apartment and sell her car. She took a break from packing to check out the Candystore, a popular Hollywood disco, where she was approached by Ron Smith, who ran modeling agencies at the time and now owns Celebrity Lookalikes. Smith was one of many friends beating the bushes to find another girlfriend for Elvis. He took her number. For several days he called Mindi, trying to get her to come to various parties. She always refused.

"Look, I'll be very honest with you," he finally said. "Elvis has broken up with his girlfriend, Linda Thompson, and he's really looking to meet some nice girls. He can't just go out and say, 'Hi, I'm Elvis Presley. Do you want to go out on a date?' It's just a party at his house. You'll be with lots of other people, and maybe you'll meet him."

At eleven o'clock that night, Mindi pulled her GT convertible Mustang with the bashed-in side door into the driveway of Elvis's Holmby Hills house. Charlie answered the door and Mindi walked in to find a dozen guys lounging on the sofa and chairs and watching TV—no other women. I knew right away that Elvis would like her. She smiled bravely as the guys barraged her with questions in their thick southern accents: "Where were you born?" "What kind of things do you like to do?" "Do you have a boyfriend?" It was the standard interview for the position of Elvis's girlfriend. They were terrified that Elvis wasn't going to find anyone. If he didn't have a girlfriend, "boss" was unhappy, and the workload increased.

As the guys were going through their routine, a very large man walked into the room. At first, she didn't recognize Elvis looming in the doorway, watching the guys grill her. He was wearing one of his little tennis hats and a sweatsuit, his usual attire when he wasn't onstage or in public. He looked at Mindi, then glanced around the room. "Honey," he drawled, "sorry I'm late, but so are you." For some reason, that struck her as hilarious. She let out a hoot, and the ice was broken. The guys laughed and slapped their thighs in relief. Everyone sat back and relaxed. All was well. The girl had a sense of humor; she thought the boss was funny.

Elvis sat next to Mindi, and did the jewelry box routine, offering Mindi incredible pieces. "Elvis," she said, looking straight into his eyes, "that's very sweet, but I don't know you. If I knew you better as time went on, perhaps I could accept this, but right now, I can't." She'd passed the second test with flying colors. Now came the third.

"Is this your car in the driveway?" Elvis asked.

"Yes."

"Well, honey," he said, "don't you think you need a new one?"

"This car works fine," Mindi answered.

"But the side's all bashed in," Elvis protested.

"So what?" Mindi came back. "I'll get it fixed." If she had expressed the slightest dissatisfaction with her Mustang, Elvis would have given her a new set of wheels on the spot. He needed a steady girl, he liked Mindi, so he wanted to give her something.

One by one, we left the room. Elvis was still shy, very much the southern boy with a new woman, so we didn't desert him all at once.

"I thought you were having a party," Mindi said when they were alone.

"No, you're the party," Elvis teased and grinned bashfully at her. They both laughed and Elvis put on his show. He entertained Mindi with a string of jokes. Then he called the guys back to help him demonstrate karate. He encouraged Mindi to take up martial arts herself. "I really like you," he confessed sweetly. They talked for hours, then Elvis took Mindi upstairs to see Lisa Marie asleep in her white round bed. "Isn't she beautiful?" he cooed. "She's my baby doll." They went to Elvis's bedroom, where he played guitar and sang a new song and read to her from the Bible and his spiritual books. The next day, Mindi told him she was returning to Europe, where she had a life and a career.

"No, you don't," Elvis said. "You're not moving now. You're staying here." They had a long talk and she accepted his invitation to go on tour with us. He asked me to call Joan, from whom I was now divorced. Joan met Mindi at Ships, a coffee shop on La Cienega Boulevard, to give her five thousand dollars to pay for having all her things sent back from Europe and her rent.

Oddly enough, Mindi had had a premonition about Elvis a few years before. She and a girlfriend named Carol were driving up Laurel Canyon one day, about to turn left on Sunset Boulevard, when they noticed a black Stutz Blackhawk.

"Look who's turning left in the lane across from us," Mindi told Carol. "It's Elvis Presley."

Star sightings are common in Hollywood, but Elvis was special. Mindi stared a few moments. His hair was slicked back and he was wearing his EP sunglasses. She turned to her friend. "Carol, I'm going to know this man," she said. "Don't ask me how, but I know that I'm not just going to meet him. I'm going to know him."

We picked Mindi up before leaving on tour. About three or four limos roared down Mindi's street, the guys screaming like banshees out the windows. Mindi and her roommate looked out their apartment window to see what the racket was about and howled.

That night Elvis asked Mindi to dye her dark brown hair jet black. He always seemed to wind up with blondes, he told her, but he preferred brown-eyed brunettes, because his mom had brown eyes and dark hair. "Just wait," Mindi asked.

"Honey, call Charlie, I want to have my hair dyed, and I want you to have your hair dyed jet black like mine," he said a few nights later, during the tour. Mindi promised she would have it done professionally when they got back to Los Angeles. Then Charlie walked into the suite carrying the dye and gloves. "Come on, honey, I want you to do your hair dark," Elvis pleaded. She stalled him once more, and he talked again about his mom.

"Were you close to your mom?" Mindi asked.

"Yeah," Elvis told her, "she used to walk me to school. She took care of me. It's hard to find a woman who compares to her."

"Do you do that even though she's passed away?" Mindi asked.

"I do," Elvis admitted. "It's not fair and I try not to, but she took such good care of me. It's hard to find the combination of a mother and a girlfriend. I never looked at my mom with that kind of feeling," Elvis qualified, too much a gentleman to say "sex" in the same breath as "mother." "But it would be nice to have someone where you can feel all those things." Mindi never did have her hair dyed.

Mindi told me about those conversations after Dee Presley's recent claims in the tabloids that Elvis had had an incestuous affair with his mother. Elvis never spoke of his mother except with love, but there was never the slightest hint of a sexual connotation in his reminiscences.

Mindi was sitting on the bed one night when Elvis came out of the bathroom. She turned to look at him.

"Hold it right there," he said. "Don't move."

"What's the matter?" Mindi asked.

"Just sitting there like that," he answered, "you remind me of Priscilla."

"Uh-oh," Mindi thought to herself, then asked aloud, "Is that good or bad?"

"Both," Elvis said. "Yeah, I'll never forget the time . . ." and he recounted an argument he'd had with his wife. "She was sitting there, pregnant, putting this oil on her body," he said. "She was always rubbing this oil on her belly and it smelled terrible." Elvis complained about the smell, and Priscilla threw the bottle of oil at him. "That woman had a temper," Elvis told Mindi. "I couldn't believe it. Come to think of it, we argued an awful lot. Boy, she was feisty."

Mindi listened without comment.

Like Elvis's other women, Mindi hated touring, the blur of day and night, the endless routine of plane to limo to hotel room to show, trying to steal an hour of rest here or there. We toured constantly throughout the seventies, playing a date at one venue, then flying to another part of the country to do the same. In ten or fourteen days, we played almost as many dates, then Elvis would return to Memphis for a few weeks' rest before we were off again. We were used to the routine, but the strain got to Mindi one night in a hotel room in Georgia. Elvis was sitting in bed reading one of his spiritual books when Mindi began banging her head against the wall. Elvis finally looked up from his book.

"Honey," he said, "what are you doing?"

"I can't take this!" she wailed. "I'm really bored, going crazy!"

"You know," Elvis said calmly, "you've got to have some discipline in your life."

"Excuse me," Mindi thought to herself, "that advice, from you?"

"Why?" she asked aloud, somewhat defiantly.

"How do you think I do this?" Elvis asked her. "Without discipline?"

"But how can you do this all the time?" Mindi cried in frustration.

"Well, honey, you're not used to this, but I am," Elvis replied, settling into his mentor role. "You have to understand that this is my business, and if you're going to be on tour with me, this is what you have to do. You have to get used to it. There's going to be a day in a city here, a day in a city there. You're not going out, you're not going sightseeing, you're not going shopping."

Like others who had spent a considerable amount of time with Elvis, Mindi craved simple, normal activities, like a walk outdoors. But he was afraid to do those things. "No, we really can't," he always said when she asked. But there were exceptions.

In 1976, just after we finished an engagement at the Las Vegas Hilton, Elvis bought Mindi a brand-new white Pontiac TransAm. We planned to fly to Palm Springs and have one of the guys drive the car there. "Can't we drive instead?" Mindi asked. So Al Strada and Dave Hebler, two new members of the Memphis Mafia, piled into the backseat, and Elvis drove the TransAm up and down the Vegas strip. He got out to fill the gas tank and introduced himself to the attendant and the customers. "Hi, I'm Elvis Presley," he announced, "and I'm here to get gas." He still loved shocking people. Then they took off for Palm Springs. During the ride, it rained everywhere except over the car. They'd look out the window and see that it was raining, so Elvis would turn the wipers on. But it was raining in patches and the windshield was dry, so he turned them off. Then he'd see it was raining and turn them on again. That kept happening until they reached Palm Springs.

In 1978, a little over a year after Elvis died, Mindi was driving down the street one sunny Southern California day. The windshield wipers suddenly turned on, then switched off, all by themselves. Mindi thought there must be an electrical short. She took the car to the Pontiac dealership, and they found absolutely nothing wrong with it. For a year and a half, the windshield wipers switched on and off for no reason. Finally, she confided in Shirley Dieu, my girl-friend.

"You know who that is, don't you?" Shirley asked.

"Yeah," Mindi said, "but I'm afraid to say it."

From then on, whenever the wipers turned on, Mindi would say, "I know you're here."

Like his other relationships, the romance with Mindi just fizzled out. Of course, Elvis already had a safety net, someone younger and more naive, whom he thought he could shape into another Priscilla.

Ginger Alden was Elvis's last girlfriend, a young woman who lived in Memphis, where he was spending more and more time between tours. Late in 1976, Elvis asked George Klein to find him another girl because Mindi wasn't working out. George had been introducing him to a lot of girls in Memphis, without success.

Ginger, with her black hair, sensuous lips, and very deep-set, beautiful blue eyes, looked a lot like Priscilla. Elvis may not have been in love with Priscilla any longer, but he still loved her looks. Another point in Ginger's favor was her quiet nature and lack of sophistication. Jo Laverne, her pushy, talkative mother—a stereotypical showbiz mom—was more eager for Ginger to be with Elvis than Ginger was herself. If you asked Ginger a question, Jo Laverne always butted in with the answer before her daughter had a chance to open her mouth. Jo Laverne had been a big Elvis fan. When her daughters were small, she took them to Graceland, hoping for a glimpse of the King on his horse. She'd even brought Ginger to the fairgrounds one night when Elvis was having a party there.

After the breakup with Linda, Elvis had begun telephoning Priscilla more often. He told her he wanted to get back together and have a baby boy. Elvis may have been toying with her, trying to convince Priscilla to remarry him only so he could dump her as revenge for her leaving him for another man. His was not just a male ego, but a southern male ego, and a superstar southern male ego to boot. Priscilla would never have remarried him anyway. So when George introduced him to Ginger, it was an opportunity to start over again; she would be a new "Priscilla."

"Come into my home, ladies," Elvis said graciously after George introduced him to Ginger and her two sisters, Terry and Rosemary. He showed them into the living room, and all three girls sat together on the long couch. Elvis positioned himself next to Ginger and offered the women drinks. George had intended to fix Elvis up with Terry, Ginger's older sister, who was the current Miss Tennessee. But twenty-two-year-old Ginger had come along, and Elvis immediately liked her. Anyone who knew Elvis could have predicted it. Terry was just as pretty, but she lacked that certain look; she was also older, less easy to mold. George and I understood that Elvis had made his choice. Terry and Rosemary did most of the talking, while Ginger sat there silently, the picture of innocence. Elvis was puffing on a cigarillo, pretending to listen to Rosemary and Terry, who were telling him that their father, Walter Alden, was the U.S. Army officer who had inducted him into the Army. As they talked, Elvis shot glances at Ginger and flashed his smile.

"Do you work, Ginger?" he finally asked her.

She seemed nonplussed, as if she couldn't believe Elvis Presley was actually talking to her. After an awkward pause, she summoned up an answer. "I'm not working right now. I do some modeling," she said, then fixed her gaze on the white carpeting at her feet. The rest of the evening passed with more casual chitchat.

Before George rose to take the girls home, I got Ginger's telephone number. I knew we'd be needing it.

Sure enough, the next afternoon Elvis called me up to his room.

"Call George and get that girl Ginger's number," he said.

"I got it from him last night," I replied with a big smile.

"Smart thinking, get her on the phone for me."

Ginger came on the line, and I passed the receiver to Elvis.

"Hi, this is Elvis," I heard him say. "What are you doing tonight?" There was a short pause, and then he said, "Why don't you just come up by yourself? I'll have one of the guys pick you up at seven." When Ginger arrived at the house, he met her at the door, gave her a little peck on the cheek, then led her by the hand to his Stutz Blackhawk.

"We're going for a little ride," he announced. Ginger said nothing. Patsy Presley Gambil, Elvis's cousin on both his mother's and father's sides, was sitting in the backseat with her husband, Gee Gee, and Elvis introduced them to Ginger. He took the driver's seat and drove to the Memphis airport, where I was waiting with the crew of the *Lisa Marie*. Elvis boarded the plane with Ginger and showed her around.

"Have a seat," he said. "Oh, by the way, we're headed for Las Vegas."

Ginger panicked. "Wait, I can't go to Las Vegas," she nearly wailed. "I have to call my mother."

"We'll call her when we get there," Elvis assured her. "Sit back and enjoy the ride."

Ginger looked dubious, as if she were wondering what she had gotten herself into. We arrived at the Las Vegas airport, where the Las Vegas Hilton Hotel had two black limousines waiting. We drove up to the back of the hotel and were met by four of the hotel's security guards. Elvis introduced Ginger to each one. Then we went up to Elvis's Imperial Suite by the service elevator. For the first time, a smile came over Ginger's face. I don't think she expected anything so grand. The ten-thousand-square-foot suite, decorated in bold strokes of yellow and black, boasted a fifteen-foot-high ceiling, a huge bar, and floor-to-ceiling windows that offered a panoramic view of Las Vegas. Elvis took Ginger's hand and led her through the entire suite, including my bedroom, Rick's room,

Sonny's room, the gigantic kitchen, the formal dining room, and the rooftop deck that encircled it completely. They sat out on the deck alone, talking all night until the sun rose, while the rest of us ordered food and watched television.

Then Ginger and Elvis headed for the bedroom, and we said our goodnights. I went straight to the gambling tables, where I contributed five hundred dollars to the hotel's coffers, and finally got to bed at about 8:30 in the morning. The next day, we didn't hear from Elvis and Ginger until after six in the evening, when Gee Gee ordered breakfast for them. They were holding hands as they came out of the bedroom. We left for the airport, boarded the *Lisa Marie,* and flew back to Memphis. It was Ginger's first trip to Las Vegas. She didn't see anything of the town or of the hotels because we had to get home to prepare for a fourteen-day tour beginning in a few days.

"Twenty-two, quiet, listens—another young Priscilla," Elvis must have been thinking. He was trying to repeat his past, but this time, with no mistakes. Of course, it was impossible: He would discover soon enough that Ginger's quiet nature was due less to shyness than to having very little to say.

By now, Elvis was living like a recluse, holing up at Graceland between tours, bored and sick of everything, and working only because he was still spending money excessively. He complained of pulled hamstring muscles when he did karate moves onstage, but instead of resting, as Dr. Nick ordered, he stubbornly insisted on doing his complete show, full-out. He'd get a hotel doctor to inject a shot of novocaine into the muscles so he wouldn't feel the pain. Dr. Nick had encouraged him to get into racquetball, and Elvis had built courts in back of Graceland. But he rarely played, and in the last few years, he had dropped karate completely. Elvis was performing poorly and he knew it. He needed more and more· reassurance that what he saw and felt when he faced an audience of screaming people was real, that they still loved him. During a stop in Hartford, Connecticut, in the middle of a 1976 tour, Elvis and the Colonel had an argument. Elvis was shaken, and he expressed concern about his performance that night. He couldn't call the Colonel because they weren't speaking for the moment, so he called Tom Hulett.

"I'll never forget what I told him," Tom says. "He was in a really down mood, saying things like, 'Tom, do you think people were happy with the show? Do they still like me?' " Tom listened.

"Elvis, I want to tell you something," he said. "I really believe this. You've got to look at yourself through my eyes. If I was standing in a hotel ballroom in the middle of two thousand people listening to a speaker, only three people could come in through the back door and make everyone sense their presence and turn around: John Kennedy, Winston Churchill, and Elvis Presley. I don't think you realize the power you have over normal people, your charisma and magnetism."

"You really think that?" Elvis asked.

"Yeah, I really feel that," Tom said. "You are the biggest entertainer there is and everybody loves you. We always sell out, and we could add shows wherever we go. We have the greatest deals. You're on top of your profession. You are bigger than you believe you are." It was true. Despite the drug abuse and the heavy toll it took on his personality, health, looks, and talent, the people loved Elvis Presley. The loyalty he had always valued in his fans was still there.

Despite such reassurances, his poor condition depressed him so much that he had to take more drugs and eat more junk to forget. Elvis never ate salads and vegetables because he was raised on fried foods and other garbage. He binged on hamburgers, BLTs, french fries, pancakes loaded with butter, applesauce, and such. Like most drug addicts, he craved sweets. During those final tours, Elvis came to resemble his mother more than ever. Before she died of alcoholism, Gladys had that same bloated look and the heavy, swollen eyelids that signal systemic toxicity.

In the last six months of his life, Elvis moved Tish Henley, Dr. Nick's nurse, and her husband, who worked on the grounds, into a trailer in back of Graceland. He said he wanted a nurse on the premises because his dad had suffered a heart attack. Tish's main role became overseeing the dispensing of Elvis's medication, ensuring that he wasn't taking all the pills at once. Tish consulted daily with Dr. Nick while they worked together at the office. He told her what to give Elvis, and she made up the pill packets.

Everyone in the inner circle was Elvis's caretaker by now, and we even hid negative reviews from him. If he gave a bad show and he asked how it was, everyone said, "Great," except for a few people like Pat Parry and Myrna Smith. "That show really stunk," Pat said sometimes. "You're fucked up," she would add, if he was obviously drugged-out. Elvis respected those who spoke honestly, but he had a hard time accepting the truth, and women got away with it more easily than men. Still, when he heard something he didn't like, he retreated to his room and took more pills.

Elvis was living in a twilight zone, but he was so set in the performing routine that he could do shows blindfolded and completely asleep. I would explain the lineup of the songs and which musicians would be there, and he was usually able to receive that information. But more and more, the Sweet Inspirations and others onstage had to pull for Elvis to get him through the show. If he hadn't received his amphetamine/B$_{12}$ shot soon enough to be up, for twenty or thirty minutes of the performance, he was sluggish. Estelle Brown once had to hold the lyrics for him onstage. If he couldn't remember a line, he'd come off stage and someone fed it to him.

Things got so bad that there were times when we almost hoped he would cancel the show. He forgot lyrics and lurched around the stage, and audience members walked out. We asked him to take time off. "Nah, I want to keep working," he insisted.

Only three times was Elvis completely unable to pull it off: The disasters happened in Baton Rouge, Louisiana, on March 31, 1977; in Baltimore, Maryland, on May 29; and, soon after that, in Houston, Texas.

In Baton Rouge, the opening act had finished and intermission was already over, but neither Dr. Nick nor I had not been able to persuade Elvis to leave his hotel room.

"Elvis, let's go, it's time to do the show," I said. He hemmed and hawed, wandering around the room, picking up objects and letting them drop, making every possible excuse because he didn't want to go.

"Yeah, I'll be there in a minute, I have to go to the bathroom," he said.

Then it was, "I have to see to something." He wasn't specific, because Elvis didn't have to explain himself to me or anyone else.

"Goddamn it," he raged, after I'd hounded him long enough. "I'll be there when I'm good and ready and the show can't go on till I get there." Finally, he admitted that he just couldn't do it. I called Tom Hulett at the venue. "You better get over here." He rushed to the hotel. Elvis didn't seem that sick, but he looked at Tom, and said, "I can't go on."

It was clear that there was nothing to be done. "Okay," Tom agreed. He turned to Dr. Nick: "Call a hospital." We would have to check Elvis in to cover ourselves. Tom had been through concert cancellations in his career; the problem was we had already started the show. The tickets were torn and thrown to the ground. We either had to refund or replay at a later date. We decided Elvis should get right into a Memphis hospital or there would be hell to pay. I got on the plane with Elvis while Tom handled the show. J. D. Sumner announced from the stage that Elvis was very sick at the hotel and unable to perform that night.

"We know all his fans will understand," J. D. said in his smooth bass voice. "He's on his way back to Memphis to be checked at the hospital. You'll read about it tomorrow in the paper." Tom called the Colonel the next morning.

"We had to cancel last night's show," Tom told him. "He was sick." The Colonel didn't have to ask what was wrong. He knew.

"Okay," he said, "you take care of the building people." We canceled the next show, the last one of the tour, and we all went home. The refunds were a nightmare. We replayed those dates about four months later.

In Baltimore, Elvis excused himself to the audience after just twenty minutes onstage.

"Jesus Christ, he's stoned!" the building manager in Houston said to Tom Hulett after Elvis struggled through a few songs and then gave up.

"I hope Tom doesn't tell the Colonel about this," Elvis said to the guys. He didn't. The Colonel was six hundred miles away in the next city. What could he do about it?

At this point, outside of his concerts, Elvis's contact with the outside world was completely secondhand, experienced through three television sets that blared continuously in his bedroom, a radio tuned permanently to gospel and country and western stations, the closed-circuit TV monitor through which he viewed images of visitors he refused to meet in person, and the guys, what remained of the Memphis Mafia.

I no longer lived in Memphis when we were off the road. For the last few years of Elvis's life, I lived in Beverly Hills. Elvis knew I didn't like Memphis, so we had come to an arrangement where I flew in a day or two before a tour and stayed a few days to tie up loose ends when we came off. I had my freedom, but I was in touch with Elvis or the guys by phone every day, acting as liaison between Elvis and the Colonel's organizations. Many of Elvis's other old friends were gone or busy with their families and lives. Much of his life had been tied to those lifelong buddies. The guys had their shortcomings, but they shared a sense of humor and a history with Elvis. Now he had lost most of them.

In his last six months of life, Elvis was especially devastated by the betrayal by Red and Sonny West and Dave Hebler, who wrote *Elvis—What Happened?* Elvis fired Red and Sonny West and Dave Hebler because he was facing several lawsuits stemming from the bodyguards' aggressive protection of Elvis. Someone would step off an elevator, look as if he *might* do something, and instead of stopping and questioning him, the bodyguards punched the poor guy out. Vernon was complaining about the lawsuits to Elvis and me and saying we should save money and fire them. Finally, Elvis caved in. "Daddy, you do it," he said and slunk off to Las Vegas while the deed was being done. Despite Red and Sonny's many years of service to Elvis and their longtime friendship, Vernon squeaked out a measly one week's severance pay and three days' notice. Understandably upset, they retaliated. The book exposed Elvis's drug habit to the world. But it also reflects genuine concern and frustration at not being able to help Elvis, particularly on Red's part. Although they had grown apart over the years, Elvis and Red had been friends since high school, and Elvis was obsessed with what he viewed as this ultimate disloyalty. Elvis talked about the book incessantly, and its imminent publication hung over his head like a dark storm cloud. After every show, the guys were a captive audience for Elvis's endless rants about "that damn book" and "those guys."

"How could they do this to me? I was their friend!" he would rail. "All those years! They're betraying me! What about my daughter, Lisa? What is she going to think when she gets older and reads what they've said about me? How could they do this? I was always out to protect them!" Elvis was terrified that the book would destroy his career, and he was constantly scheming to buy off Red, Sonny, and Dave. He sent emissaries, among them John O'Grady, our detective friend in Los Angeles. But the bodyguards were immovable. Elvis even talked to Red himself. A transcript of their taped conversation appears in the epilogue to *Elvis—What Happened?* Even there, Elvis hedges, blaming the dismissal on outside pressures. Elvis couldn't simply say, "Hey guys, I'm sorry I fired you." He had problems, he told Red, he wasn't feeling good.

Elvis—What Happened? was published only two weeks before he died, but it didn't receive the huge publicity we feared. Ironically, Elvis's death gave the book its greatest promotional boost. After August 16, 1977, sales skyrocketed.

Elvis was now surrounded by new people, kids like Rick and David Stanley and Al Strada, people who hadn't grown up with him and with whom he shared little. Elvis had too much time on his hands, time that the guys used to fill. He had problems with his kidneys, his intestines, and his pulled hamstrings, and he was even beginning to lose his hair, which had always been very thin and baby fine. He stayed in his bedroom with Ginger, but he was painfully lonely.

Ginger Alden was not working out. She complained and bitched, and her mother was always hanging around, hoping Elvis would give her something. He did give gifts to Ginger's family—fur coats, new cars—because Jo Laverne was always hinting. She learned quickly that all they had to do was hint. "Oh, my husband's car isn't running right," Mrs. Alden sighed, and Elvis gave her a new car. I assumed she was telling Ginger to stick with him, so they could get all these presents. Ginger and Elvis fought about the tours.

"I'm not leaving town," she often said, sometimes not until the last minute, and Elvis would become furious. The guys heard rumors that she had another boyfriend in Memphis. Elvis gave Ginger an engagement ring and said they were going to marry. He just wanted to see if she would accept the ring and say yes. "Oh, we're getting married," Ginger told everyone. "We're going to announce our engagement on Christmas." But I knew it would never happen.

Elvis told a different story when he sat around with the guys. "She's beautiful and nice, but I'm not about to get married," he said. Elvis just needed a beautiful girl at his side to feed his ego. He knew he was out of shape and that he wasn't a kid anymore.

Early in 1977, several months before he died, an incident occurred that proved how little he actually felt for Ginger. Priscilla and Lisa were in Memphis, visiting Minnie Mae. Elvis and Ginger were due to return from a tour that night. Priscilla wanted to leave before they got to Graceland, so she and Lisa checked into the Howard Johnson motel down the street.. But when Elvis came home, he called her there. "Listen, come back to the house," he ask. "I want to see you and Lisa." Priscilla drove back. They visited upstairs in Elvis's bedroom for over four hours, reminiscing about old times and talking about what she was doing, while Ginger waited in the kitchen. Over time, Priscilla and Elvis had become good friends through their long middle-of-the-night phone talks. They even captured some of the closeness they had shared before they became husband and wife. Elvis had none of that rapport with Ginger.

One night, after we finished a performance, Elvis took Myrna into the small back room next to the Sweet Inspirations' dressing room. He shut the door.

"Myrna, do you know what an albatross is?" he asked her.

"Yeah," she said, "something that goes around your neck and bothers you." Ginger was his albatross, he said, and he thought she was sleeping with other guys. But Elvis was too demoralized to do anything but complain.

Elvis was sick, exhausted, and numbed. He no longer saw the world as full of the challenges that once fueled his remarkable zest. The challenges *were* there; it was Elvis who had lost his taste for adventures, and with them, his reason for being.

The night before Elvis died, he called Tom Hulett. The phone rang just as Tom was leaving to join the Colonel in Palm Springs so they could fly to Portland, Maine, the first stop of the tour that didn't happen. Rick was on the line. "Elvis wants to talk to you," he said. Elvis had never called Tom at home before.

"Hi, what's up?" Tom said.

"How's the tour?" Elvis asked.

"Sold out," Tom said.

"Really?"

"Yeah," Tom repeated, "sold out."

"You're sure?" Elvis asked again.

"Yeah, we're sold out."

"Good," Elvis said. "When are you going out?"

"I'm leaving tonight to meet the Colonel in Vegas," Tom answered. "Are you okay?"

"Okay," Elvis said, as much to convince himself as Tom. "I'm playing some racquetball, getting ready for the tour. I'll see you there."

They said goodbye and hung up.

That same night, August 15, 1977, I flew to Memphis. We were scheduled to leave for Maine on the following night, the sixteenth, for the first date of a twelve-day East Coast tour. It would be the usual routine: every night a different city, with additional Saturday and Sunday matinees. I arrived at Graceland late, about ten in the evening. Sam Thompson, Linda's brother, was there. He had been hired as a bodyguard from the Memphis police force after Elvis began seeing Linda and had kept working for us after their breakup. About six foot three inches tall, thin and boyish, with a deep southern accent, Sam was quiet and intelligent, not an intimidating, brutish type like Red West. In fact, after Elvis died, Sam went to law school. Today, he's a Memphis juvenile court judge. Lisa Marie had been visiting her dad at Graceland since the end of July. One of the guys had flown out to Los Angeles, picked her up at Priscilla's Beverly Hills home, and brought her to Graceland. Lisa passed her days with friends riding in the golf cart that Elvis often drove around Graceland's grounds and down to the gate to sign autographs for the fans. Though Elvis kept reversed hours and he was on drugs most of the time, he made sure to spend time with Lisa every day, even if it was only in his bedroom. This was Lisa's longest visit with her father since the divorce, and Sam was supposed to take her back to Priscilla in L.A. the next day, August 16. Then he would meet us on the road.

Sam and I caught up on news and chatted a bit.

"Where's Lisa?" I asked.

"Elvis got her to bed at around nine-thirty," Sam answered.

"How's Elvis?"

"He's okay," Sam answered laconically. "Good days and bad days. Some days he's out of it; other days he's not."

That was normal. "Have you seen him much?"

"No, he's been up in his room mostly, going to a few movies at night."

I called upstairs to talk with Elvis, and Billy Smith picked up the intercom phone. "Not now, Joe," he said. "We're going somewhere." Soon I heard Elvis and a few others walk out the front door.

"Where are they going?" I asked Sam. "I have to talk to him tonight."

"They'll be back," Sam assured me. "He's going to the dentist." An 11:00 P.M. dental appointment was not unusual for Elvis. Apparently, Dr. Lester Hoffman filled some cavities, then called in a prescription for pain medication, which Elvis and his group picked up from the pharmacy. I was sitting in the kitchen when they got back. The car pulled up, then Elvis came in the front door and climbed the stairs to his room. I called up on the kitchen intercom.

"Elvis, is there anything you need?" I asked, my usual pretour question. "Anything special for this tour?

"No," he said, sounding alert. "Everything's fine. Call to wake me up tomorrow around five in the evening." We didn't have to leave until very late the next day, because the show wasn't until the day after. That was our entire conversation, and it was our last.

I knew Elvis wouldn't fall asleep right away. He'd sit up, reading and watching television. But he probably wouldn't come downstairs again. If he wanted anything—food, sleeping pills—he called on the intercom, and whoever was on duty sent it up. I hung around a while, discussing the tour with Sam as I ate a meal the maids cooked for me. Then I left for the Howard Johnson motel down the street. I got in bed around two o'clock, took a couple of sleeping pills, watched television for a few hours, and fell asleep.

After I left Graceland, Ginger, Elvis, and Billy and Jo Smith came downstairs again to play racquetball on the court he'd built in back of Graceland. Then they gathered around the grand piano in the music room for a group sing before he went back upstairs. Billy washed Elvis's hair in the master bathroom. They talked about the tour and, of course, the bodyguard exposé, which had been out for two weeks.

"They have never beat me and they're not going to beat me now," Elvis told his cousin in a pathetic attempt at bravado.

Elvis and Ginger went to bed at five or five-thirty on the morning of the sixteenth. Even at that late hour, Elvis generally stayed up reading, periodically downing the packets of pills prescribed by Dr. Nick to help him sleep. David Stanley was on duty. That night he gave Elvis a total of three packets containing about four or five pills each, which by then was normal for Elvis. That's what it took to put him out. He would down one packet, and if it hit him, he might sleep for a while. Or he sat up reading, fighting it. Elvis must have taken the three packets between approximately 4:00 A.M. and noon. I was told much later that Elvis also took Dilaudid that night, prescribed either by the dentist he'd visited earlier or by Dr. Nick the day before. At approximately 10:00 A.M., Ginger and Elvis were in bed when he got up. "I'm going to go into the bathroom to read a book so the light doesn't bother you," he said, and Ginger fell asleep. She woke at around 2:20 P.M. and discovered Elvis's body in his bathroom.

Meanwhile I awoke that day at around noon at the Howard Johnson motel and arrived at the house at approximately twelve-thirty. As I ate the huge breakfast the maids prepared, I asked, "Anybody hear from Elvis?" No one had. I walked to the back of the house where Elvis had enclosed an indoor/outdoor porch off the kitchen to create what we called the Jungle Room. This was our hangout spot, wild looking but comfortable. A waterfall ran down a stone-faced wall and ended in a little pond. Several inviting chairs and fake trees were scattered about. A long plush sofa covered with tiger skins faced a six-foot projection television screen. Elvis liked a tiger skin motif. His Korean karate teacher, Kang Rhee, a small bundle of coiled muscle, had dubbed Elvis "Tiger," because he fought in the style named after that animal.

I turned on the TV, sank into my favorite chair, and gazed for a few moments out the picture windows at the pastures and horses. Then I picked up the phone to confirm arrangements for the tour. I was still on the telephone at around two-thirty, when the intercom in the kitchen rang from upstairs. One of the maids picked it up.

"Who's on duty?" Ginger asked.

"Al is here," Mary replied, and passed the phone to the young man we'd hired to take care of Elvis's wardrobe.

"Al, come upstairs," Ginger said breathlessly. "I need you. Elvis has fainted."

Al ran up. A moment later, the intercom rang again. It was Al calling from the master bedroom: "Joe, come upstairs, I need your help!" His voice had the hollow ring of fear. I scaled the stairs and rushed into the bathroom to find Elvis on the floor. He had been sitting on the toilet and had fallen face forward at a slight angle, onto his knees. He seemed to have either passed out or died sitting on the toilet, then just keeled over, because he was frozen in that position, on his knees. He was wearing gold-colored silk pajama tops, and the blue bottoms were bundled around his feet. His face was smashed into the thick carpeting, his nose flattened to one side, and he appeared more bloated than usual, as if he'd choked. His eyes were closed. A book he'd just received from his barber and friend, Larry Geller, *The Scientific Search for the Face of Jesus,* was still clutched in his hand.

I turned him onto his side, away from the toilet and toward me. At the same time, out of a natural instinct to protect him from embarrassment, I yanked up the pajama bottoms. The moment I touched Elvis, I knew he was dead. He was cold and bluish; rigor mortis had set in. When I turned him over, air escaped from his lungs. "Maybe he's going to breathe!" I hoped for a brief moment. Later, I learned that the release of air left in the lungs after death is a natural reaction.

I grabbed the phone by the toilet to summon an ambulance. I caught Dr. Nick just as he was leaving on a house call. "Elvis had a heart attack," I yelled. "Get out here now!" Finally, I called downstairs to Vernon's office. Elvis's mouth was clamped shut, and his tongue bulged slightly through his teeth. I was able to stretch his body out a bit, but I couldn't force his mouth open, so I pounded hard on his chest. My thoughts were racing: How fast can we get him to the hospital? Is he going to come back? Can they bring him back? What about Lisa, the tour?

The scene in the bathroom quickly disintegrated into chaos. Charlie Hodge was crying and moaning, "Oh, Elvis, don't die! Breathe!" Vernon, who was recuperating from his heart attack six or seven months earlier, collapsed next to his son on the floor.

"Elvis, my son," he screamed over and over. "Don't leave me!" The ambulance took twenty minutes to reach Graceland from a station only a few blocks away. The paramedics burst into the bathroom just as nine-year-old Lisa Marie came to the doorway. "Get her out of here, quick!" I yelled at Ginger. As she led Lisa from the scene, Ginger told her not to worry, that her daddy would be okay. He was just sick. The paramedics, Charlie Hodge, and I carried the stretcher downstairs. We'd just put Elvis into the ambulance when Dr. Nick's car screeched to a halt in Graceland's driveway. He jumped out and into the back of the ambulance with me, Charlie, and the paramedic. He pumped oxygen through a mask over Elvis's face, while I continued pressing rhythmically on his chest. As we raced toward the hospital, Charlie and Dr. Nick kept up their chorus: "Breathe!" they pleaded. "Don't leave! You'll be okay."

The emergency team at Memphis's Baptist Memorial Hospital were alerted that someone important who had stopped breathing was coming in, so they were waiting outside. They pulled Elvis from the ambulance and ran with him into the emergency room with Charlie, Dr. Nick, and me at their heels. Charlie and I were escorted to a private waiting room near the emergency room. Dr. Nick rushed with the hospital personnel into the ER. Soon after, Billy Smith, Al Strada, and David Stanley showed up. Sam Thompson stayed behind at Graceland with Vernon, Minnie Mae, and Lisa. We waited in that room for twenty to thirty minutes, barely talking. Finally, Dr. Nick entered, his face blank and as pale as his shock of white hair. It was over.

chapter 11

peace
in the valley

"he's gone," Dr. Nick said. "He's no longer here."

Everyone burst into tears and held on to one another. We didn't discuss the cause of Elvis's death. No one mentioned it, and I doubt if anyone even thought of it. For a few blank moments, we were at a loss. We had no contingency plans. Then I put shock, grief, and confusion aside. To steady myself, I focused on my job: to do the funeral and do it right.

"Do you want to make the announcement?" Maurice Elliot, the hospital public relations man, asked me.

Dr. Nick intervened. "Wait," he said. "Don't make the announcement until I get to Graceland and talk to Vernon." He rushed out of the hospital, and the ambulance driver dropped him at the house. He didn't want Vernon to learn of his son's death over the radio. I asked Elliot for a telephone. Someone led me into a conference room off the emergency room.

My first call was to the Colonel in his hotel room in Portland, Maine, where he was awaiting our arrival. George Parkhill, the

Colonel's assistant from RCA Records, answered. I asked to talk with the Colonel.

"I have something terrible to tell you," I said. "Elvis is dead." A silence of thirty or more seconds stretched between us.

"Okay, Joe," the Colonel finally replied in equally flat tones. "We'll be there as soon as we can. You just do what you have to do. Tell Vernon we'll be there. We have a lot of work." The Colonel doesn't reveal his emotions easily, but I could tell he was shaken. Like me, he would do whatever had to be done: cancel the tour and let everyone know it was all over.

Meanwhile, the show plane was in the air, carrying band members and crew out to the East Coast. When they stopped to refuel in Texas, Marty Harrel, the trombone player, got off to find out what was going on. A message was waiting: Call the Colonel's hotel.

"Get back on the plane and return to Los Angeles," he was told. "Elvis is dead." Marty reboarded. He stood at the front. "Would everybody get off the plane," he asked. Everyone disembarked but Myrna. "They've left someone in L.A.," Myrna figured, "I'm not getting off." Marty walked to the back where she was seated. "Myrna," he said, "would you please get off because there's something I have to say, and I can only say it once." Myrna followed Marty out. He stood on the runway a moment, then cleared his throat. "I hate to tell you guys this," he said, "but Elvis is dead." Myrna began running wildly around the airfield. Someone caught her and sedated her with Valium. Everyone reboarded the airplane and flew back to L.A. As Myrna listened to the conversations swirling around her, she was shocked to realize that people who had been with Elvis as long as she, who Myrna believed loved him as much as she did, were actually furious to learn that he was dead. They were angry rather than hurt because his death affected their livelihood. As soon as they landed, Myrna booked reservations for Memphis.

My second call was to Priscilla in Los Angeles. Her sister, Michelle, answered. Priscilla wasn't home. "I've got to talk to Priscilla immediately," I told her. She was expected back any minute. "Have Priscilla call me as soon as she walks in," I repeated. I didn't tell Michelle what had happened. Three minutes later, the phone rang. "I have bad news," I told Priscilla. Again, I was abrupt. I was on overdrive and couldn't take time to find words to cushion the blow. "Elvis is dead," I said. I heard the phone clatter to the floor and Priscilla's sobs. She couldn't say a word. After a few moments, she picked up the receiver.

"How's Lisa," she asked through her tears.

"She's fine," I assured Priscilla. "As far as I know she didn't see anything. I kept her away. I'll make arrangements for the plane to come to L.A. to bring you and some others back to Graceland." Then Michelle took the phone. I told her I'd call back to let her know when the plane would be ready.

Linda Thompson was at home in her West Los Angeles apartment when her phone rang. It was Lisa Marie, who dialed Linda's number by herself from time to time, just to say "hello." Breathless and excited, Lisa sounded like a typical nine-year-old sprite.

"Linda! This is Lisa!" Nothing seemed different at first.

"I know who this is, you little goobernickel!" Linda teased.

Lisa burst out crying: "My daddy's dead! My daddy's dead!"

Linda was stunned. "No, honey, he's not."

"Yes, he is!" Lisa insisted. "Nobody knows except the people here at Graceland. He fell into the carpet and smothered to death!"

Linda knew how many times that could have happened, but she had always been there to save him. This time she hadn't been there. In her shock, Linda threw the phone up in the air. It hit the floor as she screamed, "Oh no! Oh no!" Then she realized that Lisa was sharing the most traumatic event of her life.

"Lisa, honey, are you sure?" Linda asked.

"Yes, yes, I'm positive," Lisa cried. "They just took him out in the ambulance."

"Well, maybe he's just sick," Linda offered. "You know, the times he's been sick and we'd take him out in the ambulance and he'd be all right."

"No, no!" the child insisted, her voice rising toward hysteria. "He's dead, they said he's dead!"

Linda tried to reassure Lisa, telling her how much her dad loved her. Then Lisa said she was "going to call my mommy."

Sam Thompson, Linda's brother, got on the phone.

"Linda," he said, "you'd better come home."

"Sam, he's not really, he's not dead."

"Yes, he is," Sam replied quietly.

"No," Linda said, "maybe he's just in a coma and they're taking him to the hospital."

"Linda, he's dead," Sam repeated. "Come home."

Strangely, the moment Linda hung up the receiver, every light in her apartment went out. None of the other apartments in the building experienced a power outage. The day was overcast, so she lit candles and packed by their light. Linda made no calls because she didn't want anyone to slip the news to the press. But an hour later, her phone began ringing as other people heard the news on the radio and television. The power came back, and Linda turned on the television. "Elvis Presley was found dead today in his Memphis home," they'd announce, then move on to the next news item. How dare they! Linda thought. For her there was nothing else. Shirley called Linda to let her know the plane would be ready at seven o'clock, and Vernon called, ostensibly to give Linda information but also seeking comfort from a woman he knew truly cared for his son. "The plane is coming out," he said, his voice strangled with the effort to hold back his sobs. "Go ahead and get on the plane and come on back with it."

When I called Sheila Caan, she was on page forty-two of Sonny, Red, and Dave's book. "I was sitting on the couch in my little house on Camden. I put that book down and never picked it up again," she later told me.

I asked Sheila if she was coming to the funeral. She said no. By now, she was involved in a difficult marriage to James Caan, and they had a small baby. She knew Memphis would be chaotic, and it was pointless for her to come. For four years, Sheila refused to look at any broadcasts concerning Elvis's death. "I pretended it didn't happen," she says. "I didn't grieve, I didn't do anything. I just closed that book and turned off the radio and television. Six years later, I began having dreams that his arm was on me and it was so heavy I couldn't get it off. I had to deal with the grieving then. I hadn't done it when he died, because I was already living a nightmare with my husband."

Meanwhile, the press had gathered at the hospital. When we received word that Vernon had been told, the media people were herded into a separate waiting room.

"Joe, are you ready to make the announcement to the press?" asked the hospital's PR guy.

"Yes," I said. But I just couldn't say the words. "You'd better tell them," I said. Elliot announced that Elvis had died at approximately 3:40 P.M. and further details would be forthcoming. Dr. Nick never did tell us the cause of Elvis's death, then or later. We were still so deeply into denial that no one even hypothesized that he had died of drug abuse.

The room exploded. Over two hundred reporters rushed out to hit the wire services, television, and radio stations, and call their papers. I left the hospital, trailed by flashing camera bulbs and a barrage of reporters' questions. Detective Roy Millican and Sergeant Peel took Charlie and me back to Graceland, where a crowd of fans was building swiftly. Sobbing and holding on to one another, they pressed against the tall iron entrance gates.

The first thing I did was pay my respects to Vernon. He was so dazed and grief-stricken, he barely acknowledged me. I had called ahead from the hospital to ask someone to clean the upstairs rooms. I opened the door to his bedroom, and a chill shot down my spine. The maids had made up Elvis's bed as if he were coming back. But they hadn't removed the drugs. Al Strada, Billy Smith, and I took on that job. We gathered together all the prescription drugs and the hypodermics. We filled two grocery bags, including vitamins, Aspirin, old medicine, and empty bottles, and turned it all over to Dr. Nick. Elvis was a packrat, he saved everything. When we finished, the room was absolutely clean, suspiciously so. But who was thinking clearly?

I searched Graceland for Ginger Alden, but she had already slipped away. No one even noticed. Ginger's presence had barely registered when Elvis was alive. After his death, she virtually vanished, almost as if she'd never been there.

I talked with Vernon about the funeral. "Would you help me out?" he asked pitifully. I called the funeral home that had taken care of Elvis's mother. The director, a wonderful man, came to Graceland immediately.

"Do you want the same casket we had for Gladys?" he asked. Vernon did.

"Joe, it will cost a lot of money to fly the casket in," the funeral director warned.

"Fine," I said. "Just get it done," and we had it transported from Oklahoma City. Some people have suggested a fake body was in the casket because it was so heavy. The truth is that the casket was made of solid copper; by itself it weighed over nine hundred pounds. I asked the funeral director for a fleet of white limousines. "We only have a couple in Memphis," he said. "But I'll call around the South." In one day he rounded up seventeen gleaming white limos. We conferred with Vernon on where Elvis would be buried: a plot next to his mother or a mausoleum. The director suggested the mausoleum. Vernon agreed. The mausoleum would be more protective.

Jesse Garon, Elvis's twin brother, had died in Tupelo, Mississippi, soon after their birth. I never understood why Elvis didn't have his body brought to Memphis and buried next to their mother. When a person becomes wealthy, he usually buys a funeral plot or builds a mausoleum for himself and the departed members of his family. Vernon could have done this on his own, before Elvis died. But neither man liked to think about death. They didn't even own a family plot.

I conferred with Sam Thompson and Dick Grob, both former police officers who had quit their respective forces to handle Elvis's security. I asked Dick to contact the Memphis police and the sheriff to set up around-the-clock patrols. Police were already in front of Graceland, trying to control the traffic that was rapidly knotting itself into an impossible snarl. We arranged for the funeral home to pick up the body from the hospital after the autopsy and prepare it for viewing. Elvis had reached the hospital at 2:45 in the afternoon. They would work on the autopsy all that night and release him to the funeral home in the morning.

At first, we planned to hold the service at the funeral home, but Vernon wanted it at home, in keeping with the custom of poor southern people who can't afford a funeral home. The Presleys were wealthy now, but that was the way it had always been done. I agreed because we would have more control at Graceland. I began arranging for people to fly in. The phones were ringing nonstop with calls from all over the world, and I was discouraging as many people as possible from attempting to come. "Please don't come, it's going to be impossible," I pleaded with Nancy Sinatra, as I had with many others. "Stay home." Ann-Margret refused to stay in Vegas.

"I'm coming," she said. "I want you to know I'll be there."

"Fine," I replied. "I'll have a car pick you and Roger up at the airport. Just let me know when you're coming in."

Telegrams poured in from stars and celebrities: the president, politicians, movie producers, Frank Sinatra, Bob Hope, and many others. Reporters called, but I refused to talk with them, not until Elvis was buried. The crowd of distraught fans outside the house continued to swell. "What do we do with all the fans?" we wondered. "Do we have an open casket for them to say farewell?" It was the right thing to do, I thought, and Vernon agreed. We'd line people up. They'd enter through the front door, pass by the casket in the foyer, then walk out. We'd have to set up heavy security. There was no telling how many people would want to say goodbye.

Finally, I made arrangements for the plane crew to fly the *Lisa Marie* to the West Coast. The plane would arrive in Los Angeles at seven o'clock at night to pick up Priscilla, my ex-wife, Joanie, Linda Thompson, my girlfriend, Shirley, and others. "Get whoever you can get on the plane," I told the crew.

But Priscilla had a different idea.

"I don't want anybody on the airplane, just us—my family, Jerry, you, and Joanie," she said when Shirley called to notify her of the departure time. "No one else."

"But I already told Ed Parker," Shirley protested. Ed Parker was the karate champion who worked for us on and off as a bodyguard.

"I do not want him on the airplane," Priscilla insisted. She thought Ed was a freeloader. If Ed heard Elvis was giving something away, Priscilla once told me, Ed would suddenly appear at Graceland's doorstep.

Shirley broke the news to Ed. "Okay," he said, amiably enough. "I'll fly commercial."

Priscilla also barred Linda Thompson from the *Lisa Marie*. She told Linda that she didn't want the press to see the wife and the girlfriend coming home together to his funeral. Linda caught a commercial flight at midnight.

Jerry Schilling was the first to board the *Lisa Marie*. "It was the eeriest feeling," he said. "I was all alone. I walked back to the bedroom. His pajamas were laid out and all the books were ready for him. I broke down." Then, while they were in the air, the plane's interior began smoking. The blankets in the underneath storage section had caught fire due to bad wiring. It was a really weird time.

I made certain to be at Graceland's entrance as soon as Priscilla arrived so I could call her aside. "Priscilla," I said quietly. "I have something I think you should have." I passed her the blue Samsonite case.

"Oh, thank you very much," she whispered. We didn't go into further details. Priscilla was happy to get her hands on it before someone else did. She dashed up the stairs to stow it in her room.

I knew the videotapes and Polaroids had to be weighing on her mind. Elvis was dead and the tapes could be anywhere in the house. If others were to get their hands on them, they could blackmail her or sell them. Priscilla may still have the tapes, although she once asked me about the best way to destroy them. "You can put a magnet over them and wipe them out or just burn them," I told her.

The next day, the seventeenth, the Colonel, Jerry Weintraub, Tom Hulett, and George Parkhill arrived. We arranged for Elvis to be brought to the house for the viewing. The National Guard offered assistance for the viewing and an honor guard for the funeral the next day. The police department was already out in full force, trying to control a crowd of at least fifty thousand fans who had stampeded Graceland the moment they heard the announcements of the open viewing that afternoon, from two-thirty to four-thirty. Friends and family streamed into and out of the house all day, saying hello, offering condolences, visiting, remembering, and saying goodbye. Charlie and Larry Geller went to the funeral home to fix his hair. Vernon requested that Elvis wear the white suit he'd given his son for Christmas. To go with the suit we sent a light-blue shirt and a white tie.

The casket arrived at the house around noon. We had it brought through the large foyer entrance and set up between the living room and the music room, right in front of the archway. We placed flowers around the casket. Then the funeral director raised the lid. Fear slammed into my gut. Elvis looked very bloated and chalky, and he seemed strange in the suit and tie, like a stuffy banker. I know he would have preferred a warmup suit or one of his stage outfits with the stand-up high collar.

The funeral director signaled to Vernon. He approached the coffin, assisted by his girlfriend Sandy Miller, who was a nurse. When he saw his son lying there, Vernon's knees buckled as if he were slipping into a faint, and someone held him up on his other side. "You're going to Gladys," he told his son between choked sobs. "Now you'll see Gladys, you'll be with her." I was terrified Vernon would die right there, his heart was so weak.

Minnie Mae Presley had been keeping to her room the entire time, watched over by Aunt Delta, Vernon's sister. She was strong for a woman in her eighties. But she couldn't believe her grandson was gone. We helped her shuffle to the casket. "How could he die before me?" She kept repeating in her high, quavering voice, "I'm the old one. I'm supposed to be gone." And she worried about her son. "How's Vernon, how's Vernon?" she kept asking.

The Colonel was wearing his trademark baseball cap. He wasn't disrespectful, just being himself. He refused to look at Elvis. "Joe, I want to remember Elvis when he was alive," he told me. "I want to remember good memories, great times. I don't want to go in there and see him dead." I paid my respects later. I was too busy preparing the public viewing.

By the time we opened the gates for the viewing, the summer heat was unbearable and the humidity suffocating. Police lined the long driveway, forming a huge horseshoe. They guided the fans in a single row up to the house and through the front door, where they walked by the casket we'd moved to the foyer. Some fainted. They simply collapsed the moment they set eyes on their dead idol. Others burst into tears. I stood there as all these individuals expressed shock and grief at the realization that Elvis was gone. With each person who passed, I reexperienced my own loss. "We loved you, Elvis, God bless you," many cried. Several of us stood around the back of the coffin, making sure no one went nuts. In the space of four grueling hours, thousands of people passed by, shepherded by at least two hundred volunteer police and National Guardsmen. They weren't allowed to linger, and they couldn't take pictures.

Linda Thompson was sitting on the landing of the grand staircase with Elvis's cousins, Patsy Presley Gambil and Billy and Jo Smith. They watched the fans filter through, laughing as they thought of what Elvis might have said when some character passed by, and crying as they shared a particularly poignant memory: At Memphis disc jockey Dewey Phillip's funeral a few years earlier, someone had made the clichéd remark, "Doesn't he look natural?" To which Elvis had responded, "Sonuvabitch looks dead to me!"

We had had tears in our eyes from laughter, but people thought we were crying. So as one fan wearing a neck brace struggled to bend over the casket, Linda, Billy, and Patsy stopped crying over Elvis's sensitivity and how much he loved his daughter. They looked at one another. In perfect sync, Billy and Linda burst out in Elvis-like tones, "Poor sonuvabitch is in worse shape than I am. What in the hell is he doing here?" They exploded with laughter. Elvis would have said just that.

The temperature had soared to over one hundred steamy degrees. People were scattered all over the lawn and down the streets, screaming and fainting, as nurses and ambulance crews attempted to administer oxygen and other first aid. It was surreal, something from a battlefield or a page of Dante's *Inferno*. After four hours, we ordered the police to close the gates. They shoved against the solid iron, but thousands of fans pushed back. "We'll extend it for a half-hour longer," we decided. "But that's it." After another half-hour, people were still pressing against the gates, but the police managed to close them. Slowly, the crowd thinned out. We stood in the abrupt silence for a moment before rolling the casket back to its position by the music room and preparing for more visits from personal friends.

James Brown flew in with his entourage. "I've got to see the King," he said. He walked to the back to pay his respects alone, then returned to the living room to offer his condolences. Caroline Kennedy approached the outside gate and sent a message that she would like to come in and pay her respects. Unaware that she was on assignment for a newspaper, we showed her around Graceland and took her to see Elvis. A week or so later, we were shocked to see a long newspaper article describing her visit.

Everyone had their quiet time with Elvis. Mindi Miller and my girlfriend Shirley Dieu took turns going up. "We almost couldn't get enough of it," Mindi said. Just before the casket was closed, some of Elvis's friends put little mementos inside. Shirley read a few verses from a small book, then placed it in the casket. It was their way of saying goodbye.

The moment news of Elvis's death was broadcast, all the relatives descended on the house, the most despicable bunch I've ever seen. The Smith side of the family were the worst; the Presleys weren't as bad. But they all gathered like a gaggle of clucking geese, necks stretched out, beady eyes on the lookout for what they could get. They were waiting for the will. One of them, I don't know which, cashed in on Elvis's death early by taking a photo of Elvis in his casket and selling it to *The National Enquirer.* I heard the price was seventy-five thousand dollars. Some had worked as guards or in the yard, but most didn't bother to lift a finger. Venal and self-serving, they preferred handouts, which half of them would promptly drink up. Now they were jockeying for position with Vernon. Poor Vernon was oblivious, attended to by Sandy.

That night, a group of wives and friends, including Priscilla—about twenty-five in all—went out to dinner. Sam Thompson and his wife, Louise, stayed behind to guard Elvis's body. We didn't speak much of Elvis. We actually laughed, made small talk, and to our surprise, enjoyed ourselves. We were relieved, although we didn't acknowledge it. I still can't explain that feeling entirely. We were finding our bearings, I guess, and the relief came from knowing that we no longer had to fear what might happen.

On August 18, 1977, at 3:00 P.M., the air shimmered with the heat haze of Memphis, Tennessee, in high summer. Inside Graceland, Elvis's family and friends—more than 250 closely packed sweltering bodies in all—were seated on folding chairs we had set up in the long blue-and-white living room. Vernon Presley's preacher competed for air space with the loud, futile hum of air-conditioners. Improvised paper fans waved listlessly, and eyes squinted with the effort of focusing on the pastor's eulogy. Elvis had never set foot in the man's church, but Vernon was burying his only child, and his wishes had to be honored.

"Elvis was a wonderful person," the pastor said. "He's with God now. He did the best he could while he was alive. His daughter will miss him, and so will his other family and friends." Then Jackie Kahane, the comedian who traveled on the road with us, stepped forward to tell us about the real Elvis, the wonderful, paradoxical child-man we all knew. He spoke of Elvis's close friendships, of his fun-loving nature, of his generosity and concern for others—often at his own expense—of how much we would miss him, and of how his music would live on. The Stamps Quartet sang a few hymns. Kathy Westmoreland stirred us with "How Great Thou Art" and "My Heavenly Father Watches Over Me." Jake Hess, whom Elvis considered the finest gospel tenor ever, delivered a touching rendition of "Known Only to Him."

The past forty-eight hours had been a sleep-deprived adrenaline rush, a nightmare hyperreality. After seventeen years of organizing his life, it seemed natural for me to organize Elvis's funeral. I'd handled the arrangements like a sleepwalker on fast forward, and I welcomed the distractions from the loss and grief that awaited me. I didn't want time to think. I glanced around Graceland's living room, checking who was present and mentally computing who I would assign to which limousine for the ride to the cemetery. My mind was still racing, galloping back and forth over the infinite details that had to be seen to.

To my left was Linda, blonde and lovely in her lavender spaghetti-strap sundress, and the only person there not dressed in black. She told me later that when she had gone through her clothes closet by candlelight, she picked that dress because it would have been Elvis's choice. Lavender and violet exude the highest metaphysical vibrations, the perfect choice for his send-off, she thought. A few rows behind Linda, I glimpsed George Hamilton's handsome profile. He hadn't been close to Elvis, but as a well-mannered southern boy himself, he was there for his good friend, the Colonel. Ann-Margret held hands with Roger Smith. I was happy she came, because Elvis had told me many times how much he loved her. Once Elvis loved, he always loved. Ann had told me that the day Elvis died, she'd known something was wrong. Every time she opened in Vegas, Elvis and the Colonel sent her a huge floral arrangement in the shape of a guitar. Ann-Margret had opened in Vegas more times than she could count, but the night before Elvis died was the only occasion when she didn't get her floral guitar. Ironically, it was not because Elvis had died. Elvis was still alive on the fifteenth. Someone goofed and forgot to order the flowers. Priscilla kept her gaze focused straight ahead, occasionally looking down at Lisa Marie, who leaned against her, swinging a leg back and forth. Lisa looked tired and confused.

• • •

The ceremony was over. People rose from their chairs and mopped their brows. They began looking around for someone to tell them what to do next. I pulled the list of the friends and relatives from my jacket pocket and began assigning people to various limousines. The relatives surrounded me: "I want to be in the second limousine!" "I want the third one!" I cut off their demands. Vernon had given instructions, I said, and that's the way it was going to be. They objected when they realized that many of the guys and their families were riding in the lead limousines. But they caved in because they didn't want to offend Vernon and cut themselves off from the golden goose.

Lamar Fike, Charlie Hodge, Gene and Billy Smith, George Klein, Dr. Nick, Jerry Schilling, and I carried Elvis's coffin out Graceland's front door into the muggy afternoon. The day had turned eerily still, with no hint of wind. Suddenly, a huge branch hurtled down from the tree right outside the house. It crashed onto the driveway, nearly smashing the Alden family car. We were stunned. Was it a farewell comment from Elvis? Just in case, we each broke off a piece of the tree limb as a memento. My girlfriend Shirley took the largest. A huge blanket of roses covered Elvis's casket, and we each took a rose. Later, we had the roses encased in lucite blocks. We placed the casket in the back of the hearse, and everyone got into their assigned cars.

Vernon rode in the first limo with Sandy, Grandma, and Aunt Delta. Lisa Marie, Priscilla, my ex-wife, Joan, and Priscilla's family were in the second. Shirley, some of the pallbearers, and I were in the third. Jerry and Myrna rode in a limousine with Lamar and others. The procession seemed to crawl at a snail's pace, but it took only ten minutes to traverse the three miles from Graceland to the cemetery. We passed streets lined on both sides with masses of tearful people held back by policemen, their right arms frozen in salutes.

Not much was said in our car. I was awestruck by the number of people, some of whom had come from the far corners of the globe, and by the depth of their emotion. Later, I learned that at least eighty thousand people attended Elvis's funeral. If Elvis was looking down at all the people who loved him, he had to be proud of himself. This funeral was bigger than any Mafia don's.

When we reached the cemetery, I leaped out, back in my "organize everything" mode, directing people and cars like a harried road manager. We led over four hundred journalists to a roped-off area to the side. Helicopters equipped with video cameras buzzed overhead but kept a respectful distance. Later, I held a small press conference with representatives from UP, AP, and *Time* magazine. "Absolutely no drugs whatsoever," I stated emphatically when they began probing about the cause of death. "Elvis didn't take drugs." The habit of rote denial would die slow and hard.

We removed the casket from the hearse and entered the dark mausoleum. The small stone building overflowed with flowers. Graceland had been filled beyond capacity. Even the long driveway was banked on both sides with huge bouquets. We hadn't been able to take any more at the house, so we'd ordered whatever arrived to be sent to the cemetery. The morning of the funeral, we had all the flowers from Graceland brought there as well. So many flowers had been sent that the city of Memphis had actually run out and was bringing them in from neighboring towns. Vernon's minister limited himself to a few brief words, and we filed out of the mausoleum, Vernon sobbing and near collapse. Sandy supported him on one side, with me on the other, and we put him in a car. I stayed behind to supervise departures. After everyone had left, I returned to Graceland.

We caught up on news and tried to comfort each other, murmuring the time-worn, soothing platitudes: "He's at peace now," "He's with God," "He's with his mother," "He's with his friends," "He has nothing to worry about now." We were beginning to accept that Elvis was gone, and that with all his suffering in the past few years, it may have been for the best. He was finally safe. Perhaps death would give him the privacy he had craved. But what would we do without him?

afterword

elvis lies with his mother, father, and grandmother in Memphis. A plaque by Graceland's meditation garden honors the memory of his twin brother, Jesse Garon. Every year on August 16, a candlelight ceremony is held on the grounds, across the street from the *Lisa Marie* and the *Jet Star,* both of which are on permanent display as part of the Graceland tour. Every year, more and more fans pledge love to their idol in scribbled messages that cover Graceland's vast stone wall.

Yes, Elvis came to a sad, tragic end. I told that story in this book, because it is the truth and the truth must be told. But that was only a small part of Elvis's life. We tend to remember people as they were at the end, and Elvis's last few years were certainly not his best. But the whole world didn't love him because he was unattractive, drugged-out, and mean. Except for those few years, Elvis wasn't the bizarre, tormented creature the media like to portray. Yes, there were creative and personal disappointments, but most of Elvis's life and career was exciting and full of fun. Elvis was not only blessed with unparalleled singing and performing gifts, he was extraordinary in his kindness, generosity, and insight. Elvis made it easy for us to forget who he was to the world. One afternoon, I was painting fences with him on the ranch. Then, a few days later, he was performing for almost sixty thousand people at the Houston Astrodome. "OmiGod!" I'd thought. "I forgot who this guy is!"

Almost everyone who knew the man felt the same way. Every one of us felt close to Elvis and, even more pertinent, we each *knew* that he understood us in a way no one else did.

Success and show business are wonderful, but they bring tremendous responsibility and temptation. Everyone's feelings are tuned to you and only you. You walk into the kitchen to have breakfast, and everyone there is looking at you, waiting to see how you feel and what you're going to say and do. Elvis loved being Elvis Presley and he loved his lifestyle. He had fun! He liked certain people, and he wanted them around. He loved movies, and if he wanted to see the same reel three times, the great thing was, he could! If he wanted to ice skate, he rented the rink!

Elvis enjoyed his privileges fully and he was grateful. But he never forgot who he was and where he'd come from. He tried to use those gifts to make himself and others happy. If he showed any favoritism at all, it wasn't to the wealthy and powerful, but to the needy and helpless.

"Who was Elvis?" people ask me.

"He was a good guy," I say. "There was no harm in Elvis, but there was an awful lot of love." What more can I tell them? That he got mixed up in a business that destroyed him? That he had a medical problem that wasn't recognized at the time for what it was? That he was caught in a world that few of us could navigate successfully?

Elvis was happiest when faced with a challenge, when he didn't know if he could make it or not. Who knew that after eight years of making movies, people would accept him again in his 1968 comeback special? The next year, he walked onto a Las Vegas stage—his first live concert in the town where he had bombed many years earlier—and he inaugurated the most successful phase of his career.

Because of Elvis, his friends had the opportunity to know other extraordinary people of our times. Yet none could match him. Today, the legend of Elvis Presley is so indelibly engraved in the mass consciousness that his image appears on U.S. postage stamps. In 1993 alone, two critically praised boxed reissues of his music topped the pop charts. As I recollect my life with Elvis, it seems that not a day goes by without mention of his name. Nearly two decades after his death, Elvis Presley still reigns unchallenged as the King of rock 'n' roll, the greatest superstar the world has ever known. All the crude jokes and ugly rumors can't change the fact that there never was anyone like him and there never will be another again. Elvis was the most extraordinary ordinary man.

index

joe esposito was Elvis Presley's close friend for almost twenty years. He has been interviewed about life with the King on radio and television, including *Geraldo, Nightline, Good Morning America, Larry King Live, Entertainment Tonight,* and *The Joan Rivers Show*. He writes a regular column in *Elvis International* and has managed concert tours for performers such as the Bee Gees, Karen Carpenter, Wayne Newton, and Michael Jackson, among others. He lives in El Dorado Hills, California.

elena oumano is a freelance music journalist who has written for the *Los Angeles Times, The Village Voice, New York Newsday,* and *LA Weekly*. Her books include *Film Forum: 35 Top Filmmakers Discuss Their Craft*. She lives in Los Angeles.

Printed in the United States
By Bookmasters